PLACE

South African Literary Journeys

PLACE

South African Literary Journeys

Justin Fox

PLACE
Justin Fox

Published in 2023 by Penguin Random House South Africa (Pty) Ltd
Company Reg. No. 1953/000441/07
The Estuaries No. 4, Oxbow Crescent, Century Avenue, Century City, 7441, South Africa
PO Box 1144, Cape Town, 8000, South Africa
www.penguinrandomhouse.co.za

© 2023 Justin Fox

All rights reserved.
No part of this book may be reproduced or transmitted in any form or by any means, mechanical or electronic, including photocopying and recording, or be stored in any information storage or retrieval system, without written permission from the publisher.

First edition, first printing 2023, second printing 2023 (reprinted twice)
 3 5 7 9 8 6 4

ISBN 978-1-41521-106-9 (Print)
ISBN 978-1-4152-1131-1 (ePub)

Cover painting 'Overberg Landscape' by Erik Laubscher, © The Erik Laubscher Heritage Trust and Estate, photo courtesy of Strauss & Co Johannesburg
'All That Was Left of Them (17th Lancers at Modderfontein)' painting (page 81) by Richard Caton Woodville (jnr)
Dalene Matthee photograph (page 179) by Amanda Matthee
Zakes Mda photograph (page 201) by Joanne Olivier

Cover design by MR Design
Text design by Stephen Symons
Set in Minion Pro

Printed and bound by Novus Print, a Novus Holdings company

CONTENTS

1. Spirits of Place   1
2. Moonlight Serenade: Olive Schreiner's Eastern Karoo   15
3. Jock Befok: Sir Percy FitzPatrick's Lowveld   43
4. Band of Broers: The Long Ride of Deneys Reitz   73
5. The Soul of the White Baboon: Eugène Marais's Waterberg   101
6. Fireside Englikaans: Herman Charles Bosman's Marico   129
7. Alone in All that Vastness: JM Coetzee's Moordenaars Karoo   149
8. Like Wings Without Bodies: Dalene Matthee's Knysna Forest   179
9. Red in Truth and Lore: Zakes Mda's Wild Coast   201
10. Rock, Paper, Pen: Stephen Watson's Cederberg   227
11. Praesidio   261

    Bibliography   271

    Acknowledgements   281

BOTSWANA

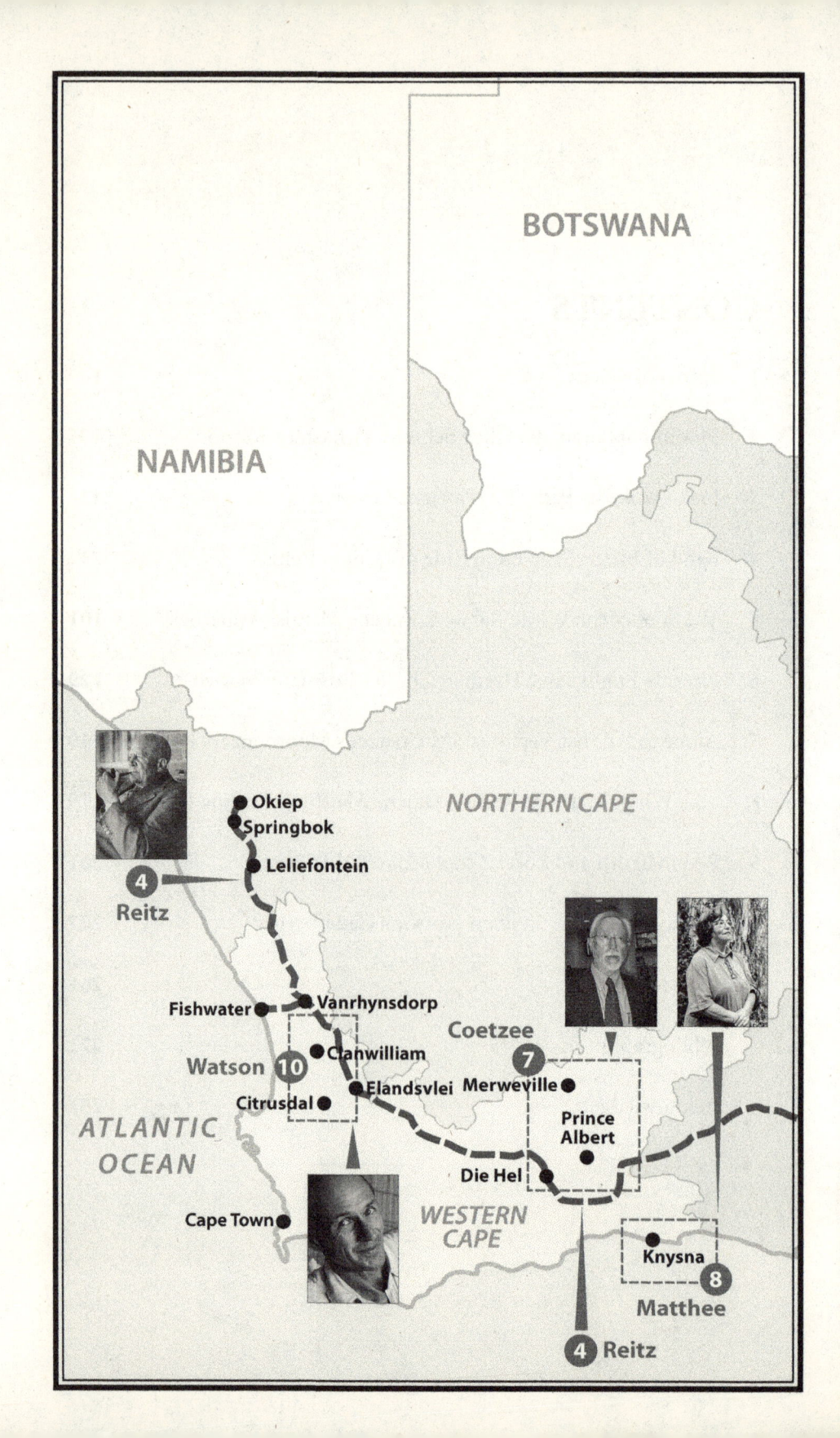

NAMIBIA

NORTHERN CAPE

Okiep
Springbok
Leliefontein

④ Reitz

Fishwater Vanrhynsdorp
Watson ⑩ Clanwilliam   Coetzee
Citrusdal Elandsvlei Merweville ⑦
                        Prince
ATLANTIC   Albert
OCEAN
                        Die Hel
Cape Town   WESTERN
                        CAPE
                                    Knysna ⑧
                                    Matthee

④ Reitz

ZIMBABWE

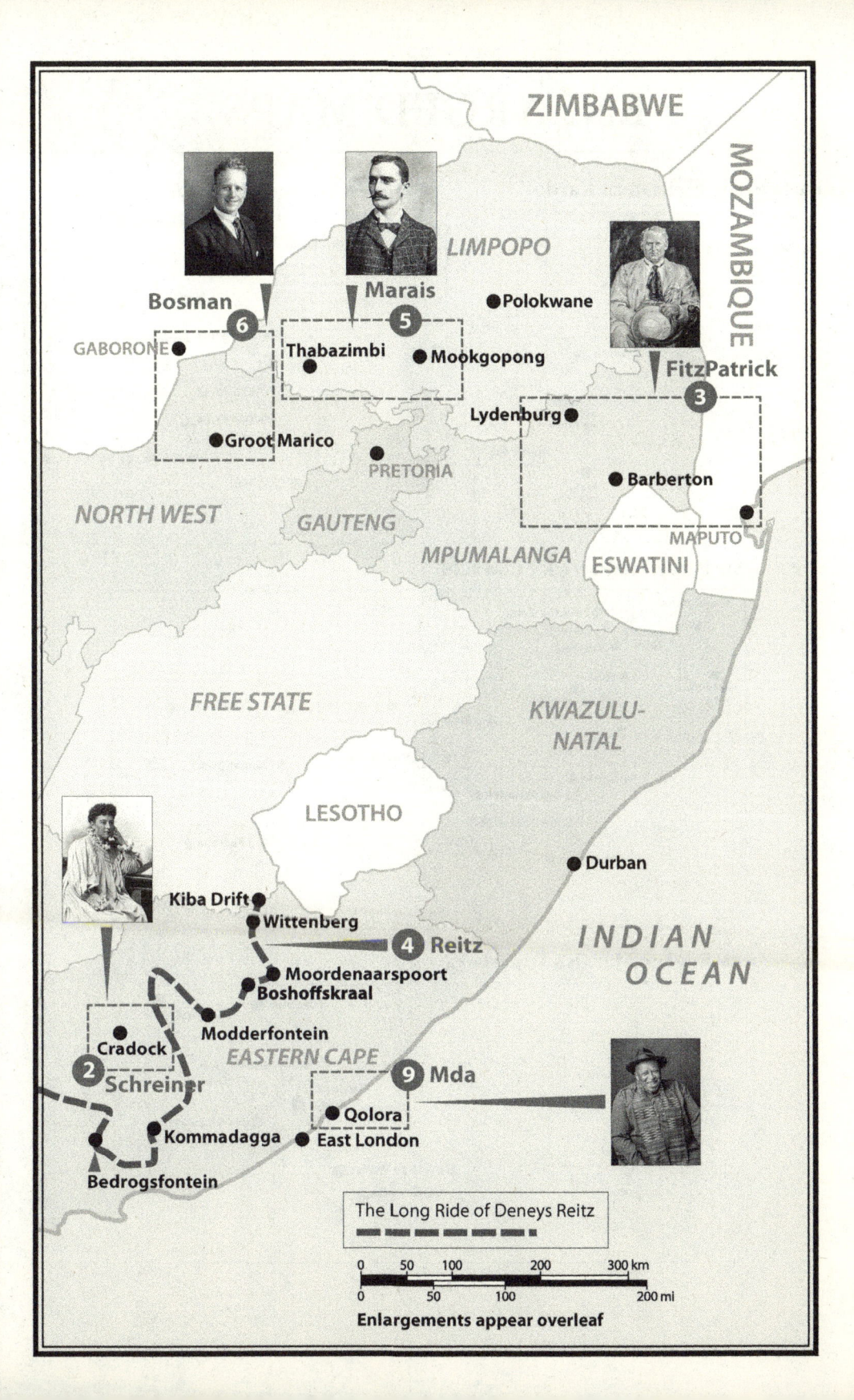

MOZAMBIQUE

LIMPOPO

Bosman
Marais
● Polokwane

GABORONE
⑥
⑤
FitzPatrick
● Thabazimbi
● Mookgopong
③

● Groot Marico
● Lydenburg

NORTH WEST
● PRETORIA
● Barberton

GAUTENG
MPUMALANGA
MAPUTO

ESWATINI

FREE STATE

KWAZULU-
NATAL

LESOTHO

● Durban

INDIAN
OCEAN

● Kiba Drift
● Wittenberg
④ Reitz
● Moordenaarspoort
● Boshoffskraal
● Modderfontein

EASTERN CAPE

● Cradock
② ⑨ Mda
Schreiner
● Qolora
● Kommadagga
● East London
● Bedrogsfontein

The Long Ride of Deneys Reitz
- - - - - - - - - -

0   50   100   200   300 km
0   50   100   200 mi

Enlargements appear overleaf

ENLARGED MAPS

Olive Schreiner's Eastern Karoo

Stephen Watson's Cederberg

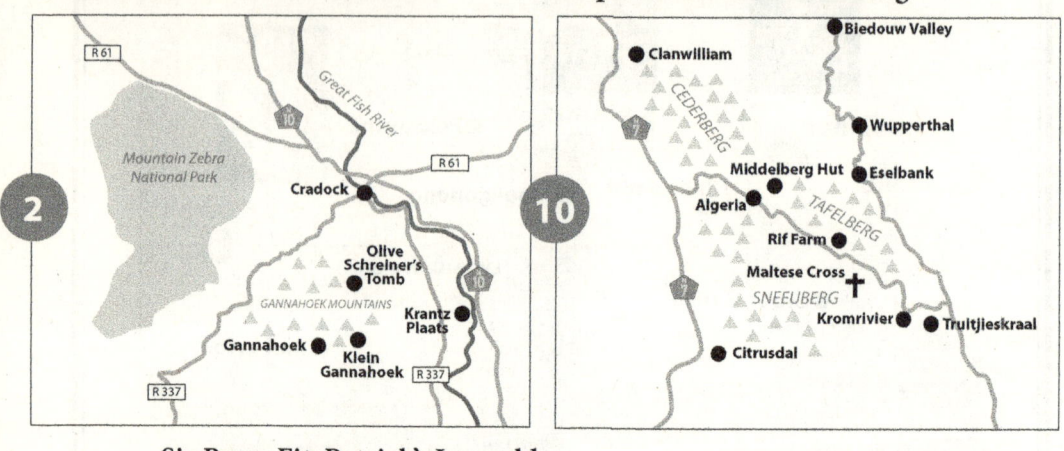

Sir Percy FitzPatrick's Lowveld

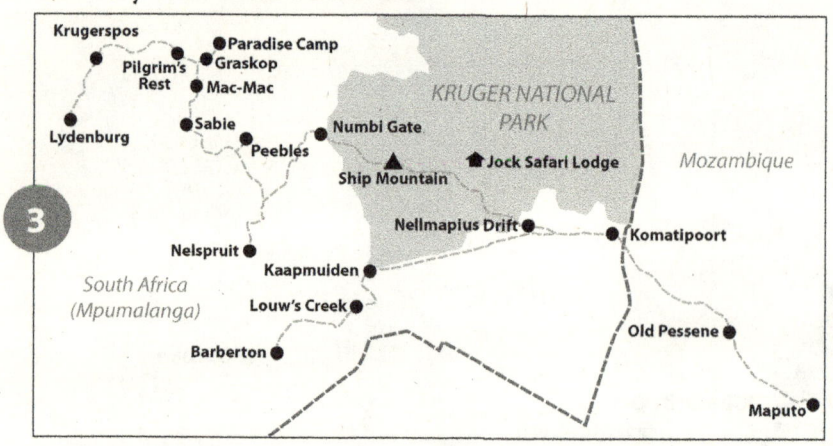

Eugène Marais's Waterberg

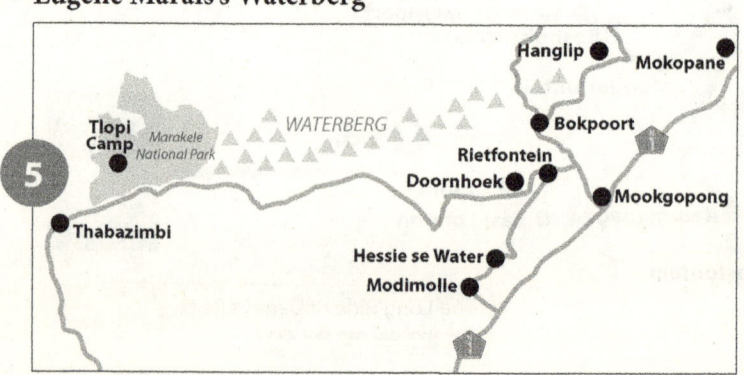

Herman Charles Bosman's Marico

JM Coetzee's Moordenaars Karoo

Dalene Matthee's Knysna Forest

Zakes Mda's Wild Coast

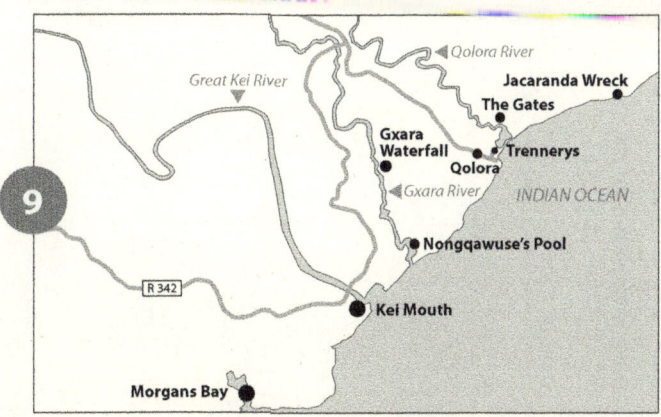

In memoriam

Uys Krige

Before it can ever be a repose for the senses, landscape is the work of the mind. Its scenery is built up as much from strata of memory as from layers of rock.

    – Simon Schama

In Spanish, *la querencia* refers to a place on the ground where one feels secure, a place from which one's strength of character is drawn … a place in which we know exactly who we are. The place from which we speak our deepest beliefs.

    – Barry Lopez

SPIRITS OF PLACE

The muleteer helps me into a creaking saddle, clicks his tongue and we set off down a stony track. The day is already warm and the line of donkeys emits a musty smell. Above and below the path on terraces lie groves of olive trees; far below is the glittering sea. My big brother is on the donkey in front of me, my big sister on the donkey behind, all three of us giggling at the jouncing ride. Upon reaching the jetty, we dismount beside a brightly painted caïque bedded in emerald water, its engine softly grumbling. We climb aboard and cast off. The old captain, Georgios, is at the tiller and sings under his breath as we chug along the coast, around a headland and into an enchanted bay.

The caïque coasts towards the beach until its bows nudge the pebbles and we clamber over the side. Dad calls out to Georgios, telling him when to pick us up that afternoon as the caïque reverses and heads back to town. The beach is enclosed by a drystone wall; behind it are olive trees and goats resting beneath gnarled boughs. Our family is alone on the beach. We swim and snorkel in warm, kaleidoscopic water, build castles out of pebbles and snooze in the shade.

At midday, we walk to a whitewashed cottage at the end of the beach where a bent woman dressed in black with a radiant smile serves us lunch – dolmades, spanakopita and peach juice, home-made yoghurt and honey – under a vine pergola. As we have our a last swim, Georgios comes nosing round the headland, the dull thudding of his engine echoing off the hillside. We climb aboard and motor back to town, towards the setting sun – happy, bleach blond, sun-kissed. I am six years old and there is no place in the world I'd rather be. Will I ever live such golden days again?

The Fox family tour of Europe in 1973 culminated in two months on the islands of Patmos and Santorini. We were joined by my sister and brother, who'd been studying and travelling abroad, as well as by various friends and family members who arrived by air, ship or donkey. For a child who'd fallen in love with islands and boats, Greece was a newfound Elysium. There were voyages on ferries and caïques, daily mule rides to beaches and monasteries, a visit to a bubbling volcano and Greek dancing at the taverna each evening. I felt and knew this to be 'home', albeit a transient and mobile one: my family united in an island setting, with me, the laatlammetjie, doted upon, contained yet free. Forever after, my 'season in paradise' has been clearly defined as that Grecian summer of 1973.

The places loved in childhood become places of the heart, sanctuaries to which you can return in memory and anchor in the comfort of their lee. For the rest of your living days, there will be triggers – sights, sounds, smells – that spirit you back to that time, that place. Paradise for me, then, is a whitewashed village, drystone walls, a chapel's tolling bell, a kraal with sheep or goats, the scent of pine, basil and leather, barren mountains overlooking a turquoise sea, a tinkling stream of crystal water and the persistent song of cicadas.

Soon after returning from Greece, my parents took me to the Cederberg for the first time. Rounding a bend at the top of Kouberg Pass and seeing Wupperthal far below – an oasis of thatched cottages encircled by mountains – brought a jolt of recognition. Everything about the village was familiar: the whitewashed houses, the chiming church bell, donkey traffic, sheep grazing the slopes, the clear waters of the Tra-Tra River and arid hills covered in fragrant vegetation.

There were other places of childhood topophilia (from the Greek *topos*, place, and *philos*, loving), such as Kanetvlei farm in the Hex River Valley, visited each autumn after harvest when the vines were scarlet – its Cape Dutch architecture and snow-capped peaks, its caves of rock art and sheep returning to the kraal each evening, backlit by dusty sunlight. There were visits to my artist uncle, François Krige, in the Klein Karoo village of Montagu and walks to thermal rockpools through sandstone kloofs echoing with the bark of baboons. There were weekends in Arniston with its fishermen's cottages on a bluff overlooking a luminous bay where brightly coloured fishing boats were launched each morning and returned each afternoon laden with silver cargo.

Children respond instinctively to beauty, an imprinting that stays with them for life, and powerful early encounters with place help to mould their sensory palates. Indeed, our habits, customs and thoughts, as well as our language, tastes and perceptions, are shaped by the 'terroir' we first inhabit. In her essay 'The Spirit of Place', poet Alice Meynell suggests that there is no 'more delicate perceiver of locality than a child. He is well used to words and voices that he does not understand, and this is a condition of his simplicity; and when those unknown words are bells, loud in the night, they are to him as homely and as old as lullabies.'

Douglas Pocock develops this idea in 'Place and the Novelist': 'Although a hierarchy of places emerges as our engagement with the world enlarges beyond our earliest activities, a crucial and indelible bond is established with early place or "home" as we most commonly use the term. It remains the centre of our egocentrically-ordered cosmos, containing our own unique, unrepeatable beginning. We may move, but we cannot begin again a second time ... In a sense we are rooted and grounded in place, by place.'

Our childhood sense of wonder, the capacity to see with fresh eyes, is unique and precious. We do not choose where we are born, but so potent is the imprinting by the environment that few of us wish to have been born elsewhere. Even hardship and sorrow play a part in deepening our love of place. This intense feeling of harmony with our first patch of earth contributes to a sense of wholeness and of 'having a place'. In a sense, we become endemics, adapted to our particular corner of the globe. Seen in this light, our beings have true meaning and value only in their proper home, in a symbiotic relationship with their landscape and ecosystem, with the fauna, flora and topography of their place.

Contemporary neuroscience has begun to explore the mechanics of our sense of locale. Researchers have identified 'place cells' in the hippocampus that store memories of specific locations, and 'grid cells' that orchestrate these memories in ways that allow us to find our way around. Cognitive psychologists tell us that the brain is only fully developed in late adolescence or early adulthood, a lag phase that allows us to adapt uniquely to our environments and develop into niches. That period also tunes our brains in a particular way to the locales of our formative years. In other words, we adapt neurologically in a deep and embedded way to place. This might help explain why people are so at home in certain environments, and why the act of emigration or exile can leave them feeling profoundly at sea.

The story of who I am – my very sense of self – depends on the places my story is set. Such sites hold my memories and are integrally linked to my sense of identity. The thoughts that seem to belong to me most intimately, in so far as they concern my own life story, are lodged as much in place as in my mind. The same applies to cultural narratives of every conceivable kind, literature included.

All our founding narratives are set in the aspic of place and, in this respect, they become sacred to us. 'Home' is an irreplaceable centre. Particular houses, gardens, topographies and scents are so deeply familiar that body and place, body and home, appear inseparable. This is especially strong and true for the places of childhood, but it applies throughout our lives.

Landscapes shape our personalities. The different geographies of South Africa have helped make the inhabitants who they are. There's the Cape with its fickleness – one minute a Mediterranean idyll, the next a storm-lashed Atlantic crag; the Drakensberg with its moods, drama and churchliness; the Lowveld is steamy, sultry and fanged; the Karoo is an expression of heat, dust and vastness. I am a product of Cape Town, of a western seaboard, a place of sunsets, mountains, beaches and an ocean deeply blue and capricious. I have a visceral response to the fynbos and strandveld, granite and sandstone, vineyards and shorelines of this place, my place. How could it be otherwise? How could I be otherwise?

While travelling, there are moments when we come upon a locale that provokes an instinctive response. Heart, mind and body seem in alignment: we are suddenly an animal in our natural environment and react with a sense of profound recognition, even love. Some such places hold a more general appeal for humans. It could be the shape of the landscape, the quality of light, the way buildings occupy the terrain, or it could be something compelling about the locals – their dialect, customs or cuisine. In this, there is an echo of pilgrimage in many cultures down the ages: the journey to, or search for, a special place associated with spiritual fulfilment or eternal life. Religious historian Philip Sheldrake notes how in ancient myth, such places were often associated with human beginnings – the site where ancestors or gods originated, or even a former paradise. As such, the physical pilgrimage was the acting out of an inner, spiritual journey.

Many of us travel in order to experience such encounters with the 'spirit of place'. Some environments seem to have absorbed the layers of history played out upon them in a particularly favourable way. In turn, their storied, gravitational pull appears to have exerted a pleasing influence on their inhabitants. Spirit of place is an invisible force that affects everything within and about the locale, and is often a magnet for artists and writers who are drawn to its unique character, its history and its residents, both past and present.

The survival of our species has depended on humans having senses that are finely tuned to all aspects of geography and nature. The location of rock-art sites, stone circles or burial mounds reminds us of the importance of landscape to the ancients. Across cultures and continents, there has been the belief that certain places are occupied by particular spirits.

Since the dawn of human time, our species has imbued such sites, particularly those that hold innate energy, with religious significance.

Indigenous cultures have always been deeply concerned with the spirits of places. For Aboriginal Australians, landforms, plants and water sources were places of tremendous power reaching down through countless generations. For many American tribes, certain sites informed their comprehension of the world, as anthropologist Keith Basso explains: 'When places are actively sensed, the physical landscape becomes wedded to the landscape of the mind, to the roving imagination, and where the mind may lead is anybody's guess.' For the Celts, elements in the landscape were seen as portals into a spiritual realm and they were able to identify what they called 'thin places', where the membrane between this world and the other world was decidedly permeable.

In classical Rome, the genius loci was the protective spirit of a place, with altars dedicated to such genii and sacrifices made to them. It was believed that the genius imbued the site with its personality, giving it a particular character. The inhabitants of ancient India, Indo-China and southern China believed in similar spirits – disembodied human souls found in all things. Spirits of place continue to be recognised by some of the world's main religions: Shinto has its Kami spirits of the landscape, Hinduism has its Dvarapalas and Lokapalas. Down the ages, a range of 'beings' have come to be associated with the spirit of a place, such as guardian angels, ghosts, fairies and elves. The phenomenon of energy fields can also be seen as a manifestation of pantheism or panpsychism – the idea that all things, even inanimate, have their own consciousness.

In contemporary usage, 'genius loci' usually refers to a location's distinctive atmosphere rather than its spiritual dimension, although a vestige of belief in its sacred character persists. The genius is often cherished in folk tales, festivals or celebrations, and invoked by artists and writers. Thus, the spirit of place exists not only in the physical environment, but also in the invisible web of culture (stories, memories, beliefs, rituals, histories) and interpersonal aspects (the presence of family, friends, kindred spirits, past inhabitants). It is what differentiates it from all other places, influencing the behaviour, attitudes and beliefs of those inhabiting or visiting it. Indeed, it is the very soul of a place.

SPIRITS OF PLACE

If there is any universal truth about stories and their tellers it is that they are, in every sense, bound to place. All narratives must happen somewhere: stories issue from geography. For some writers, landscape is central to the narrative, impregnating the writing with its presence. What would Wordsworth be without the Lake District, Thoreau without his Massachusetts woods, Camus without his sun-drenched Mediterranean shore, Durrell without his Grecian isles? In his landscape memoir, *Island Home*, Tim Winton comments on the centrality of place (Western Australia) in his writing: 'I persisted with place as a starting point for all my stories. For me a story proceeded from the logic of an ecosystem. When I began a piece I never knew where I was headed, but I followed the contours of the country my characters were in and found my way to the nub of things.'

All ur narratives are deeply rooted in geography. Homer and Virgil both treated place as sacred to a god or guarded by a spirit. In the *Odyssey*, Odysseus and his men pay a terrible price for slaughtering cattle on the island of Helios because the animals are sacred to the god of the sun. As if to forestall a similar fate, the first thing Aeneas does when he and his men land in Latium is to pray to the genius loci.

Even after Christianity and the Enlightenment's debunking of paganism, thereby consigning spirits of place to the rubbish heap of superstition, poets continued to feed their imaginations on the genius loci. Coleridge and Wordsworth were captivated by the idea of the spirit of place taking the form of a host. To damage, steal or kill anything from that place (such as slaying an albatross if you happened to be sailing the South Atlantic) violated the laws of hospitality and provoked retaliation. In an age of revolutionary industrialisation and the initiation of a prolonged assault on nature, the Romantics were acutely concerned with ways to 're-enchant' the land in order to re-establish the spirit of place.

In *Topographies*, Joseph Hillis Miller contends that writers typically take existing landscapes and alter, colour and add to them. In other words, through art, place is reimagined, recast and recreated. This act of transformation in turn affects the way readers experience those environments. 'Mississippi is partly what it is because of Faulkner's Yoknapatawpha novels,' he writes. 'Dorset has been made what it is in part by way of Hardy's Wessex, Salisbury by way of Trollope's Barset novels, London by Dickens, Paris by Balzac and Proust.'

The rise of the novel during the Nineteenth Century saw the development of a close symbiotic relationship between place and character. A writer's choice of location deeply influenced the voice, tone, style and the way characters viewed the world. Many novels of this period seem to grow from the very soil upon which they are set, so imbued are they with the spirit of the place. Characters are rendered as functions of, subject to, or children of the landscape. In some cases, landscape acquires the individuality of a character; in others, the characters mirror the personality or mood of the landscape.

Thomas Hardy classified one set of his Wessex writings as 'novels of character and environment', referring to the 'inevitableness' of both in 'working out destiny'. In Hardy, the close connection between character and place (rural and natural, not urban) helps to fashion identity, made explicit in his description of the relationship of the hills and dales of Blackmoor to Tess of the d'Urbervilles: 'they seemed a part of her own story. Rather they became a part of it.'

The novels of DH Lawrence are also uniquely imbued with topophilia, exhibiting an acute sense of what he called the 'life-quality' of nature and landscape, as well as a vivid awareness of genii loci and a passion for ancient places. His *Studies in Classic American Literature* begins with an essay, 'The Spirit of Place', in which he states that not only does a community permeate a given place by settling there, it is also influenced by that place during the process of building its own customs, traditions and identity, so that its culture is shaped by its setting.

'Every continent has its own great spirit of place,' Lawrence writes. 'Every people is polarized in some particular locality, which is home, the homeland. Different places on the face of the earth have different vital effluence, different vibration, different chemical exhalation, different polarity with different stars: call it what you like. But the spirit of place is a great reality.' He goes on to suggest that it is the business of art, and the novel in particular, to reveal this complex relation between humans and their environment.

No writer took this injunction more to heart than Lawrence Durrell, who can be thought of as fundamentally a writer of place. In the article 'Place and Durrell's Island Books', Alan Friedman quotes Durrell: 'I think the Greek landscape is absolutely saturated by intimations of the basic type of mind that grew up in it, and in Greece you feel the pagan world is very close.

Where I live now, in the South of France, you feel something equally strong – you feel Nostradamus, the Provençal singers, the intense savagery, and a different sort of mysticism. In Dorset, where I was living last year, the Druids were pretty close, I thought.' Friedman contends that in Durrell's writing the setting embodies, parallels, even motivates both the intrinsic and extrinsic workings of the characters.

In *Spirit of Place*, a collection of letters and essays on travel, Durrell admits to 'seeing "characters" almost as functions of a landscape'. In the same collection, he avers: 'What makes "big" books is surely as much to do with their site as their characters and incidents ... When they are well and truly anchored in nature they usually become classics ... They are tuned in to the sense of place. You could not transplant them without totally damaging their ambience and mood.'

Durrell's writing is replete with 'environmental determinism'. However, the idea that national and personal characteristics are influenced by the natural environment (for instance, that the temperate climes of Northern Europe were responsible for the strong work ethic and rational thought that justified imperial expansion into regions where hot climates led to laziness and indolence) has been widely discredited. This kind of thinking has been blamed for contributing to the rise of fascism and various forms of racism. Nevertheless, the effect of place on character cannot be denied; the trick is to avoid understanding it in simple terms, but rather as a product of complex interactions between people and geography that have many possible outcomes.

Durrell writes: 'As you get to know Europe slowly, tasting the wines, cheeses and characters of the different countries, you begin to realise that the important determinant of culture is after all – the spirit of place.' He did not believe that the British character, for example, had changed much over the centuries, and 'as long as people keep getting born Greek or Italian or French their culture-productions will bear the unmistakable signature of the place.' He argues, controversially, that if you exterminated the French and resettled the country with Tartars, within two generations the national characteristics would return, including restless metaphysical curiosity, passionate individualism and tenderness for good living. 'This is the invisible constant in a place with which the ordinary tourist can get in touch just by sitting quite quietly over a glass of wine in a Paris bistrot.' Durrell's theories are certainly contentious, but they do find their truth in fiction.

———✳———

My proposed literary journeys for this travelogue will take me to the mountainous, moonstruck eastern Karoo of Olive Schreiner, to the towering Drakensberg escarpment and big-game Lowveld of Sir Percy FitzPatrick, to the vast emptiness of the open veld evoked by Deneys Reitz, to the pioneer highlands of Eugène Marais's Waterberg, to the dreamy bushveld of Herman Charles Bosman's Marico, to the plains of thirst, dust and heat of JM Coetzee's Moordenaars Karoo, to the ancient forests of Dalene Matthee's Garden Route, to the rondavel-topped hills and subtropical shores of Zakes Mda's Wild Coast, and finally to the sandstone heights of Stephen Watson's Cederberg.

My choice of literary works is all about places of the heart, both for the authors and for myself. The selection is personal, reflecting my own literary and literal geographies. In some cases, such as with Deneys Reitz, I will closely pursue storylines, following a forensic trail and trying to sniff out the book's precise locations; in other cases, such as with Stephen Watson, my focus will shift to the author's intellectual and emotional response to a particular locale. The works I have chosen depict South African landscapes that have remained wild and largely unspoilt, rather than built environments. In each instance, setting is no mere backdrop, but an integral part of the work and a reflection of the author's heart-land.

Our imaginations, coloured by experience and culture, fill and shape the landscapes we inhabit. My own cultural map of South Africa is a patchwork comprising disparate scraps of literature, art, television programmes, music, film and photographs. Such a 'map' would include evocative poems of place, such as 'Drummer Hodge', 'Winternag', 'Plaashek', 'Sweetwater' and ''n Handvol Gruis', as well as short stories like 'The Pain', 'The Coffin' and any number of Bosman yarns. It would contain fragments of Butler, Paton and Palmer as well as the heart-wrenching, place-rooted songs and dances of maskandi, boeremusiek and rieldans – all of it mixed into the potjie along with my own travel memories, many of them from journeys undertaken at a young age when my mind's doors were wide open and the topophilic winds blew new and strong and true.

My maverick alternative to the AA Atlas – my 'Groot Justinian Africana' map – would also contain narratives of the countless people who have traversed or inhabited the landscape. In his article 'The Ghosts of Place', sociologist Michael Bell contends that 'a common feature of the experience of place is the sense of the presence of those who are not physically there.' This certainly rings true for me. Often when I'm alone in the veld, I find myself listening for echoes and looking for the shadows of its hosts – early hominids, San hunter-gatherers, trekboers – and picturing their stories as they play out against the telling almanac of earth and stone. Bell suggests that we construct places around the 'ghosts' we sense inhabiting them: family members who have passed, ancestors or figures from history. As such, these ghosts are versions of the genii loci.

Every person brings their experience and imagination to a locale, thereby infinitesimally changing and amplifying it, adding a brushstroke to the great canvas, contributing a thread to the story of that place. Whether it's a poem, a painting or a photograph, each act adds to and deepens the collective experience of place. One could think of this in Cubist terms: each individual facet offering a slightly different dimension to the overall picture. Looked at in this way, a landscape can be read on many levels and from many angles – ranging from geological to historical, mythical to cultural – with its layers blending and rhyming with the viewer's discretion and taste.

I am drawn to the idea of songlines, or the 'footprints of the ancestors', imaginatively articulated by Bruce Chatwin in his famous book, in which he describes the Aboriginal practice of 'singing up the land' as they travelled across Australia, chanting about topographical features as a form of oral mapmaking, navigating vast distances through song. As Chatwin puts it, the Australian continent could be visualised as 'a spaghetti of Iliads and Odysseys, writhing this way and that, in which every "episode" was readable in terms of geology.' It was through song that you found your way across the great expanse, with the result that storytelling could be thought of as the equivalent of wayfaring. With this in mind, I began to think of the series of literary journeys I was about to undertake as my own version of 'singing up the land', using the narratives of books for guidance.

I also began to picture the map of South Africa as a thickly braided quilt of culture lines, a great web laid over the landscape. Broadening the concept of songlines, or story lines, such a map would include *all* routes, from ancient footpaths to modern highways, many of them densified by narratives: oral histories of the San and Khoi, Bantu founding myths and Mfecane tales, the accounts of runaway slaves and indentured labourers, gold-diggers, big-game hunters and empire builders. It would include the stories of modern wanderers – backpackers, aid workers, campervanners, refugees – all of them leaving faint, palimpsestic tracks.

In the realm of writing, the first descriptions of South Africa were nautical accounts of the coastline by early navigators, then came the diaries, letters and documents of VOC officials and later colonisers. There were popular makers of fiction such as Rider Haggard and famous chroniclers such as David Livingstone, Winston Churchill and Mahatma Gandhi. All of them were mapmakers, all of their writing rooted in and giving colour to place. These threads of experience and narrative were amplified by literal mapmaking and scientific study, and deepened by art, a process gathering breadth and weight over time. Every single person adds to the story, recording routes and tales on Facebook and Twitter, Instagram, YouTube and TikTok, or simply by being present. There are even fuddy-duddy anachronists – such as yours truly – who still employ ancient recording devices such as pen and paper as they travel the South African road.

———✳———

In 1936, Herman Charles Bosman gave his impressions of Paris in *The South African Opinion*: 'The city in which a genius has lived becomes recreated into something that is more than the inanimate background to his sorrows. The streets through which he has walked much. The scenes amid which the incomparable patterns of his life unfolded. Above all, the places where sublime inspiration came to him. It doesn't matter what happens to such places afterwards. That spot on the earth's surface remains impregnated with the spirit of beauty that is forever rich and rare.'

In *A Writer's Diary*, Stephen Watson recalls a conversation with a friend, 'BL', who told him she could not really find Cape Town beautiful because, unlike a city such as Paris, it did not have a Baudelaire or Utrillo. In other words, it had never been properly transformed into the kind of place of the mind and imagination that Bosman had described. 'The beauty of the place thus remained on the level of the merely spectacular, the touristic.'

In researching this book, I have sought the occasions where literature and landscape have proved the lie to BL's assertion, where writers have been enchanted and inhabited by a landscape, where geography is rendered as a successful blending of reality and the imagination ... places that Bosman tells us are 'impregnated' by the beauty evoked by writers.

Each corner of South Africa I visit has a unique atmosphere and character fashioned by its fauna, flora and geology, its weather and seasonal moods, its architecture, people and history. These elements are woven together, feeding off each other to forge a unified sense of place greater than its constituent parts. My conviction is that it is to literature in particular that we must turn, rather than merely the 'facts' of geography or history, for the fullest appreciation of such locales.

During these journeys, we will encounter writers whose words and works have helped to define, broaden, deepen, complicate, vivify and ultimately alter our experience of place. All the books chosen are in a sense love letters to South Africa, saturated with a passion for the land. Indeed, the intoxication of landscape cuts deep for many local authors. In *A Season in Paradise*, Breyten Breytenbach writes of his return to South Africa after many years abroad: 'This earth speaks as no earth anywhere else, my people lie buried in this ground ... I love this soil, this land with its people, as the eye loves the light.' Watson also expresses his singular attachment to the land in *A Writer's Diary*: 'You are sustained first and last by this love and by the deep inner assurance, in the face of no matter what historical or personal distress, not least the cynicism of others, that this love is real and worthy of your deepest passion.'

———✳———

It is wonderfully rewarding to engage with the land through the pages of great books, but it's even better to put boots on the ground, text in hand, and experience first-hand something of the authors' relationship with place, to hear the voices of their characters in situ.

This travelogue was conceived as my own love letter to South Africa, marrying places and books that speak to my heart. However, the long period of researching this project has coincided with a growing disillusionment with my homeland, a period that has seen a dramatic increase in crime, corruption, economic depression and the erosion of things I hold dear. It has brought me to the crossroads of possible emigration. JM Coetzee and Stephen Watson present two alternatives: both grappled with the push-me-pull-you nature of living here. In the end, Coetzee opted for the peaceful middle-waters of Australia. After travelling abroad and wrestling with the idea of emigration, Watson concluded that he could never be separated from the landscape he loved, no matter how burning the urge to leave.

I worry that my privileged, white, male, middle-aged, middle-class way of apprehending and appreciating the land is increasingly anachronistic, out of step with a nation heading all-sails-set in another direction. Nature, wilderness, cultural heritage, literature, traditional ways of life and architecture, conservation in all its forms, are under threat from multiple forces in today's South Africa. What's to be done? In the short term, going on a series of walkabouts and seeing what was what in the lands of love and literature did not seem like too bad an idea. As to the bigger decisions, I resolved to kick that can down the farm road for a later reckoning.

Let us, then, set off together on a series of journeys around South Africa with an old kitbag full of books instead of maps to guide us. Let us follow meandering paths through the landscapes of literature, and celebrate how local authors, characters and readers are shaped and inspired by place ... and how this beloved land continues to be shaped by the joyful vagrancy of our footloose imaginations.

———✳———

MOONLIGHT SERENADE

Olive Schreiner's Eastern Karoo

We hike the last stretch to the top and come to a halt beside the grave. A chill wind teases the rooigras and wild sage; clouds cast blue dapples upon a sweeping Karoo tableau. Far below and in every direction lie koppies and valleys veined with green seep lines and dotted with karee and wild olive trees. This exposed mountaintop is the final resting place of Olive Schreiner.

In accordance with her wishes, the famous novelist, along with her husband, Samuel Cronwright, their baby and their dog, was buried here on Buffelskop, a rounded summit in the Bankberg range fifteen kilometres south of Cradock. Due to the ground being too rocky for digging, the tomb is in the shape of a domed sarcophagus.

At last, I am standing beside the final resting place of the mother of South African literature, a site that marks the symbolic beginning of my literary quests.

———✳———

Before Olive Schreiner (1855–1920), 'South African literature' comprised an assortment of travel books and journals, the poetry of Thomas Pringle and a handful of crude adventure novels. With Schreiner, we encounter the first indigenous fiction of international stature. The Eastern Cape locus of *The Story of an African Farm* has been imprinted on the landscape of our nation's letters. Schreiner's corner of the Karoo, so powerfully evoked in the novel, is a wild realm of windswept grasslands, flat-topped koppies and rugged mountains – a sublime environment that tugs at the heartstrings. Embarking on the first of my literary journeys, I wanted to visit the places that served as inspiration for her great novel and learn how the alchemy of her imagination had transfigured and immortalised these spaces.

African Farm is usually thought of as a novel of ideas – religious, political, philosophical, feminist – with some remarkable characterisation, but it is also, I would argue, a landscape novel whose characters are rooted in and shaped by the eastern Karoo. Schreiner was the first South African writer to truly capture the brooding spirit of this land, its compelling fascination, its light and moods, its vastness, and its powerful effect on the soul. Her novel brims with a love of the veld and is everywhere populated with the typical flora of aloes, milk bushes and kiepersols, with beetles, butterflies and cock-o-veets (bokmakieries), and always set against the commanding backdrop of ironstone koppies and blue-domed sky. We see the dreamy beauty of a moonlit homestead, taste the dusty heat of the drought-wracked veld, smell the incense of mimosa blossoms and hear the haunting call of the southern boubou.

My own visits to the Karoo as a child have left a similarly indelible impression. For me, it's the clank and splash of a Climax windmill, the gruff barking of baboons in a kloof, horizons punctuated by flat-topped koppies, willow-lined watercourses, blue mountains and a spare vegetation of scrub and succulents. In winter, the cold eats into your marrow, snow decks the peaks and frost greets the dawn. In summer, the cicada-shrill heat drives every creature into the shade and the land shimmers with fata morgana. A place of extremes: once the Karoo has sunk its barbs into your flesh, you're hooked for life.

Schreiner spent her early childhood moving from town to town in the Eastern Cape. After her father's insolvency and the collapse of the family home, she ended up in Cradock in 1867 at the age of twelve. Her eldest brother, Theo, had taken up a post as headmaster of a local school. They were joined by her older sister, Henrietta, and younger brother, Will. The Schreiner siblings lived in a small house on Cross Street until 1870, when Theo and Will set off to seek their fortunes on the diamond fields. Henrietta stayed on in Cradock to run a school, while Olive left to become a governess in Barkly East. She returned to the district in 1875 to work for the Fouché family at Klein Gannahoek, where she began writing *The Story of an African Farm*. The novel progressed slowly as she moved from one governess posting to another in the region: to the Martins family at Ratelhoek in 1876, to the Cawoods at Gannahoek in 1879 and later that year, back to the Fouchés, now residing at Leliekloof.

By 1880 she'd finished the manuscript, and the following year set sail for England, where she remained for the rest of the decade. Published in 1883, *African Farm* was an immediate success, bringing her into contact with

London's intellectuals and writers – notably Havelock Ellis, Rider Haggard, Edward Carpenter and Eleanor Marx, daughter of Karl – influential figures who helped shape her social and political ideas. In 1889, she returned to the Cape a famous woman and became a prominent intellectual, adopting progressive causes ranging from pacifism and feminism to socialism and the fight against racism.

Although I didn't know to what extent the farm of Schreiner's novel was a fabrication of her imagination, I nevertheless wanted to find if not the exact homestead, then at least the milieu of *African Farm*. After initial research, and a series of emails and phone calls, the prospective journey began to take shape. More precisely, it was embraced by a group of Eastern Cape curators and researchers, and it appeared that I would simply need to fall in with an itinerary they were devising for me. The team at NELM (National English Literary Museum, now renamed Amazwi), based in Grahamstown (renamed Makhanda), was particularly helpful. When its Schreiner experts began lobbing reading lists, photographs and academic papers in my direction, I knew I was in just the right hands.

I set off up the N1 from Cape Town one grey autumn day, bound for the eastern Karoo. After a leisurely day's drive, I took a right at Hanover, approaching Cradock from the northwest. Coming over a rise, the town was laid out below me in a crook of the Great Fish River where the Karoo's characteristic open plains give way to hill country and mountains. For a small platteland town, Cradock has produced a disproportionate number of illustrious sons and daughters, from leaders such as Paul Kruger, Sir Abe Bailey and Matthew Goniwe to writers such as Guy Butler and Etienne van Heerden. The town was founded by Sir John Cradock in 1812 as a frontier stronghold and developed into an attractive settlement with fine vernacular architecture and streets wide enough to turn an ox wagon.

The Cradock that Schreiner encountered in the 1860s was a pleasant Karoo dorp of whitewashed houses, garden plots filled with fruit trees, and roads lined with willows, cypresses and sluits gurgling with water. The town centre had a large square where wagons would unload produce from the countryside: animal skins, pumpkins, firewood and bags of mielies.

The square was flanked by the Victoria Hotel, the social hub of Cradock where men gathered each morning on the stoep to drink brandy and soda, smoke and gossip.

Schreiner had grown up in villages further east and Cradock offered a harsher and more spectacular environment than she was accustomed to. But the adolescent soon grew to love the stark beauty of her new home and was captivated by the colours of the landscape, the shimmering greys of a midsummer's day, the luxuriant greens and mimosa yellows after rain, the golden sunsets when the mountains matched the sky for splendour.

I checked into a self-catering cottage on Mark Street, one of the Victorian Tuishuise, restored and furnished with antiques by Sandra Antrobus, owner of the adjacent Victoria Manor Hotel. The houses have wide verandas with curved, corrugated-iron roofs painted with colourful stripes. Originally belonging to village folk and craftspeople, many tuishuise were later bought by farmers as town residences, especially for Nagmaal visits.

Victoria Manor was one of the first hotels on the eastern frontier and Schreiner was a regular patron. Although it was burnt down, rebuilt, restored and adapted over time, wandering its creaky-floored interiors you still get a strong sense of its long history. You almost expect a transport rider or gold prospector to walk through the door, dust off his hat and order a whisky. The rooms have gleaming antiques and Victorian paintings; the scarlet-walled dining hall has polished silverware, candelabras and vases overflowing with roses. The receptionist confided – conspiratorially, sotto voce – that Boer prisoners of war had been incarcerated in the basement as though it were current town gossip rather than century-old history.

In the late afternoon, I took a stroll through town, admiring the lovely mix of Karoo-style cottages, gabled Cape Dutch houses and Victorian buildings decked in cast-iron broekie-lace. On Bree Street, I passed the Wesleyan Methodist Church (1842) and St Peter's Anglican Church (1858), coming at last to the grand NG Kerk whose clocktower dominates the town. Its consecration in 1868 was the event of the year attended by more than 2 000 people. This temple-like church – a replica of London's St Martin-in-the-Fields – is a neoclassical sandstone edifice with elegant proportions, yellowwood interiors and a pulpit of Burmese teak.

Admiring its handsome façade, I was reminded of Schreiner's description of reluctant churchgoing in *African Farm*: 'The townspeople rustle in their silks, and the men in their sleek cloth, and settle themselves in their pews, and the light shines in through the windows on the artificial flowers in the women's bonnets ... We wish our father hadn't brought us to town, and we were out on the karroo ... Would it not be more worship of Him to sit alone in the karroo and kiss one little purple flower that He had made?'

Next morning, I visited the Schreiner House, an attractive, flat-roofed cottage with green shutters, flagstone stoep and vine pergola. The museum is a satellite of Amazwi and has four main rooms and a stoepkamer, with a kitchen garden and cistern out back. I met curator Brian Wilmot on the veranda. 'Welcome to the world of Schreiner, glad you got here safely from the Big Smoke,' he said, shaking my hand firmly and ushering me into his stoepkamer office.

Brian has dark, bushy eyebrows framed by round spectacles and the white handlebar moustache of a military man. A former curator of the Albany Museum in Makhanda, he moved to Cradock as a form of semi-retirement, although you'd hardly believe it given the Schreiner museum's many activities. Brian prepared two cups of instant Nescafé (half powder, half water, I noticed with apprehension) while relating the history of the house. My coffee tasted vaguely of dynamite and left me shaking and mildly hallucinatory for the rest of the morning.

'Restoration required a good deal of detective work,' said Brian. 'The house had been much altered over the years, no original doors or windows survived, the floors were of concrete and the fireplaces had been removed.

The idea was to restore the building to the period of Schreiner's habitation in the 1860s.'

'Which was Olive's room?' I asked.

'We're not sure, but it's highly likely that this stoepkamer was hers. For a budding author, it would have been a lot quieter than the main house. She wrote some of her early short stories here. Locals used to see her pacing up and down the street outside, muttering to herself, no doubt teasing out her plots. Come, let me show you around.'

We walked through the two front rooms – one had served as the parlour, the other as a bedroom – with their wide-beamed, yellowwood floors. Brian pointed out exhibits depicting Schreiner's life and a shelf with books from her personal library. I ran my eye along the spines: Darwin, Gibbon, Goethe, Huxley, Ruskin. There was a living-dining room at the end of a central corridor and a kitchen with a misvloer and large hearth. 'The turquoise walls might look a bit odd, but back in the day they used to mix arsenic with the paint to repel flies, hence the colour,' explained Brian.

The cottage must have felt somewhat claustrophobic for a spirited girl such as Olive. Her older brother and sister were disciplinarians and devout Christians, forcing her to attend church despite her growing atheism. The social life of Cradock would have been no less constricting, its townsfolk seeking to uphold 'English standards', keeping up with the fashions of the home country, hosting tea parties and concerts by lamplight, cricket on the weekends and genteel parlour conversation. Little of this appealed to Olive; however, the well-stocked local library did provide the intellectual stimulation she craved. John Stuart Mill's *A System of Logic* and Herbert Spencer's *First Principles* (which she first read in 1871) were important works, helping her develop the philosophical and spiritual groundwork for her later writing.

The town's English inhabitants held themselves aloof from the Dutch and black populations, and turned their backs on the African wilderness at their doorstep. This was a time when wild animals and even San were still hunted in the kloofs, when skirmishes with the Xhosa were commonplace and the harsh climate exacted a heavy toll on farmers. Crinolines and top hats, drawing-room poetry and good manners were bulwarks against the wilds beyond. Schreiner was to rebel against the strictures imposed by church, society and family, and her rejection of English prejudice was reinforced when she took up various governess posts on Dutch farms, growing to appreciate the simple Boer way of life.

Brian had returned to his office, leaving me alone in the parlour to mull over the exhibits. I pictured Olive sitting reading, the sounds of her siblings echoing from the other rooms. An early photo on the wall fleshed out my imagining. There she sat, dressed in her pinafore, a short and feisty teenager with long brown hair and dark, mesmerising eyes. She appears intense, rapt in a world of her own: there's so much raw talent in there that wants out. Olive gets up abruptly and exits, slamming the front door behind her. From the window, I can see her pacing back and forth, head bowed, muttering. She strides to the end of Cross Street and stops to look out at the veld, taking in the magnificent view of the Bankberg and Gannahoek mountains to the southwest. Among those peaks is Buffelskop, which will one day mark her final resting place.

The Story of an African Farm is a novel of contentious ideas written in an experimental style with a surprisingly modern, episodic structure. There are frank portrayals of free thought, premarital sex and transvestism – all radical topics at the time. The narrative turns around the lives of three characters – Lyndall, Waldo and Em – first as children, then as adults. Waldo is the son of the affable and gentle farm manager, Otto Farber. Tant' Sannie is the ignorant and tyrannical owner of the farm; Em is her stepdaughter and Lyndall her orphaned niece. The latter most closely resembles Schreiner, a headstrong and precocious girl who riles against the conservative milieu in which she finds herself.

Despite its loose structure, the book can be divided into three sections. The first deals with the childhood of its three protagonists, charting Waldo's increasing disillusionment with Christianity and the development of Lyndall's ideas about feminism and free thought. Waldo and Lyndall become soulmates; Em remains a cheerful, friendly and unquestioning child. The antagonist of this section is an itinerant Englishman, Bonaparte Blenkins, who passes himself off as a wealthy businessman fallen on hard times. His real aim is to win Tant' Sannie's hand in marriage and so acquire the farm. He is cruel to the children and manages to get Waldo's father fired, the old man dying of a heart attack soon after, but Tant' Sannie eventually discovers

Bonaparte's chicanery and boots him off the farm.

The second section deals primarily with Waldo's transition from dogmatic Christianity to despairing atheism. As a child, he is oppressed by the idea of a wrathful God and tormented by notions of Hell and damnation. A period of anguish is followed by a turn to atheism, which is succeeded by his falling for the beauty of nature and the initiation of worship of the natural world.

The final section concerns the three characters as adults. Em takes over the farm when Tant' Sannie remarries, while Lyndall and Waldo depart on separate journeys. Lyndall falls pregnant along the way but, as a feminist, makes a pact with the father of her child that they will travel together but not marry. Waldo becomes a transport rider for a time, but eventually returns to the farm where he learns of Lyndall's death and he too dies, presumably of a broken heart. The narrator suggests that both their spirits are returned to the 'Universal Unity'.

The novel offers a sustained criticism of orthodox Christianity, which Schreiner rejected as a young girl after the death of her infant sister. Her faith was replaced by a tough atheism that was later tempered by a form of freethinking mysticism. From an early age she turned to the natural world, and her immediate Karoo environment in particular, for solace. In a letter to Francis Smith in 1907 she writes: 'My childhood was so very bitter and dark, but I cling to the memories of it and especially the places I lived at, they were so unutterably lovely and it was in nature I found all the joy and help I had in those lonely years.'

Similarly, as children her characters Lyndall and Waldo are beaten to instil the piety demanded in a Calvinist household but, like their creator, both rebel and try to fashion an alternative philosophical and spiritual path. Schreiner greatly admired Spencer's *First Principles*, which addresses the conflict between Christianity and an emerging rationalist science. The book presented the novelist, and by extension her two protagonists, with a middle path between the extremes of parental dogma and atheism. She noted how Spencer helped her 'to believe in a unity underlying all nature', and through his writing she came to understand that all matter was 'alive', that the social order reflected a deeper biological order and that progress was a natural law underpinning all organic creation.

———✳———

MOONLIGHT SERENADE

On my second day in Cradock, Brian introduced me to Basil Mills, senior education officer at Amazwi, who had driven up from Makhanda to spend a few days showing me the Schreiner sites. Basil is a shaggy, golden bear of a man with a mischievous twinkle in his eye, a large moustache, blond hair to his shoulders, matching khakis and an ever-present leather bush hat. He looks as though he's stepped straight from the pages of a Rider Haggard novel. Apart from his work at Amazwi, Basil is a jack of many trades and has spent time as an archaeologist, geologist, builder, artist, historian, farmer, battlefield re-enactment participant and reptile tamer.

Brian had filled me in on the background of my prospective guide. As a boy, Basil spent his school holidays on horseback roaming the Cradock district, often sleeping rough in the mountains for weeks at a time. There are plenty of colourful anecdotes, such as Basil becoming the star of medieval jousting competitions in Europe, or helping to round up the last wild mountain zebras for relocation to the national park of the same name, or getting himself banned from a Cradock hotel for riding his horse into the pub to order a drink.

Basil is also a man of great generosity. On the basis of one phone call, he'd dropped what he was doing to come and help a stranger with his research. And I could hardly have asked for a better Schreiner guide, as Basil had been involved in the restoration of the Schreiner House and conducted an archaeological dig at Klein Gannahoek, the place where *The Story of an African Farm* is thought to have been penned.

First up, Basil suggested we visit Krantz Plaats, the farm once managed by Schreiner's then husband-to-be, Samuel (Cron) Cronwright. Soon after returning from England, Olive was staying with her friends the Cawoods at Gannahoek, where she met a handsome young farmer from the district. The attraction was immediate and mutual. Olive and Cron were married on 24 February 1894 in Middelburg, after which the couple took up residence at Krantz Plaats. Ironically, when Waldo first finds work in the novel, it was this particular farm that Schreiner had had in mind. In life, she had found a partner who matched her fictional soulmate.

With Basil at the helm, our 4x4 bounced along an overgrown track south of Cradock and drew to a halt near the remains of a house beside the Great Fish River. Apart from some foundations and a section of wall, there was nothing left of the homestead. I recalled a letter to her mother in which Schreiner describes the couple's arrival at the farm straight after their wedding: 'As we drew up before the long dark house, Cron's two dogs, Daphne and Maggie, ran out to meet us, barking and rejoicing; in the voorhuis we found the table laid and a nice fowl on it that Cron's mother had sent up for us ... We rested through the heat of the day, but in the afternoon Cron and I went down to the river and looked at the mimosa trees growing there.'

Basil led me to the edge of a low cliff and we looked down on a bend in the Great Fish lined with tall reeds and mimosas. It was a crisp autumn morning with mist smoking off the land and the sky a deep, navy blue. We scrambled down a rocky slope to the water's edge. 'I've brought along some photocopies of pictures from Cron's album,' said Basil, opening a folder. 'Here's one of him, Olive and Daphne the dog on the riverbank. If you look closely at the shape of the rocks in the pic, you can see this is exactly where they were standing.'

The photograph was taken shortly after the wedding, at their favourite bathing spot. Cron wears a black suit and stands with his hands in his pockets, a dashing fellow with a bushy moustache, looking confident and able – a man of action. Olive is in a black dress and sits beside him staring into the distance appearing introspective, perhaps resigned, but content. She was thirty-eight, had travelled abroad, been fêted as a renowned novelist, but now she had returned to her roots, to a farm in Africa, to settle down with the man she loved. There is much hope captured in this image. Ill health, depression, miscarriages, the death of her baby and war lay in the future, but here at Krantz Plaats, for a few brief months, she was to experience undiluted peace and happiness.

---※---

My particular interest in *African Farm* lies in its treatment of the Eastern Cape landscape and the connection between Schreiner's spiritual beliefs and the natural environment. Her awareness of the emotive power of her surroundings came early in life. In *Thoughts on South Africa*, she suggests that our instinctive response to a particular terrain, to the spirit of place, sends its roots deep into the psyche at a young age: 'There is a certain knowledge of land which is only to be gained by one born in it, or brought into long-continued, close, personal contact with it, and which in its perfection is perhaps never obtained by any man with regard to a country which he has not inhabited before he was thirty.'

Inspired by the Romantic notion of the sublime, Schreiner goes on to define the elements of the land she loves:

> Nevertheless, through the whole of South Africa there runs a certain unity. It is not only that geraniums and plumbago, flat-topped mountains, aloes and cuphorbla are peculiar to our land, and that sand and rocks abound everywhere; nor is it even that the land is everywhere young, and full of promise; but there is a certain colossal plentitude, a certain large freedom in all its natural proportions, which is truly characteristic of South Africa. If Nature here wishes to make a mountain, she runs a range for five hundred miles; if a plain, she levels eighty; if a rock, she tilts five thousand feet of strata on end; our skies are higher and more intensely blue; our waves are larger than others; our rivers fiercer. There is nothing measured, small nor petty in South Africa.

Throughout her life, she gained inspiration and strength from the landscape of her youth and keenly lamented any separation from it. After returning from England, she wrote to Havelock Ellis: 'I love the Karoo. Do you know the effect of this scenery is to make me so silent and strong and self-contained, and it is all so bare, the rocks and the bushes, each bush standing separate from the others, alone by itself.' Schreiner derives an inner stillness from the land, and its 'bareness' embodies a form of purity. She identifies with the hardy individuality of each bush, facing the elements 'alone by itself', just as the lonely artist must do, or someone who has charted a spiritual course outside orthodox Christianity.

In her preface to *African Farm*, she contends that the local artist must 'sadly squeeze the colour from his brush, and dip it into the grey pigments around him' to 'paint what lies before him' and not the 'encounters with ravening lions and hair-breadth escapes' that were the fare of writers such as Rider Haggard who fictionalised the derring-do of colonial adventurers. True to her injunction, she foregrounds the 'grey pigments' of the Karoo landscape in her novel, elevating it from backdrop to abiding, affecting presence.

By the late 1600s, Dutch settlers could begin to claim a degree of identification with the land they'd colonised. The first wave of British settlers arrived in 1820 and it also took them half a century to find a proper place here and start reimagining the landscape in terms that were not derivative of the homeland. In Schreiner, we have an Englishwoman who feels totally in sync with a land that does not hold the threat and alienation it did for a previous generation of British settler; it is the home of an English-speaking native.

Schreiner's farm is embedded in – and almost an emanation of – the landscape. The stones of the kraal match the ironstone boulders of the koppie; the red walls of the homestead grow from the red earth around it. Soil clings to Waldo, symbolically linking him to the land. Place is as much a part of the characters as they are of it, and neither has pre-eminence over the other. In the spirit of the Romantics and Nineteenth-Century English regional novelists, we see how the mood of Schreiner's protagonists is reflected in the landscape. When a character feels oppressed by God, this is mirrored in the brutality of nature; when they sense the benediction of natural spiritualism, the landscape grows more benign. In fact, the land exerts such power that one might think of it as an extra character. Just as in Thomas Hardy's *Return of the Native*, where Egdon Heath is a potent force, the Karoo is one of the novel's protagonists, helping to shape the consciousness of its inhabitants.

Schreiner uses the landscape as a symbol of both freedom and, ultimately, transcendence. Its wide-open spaces and emptiness provide an escape from the constraints of society, gender politics and religion. The Karoo of her mind is a realm for the free play of ideas, provocative exploration and the expression of her own identity. It's a place of the imagination and the heart – a personal, internal Karoo that is both the setting and catalyst for self-discovery, a realm outside society and even time.

Her biographer Karel Schoeman contends that Schreiner transforms the Karoo into a 'symbol of the physical and spiritual freedom that neither she in the South Africa of the [eighteen] seventies nor Lyndall in the context of the novel could ever enjoy.' Consequently, hers is a Karoo 'to be found on no map ... a subjective Karoo, intensely experienced and depicted with equal intensity, which transcends the incidental limits of the actual landscape of the spirit and of the heart.'

From a spiritual perspective, the Karoo becomes an emblem of Nature.

Early in the novel it is presented as blind, cruel and without purpose, an embodiment of 'survival of the fittest'. This idea is given expression when a dog attacks a beetle, destroying its dung ball and biting off the insect's hind legs and head. 'And it was all play, and no one could tell what it had lived and worked for. A striving, and a striving, and an ending in nothing.'

But by the end of the chapter 'Times and Seasons', Waldo no longer looks at nature as a manifestation of a blind and cruel God: 'There on the flat stone, on which we so often have sat to weep and pray, we look down and see it covered with the fossil footprints of great birds, and the beautiful skeleton of a fish.' Here scientific romanticism offers an alternative form of spirituality in which humans are viewed as part of Nature.

Renowned Schreiner scholar Dorothy Driver has noted how Waldo begins to see the rocks not as 'a blur of brown' but as existing in geological time, their 'bands of smooth grey and red methodically overlying each other.' He senses that the stones are talking to him, 'speaking of the old things, of the time when the strange fishes and animals lived that are turned into stone now, and the lakes were here; and then of the time when the little Bushmen lived here.' He looks anew at a bietou plant and realises that its 'flower has been for us a mere blur of yellow; [but now] we find its heart composed of a hundred perfect flowers, the homes of the tiny black people [beetles] with red stripes, who move in and out of their little yellow city.' His eyes have been opened: 'Every day the karroo shows us a new wonder sleeping in its teeming bosom.'

However, for Waldo, as for Schreiner, rejecting Christianity and embracing nature opens the door for the kind of amorality implied by 'survival of the fittest'. In contemplating nature, the narrator fearfully asks: 'How are these things related that should exist between them all? Is it chance?' From the terror of this idea, there is an immediate recoiling to the more comforting: 'Not a chance jumble; a living thing, a *One*. The thought gives us intense satisfaction, we cannot tell why.' Schreiner had found a belief system that avoided the realities of crude Darwinism, of nature red in tooth and claw. 'And so, it comes to pass in time, that the earth ceases for us to be a weltering chaos. We walk in the great hall of life, looking up and round reverentially … The life that throbs in us is a pulsation from it; too mighty for our comprehension.'

Perhaps nowhere in the novel are the contrasting realms of the rational and the spiritual more clearly embodied than in Schreiner's treatment of light. The hot, blinding sunlight of midday that beats down from a cloudless sky represents the world of reality. It is oppressive, unyielding, merciless. By contrast, the mellow, modulated light of early morning and late afternoon – notably the 'yellow sunshine' at the moment of Waldo's death – presents a more benign nature that reveals its metaphysical qualities.

As a child, Schreiner had an experience, described in her essay, 'The Dawn of Civilization', that tells us much about her attitude towards the symbolic power of light. After a sleepless night of worrying about the suffering and injustice of the world, she goes out at dawn to walk beside a river coursing through a deep valley. Then the sun rises, bathing the scene in soft light, 'and, as I looked at that almost intolerable beauty, a curious feeling came over me. It was not what I *thought* put into exact words, but I seemed to see the world in which creatures no more hated and crushed, in which the strong helped the weak, and men understood each other.'

Waldo experiences a similar revelation in a similar setting when he walks along a dry riverbed in the golden light of sunset, the banks rising above him 'like the sides of a room', each drop of water falling on stone with the sound of 'a little silver bell'. The trees are motionless, save for one, which shakes and trembles against the skyline. Waldo is deeply moved: 'Does it seem strange to you that it should have made me so happy? It is because I cannot tell you how near I felt to things that we cannot see but we always feel.' The crucifix-like tree, the tolling bell and the room that reminds us of a church partake of Christian metaphor, but this is instead the cathedral of nature where the unity and harmony of all life and all matter are worshipped.

Above all for Schreiner, it is the light of the moon that offers transcendence. The oft-quoted opening scene of the novel presents the possibilities:

> The full African moon poured down its light from the blue sky into the wide, lonely plain. The dry, sandy earth, with its coating of stunted 'karroo' bushes a few inches high, the low hills that skirted the plain, the milk-bushes with their long, finger-like leaves, all were touched by a weird and almost oppressive beauty as they lay in the white light.

Here it is a non-human character, the Karoo moon, whose mystical light transforms everything it touches. Even a humble clump of prickly pears 'lifted their thorny arms, and reflected, as from mirrors, the moonlight on their broad, fleshy leaves'. The light 'etherealises' a brick wall in front of the house and turns a zinc roof to 'burnished silver'. This is not the benediction of a Christian God, but that of Nature and of the Universal Unity. For Schreiner, there is a life force, represented by the moonlight, running through and connecting all things.

As the scene unfolds, the narrator guides us into the farmhouse where 'white moonlight' floods a bedroom, 'bathing' the sleeping Lyndall. Some inhabitants toss about in the wash of bad dreams, while for others the moon's balm pouring through the windows hides all defects, symbolically conflating moonlight with dream worlds and transfiguration. It represents the realm of the imagination and intuition, as well as the non-rational and spiritual. The moonlight is the very embodiment of the metaphysical aspect of Nature that offered Schreiner an escape. Where the harsh sunlight of reality proposes a Darwinian world of amoral survival, the moon's 'loving' light offers transcendence.

Later in the novel, Schreiner gives flesh to her spiritual beliefs in the 'Allegory of the Hunter' in which a man spends his life climbing a mountain in search of the White Bird of Truth, but finally dies grasping a single feather dropped by the elusive fowl. Not only is this a metaphor for the artist's struggle for truth and grace through métier, but it presents a model for how to live a non-Christian and yet spiritual life.

At one point, the narrator describes a child's powerful recognition of the Karoo's beauty in the form of an epiphany. There's been a thunderstorm and the ground is covered in hail, but the clouds have receded to reveal a rainbow. An 'unutterable longing' comes over the child, who wants to possess the scene: 'we want it, we want – we do not know what. We cry as though our heart is broken.' In this early encounter with the sublime, the child (or 'everychild', implied by 'we') has a boundless capacity for awe. Everyone, Schreiner suggests, has the capacity to appreciate nature's beauty, to understand its spiritual force, and perhaps, like the child, deep down we all yearn to merge with the natural world.

For Lyndall and Waldo, as for Schreiner, it is the land with its fauna and flora, its sunlight and moonlight, that guides their spiritual journeys and brings them to a degree of peace through an understanding of their place in nature, culminating in deaths that enact a merging with the land. In order to ultimately overcome the restrictions of the body, Schreiner imagines death as a mystical undoing, such as that which occurs when Lyndall blends into the Grey Dawn. The merging of Lyndall's body with the landscape symbolises total immersion, the longed-for unification between self and place.

In like manner, as Waldo basks in late afternoon sunshine at the moment of his death, he finds deep satisfaction in contemplating nature: 'There are only rare times when a man's soul can see Nature.' He examines an ice-plant beside him and, as the sun shines through it, marvels at 'every little crystal cell … and it thrilled him.' Only when 'the old hope is dead, when the old desire is crushed, then the Divine compensation of Nature is made manifest. She shows herself to you. So near she draws you, that the blood seems to flow from her to you.'

Only in death, or a living death where 'being' is bled of all 'becoming', is one able to become one with the natural world. For a brilliant young woman trapped in the straitjacket of conservative, Victorian, colonial society, it is appropriate that Schreiner (and Lyndall) found salvation in this ultimate merging with Nature.

---*---

Schreiner began writing *The Story of an African Farm* at Klein Gannahoek, but it is not known how much of the first draft was completed there. Cronwright's insistence that this was the 'home' of the book, and not any of the other farms where Schreiner worked as a governess, may be due to the fact that it was adjacent to his own beloved Krantz Plaats. Even if some of the manuscript was completed elsewhere, the novel's genesis was at Klein Gannahoek and much of the story's setting and environment found inspiration there.

Schreiner started working as a governess for the Fouché family in February 1875. She was about to enter one of the most contented and productive periods of her life, when relative independence and privacy allowed her to focus on developing her creativity. In a letter to Miss McNaughton, whom she had met while working as a governess in Colesburg, she wrote:

> The six months I have passed here [at Klein Gannahoek] have been the most uninterruptedly happy of my whole life ... This is a wild beautiful place. The farmhouse is perched high up on the side of one of the mountains and the bush which comes down to the garden is as unman-defiled and wild as one can wish, and I have only to teach for five or six hours a day and the rest of my time I can spend out of doors or in my own little room studying.

As Virginia Woolf famously avowed, having a room of one's own and an income are essential requirements for women writers. Schreiner was able to explore the veld on her own, something that would have been awkward for an unchaperoned Englishwoman in a town setting. Her letters and diary entries of the period show a growing love for the landscape. From her hosts, she learnt the names of plants and animals and took an interest in the area's geology and palaeontology. A diary entry of 25 March 1875 is typical: 'It is such a glorious morning but I won't go out, I must write. Through the door I can see the hills casting such beautiful shadows and I think I never saw the light through the branches of a tree look so beautiful as it did through the apple and apricot trees in front of the house.'

Klein Gannahoek lies some thirty kilometres south of Cradock overlooking a picturesque valley dotted with kiepersol and sweet-thorn acacia trees with the muscular Gannahoek Mountains as backdrop. Basil drove me through ganna-veld alive with springbok and black wildebeest until we came to a rough track that led up a slope to the ruins of the farmhouse. My imagination immediately began to conjure scenes from the book: Waldo striding to the ostrich pens with a bag of mielies slung over his shoulder, a faithful white dog with a yellow ear at his heels; merino sheep being herded into a kraal; Lyndall and Em dressed in blue pinafores and homemade veldskoens relaxing in the shade of a wild olive tree.

'This is all that's left of the Fouché homestead,' said Basil as we parked beside the ruin and got out. 'With the help of funding from NELM, I spent ages clearing the site and wrote a paper about it for *Southern African Field Archaeology*. I thought this place was really special and needed to be recorded. As far as I'm concerned, this is the birthplace of the South African novel. Being here on my own was quite magical, sleeping under the stars, communing with Olive.'

As we walked around the site, my thoughts oscillated between Schreiner's and Lyndall's worlds, trying to superimpose both the real and the fictional farmhouses onto the ruin. Here was the novel's 'great open waggon-house' with its zinc roof and 'outbuildings that jutted from its side', the 'stone-walled "sheep kraals" and Kaffir huts'. Nearby was the ravine in whose boulder-strewn stream Olive used to wash … or was it Lyndall? All that remained of the outbuildings was rubble, overgrown with weeds. Behind them the ground rose steeply towards a dam, and beyond lay bushy slopes culminating in cliffs.

In the novel *From Man to Man, or Perhaps Only* Schreiner provides a description of what is doubtless the Klein Gannahoek landscape:

> In the bush that covered the mountain sides were leopards, who came down at night and carried off lambs from the kraals; in the tall trees in the bush were little grey, long-tailed monkeys, and wood-doves, and cock-o-veets, who cried and called all day; in the rocks that crowned the mountain troops of baboons climbed and fought; and down in the valley among the thorn-trees were mier-kats and great tortoises, and hares who paid visits to the lands.

Basil led me past the remnants of ostrich and sheep pens, a fenced-off graveyard and a grassy patch that had once been an orchard of orange, lemon and fig trees, before circling back to the ruined house.

'From the outline of the foundations, Olive's descriptions and Cron's photographs, I had a pretty good idea of what the building looked like in the 1870s,' he said. 'My task was like a jigsaw puzzle and I loved piecing it all together. The house faced east, with a thatched roof, open stoep and shuttered windows.'

All that remained of the homestead were bits of the stone-flagged stoep, a clay-brick wall and some foundations. 'This would have been the voorkamer which served as a general living area,' said Basil as we paced the outline of the floor plan.

In *Thoughts on South Africa*, Schreiner describes an early morning scene in a voorkamer that must surely be Klein Gannahoek:

> In the front room, as we enter, we find the father already up,

leaning over the half-door with the pipe in his mouth to scan the darkness; the Kaffir maid has come and made fire in the kitchen, you can hear the crackling of the wood in the large room, and the eldest daughter slips out of her chamber and takes the tallow candle from the table to go to the back and make coffee. Presently the house-mother and the younger children, the last still without their jackets and dresses, come in and sit about the room, some holding their vel-schoens sleepily in their hands. Through the top of the open door you can see a streak of grey dawnlight along the far-off horizon and by the time the coffee comes it is almost light in the room; the tallow candle is blown out, and except in the dark corner, you can see all the faces.

Above the front room lay the loft, now wide-open sky. It was from up there that Tant' Sannie overheard Blenkins courting her niece, precipitating his ejection from the farm. It was also in the loft that Waldo found his treasure trove of books, and Gregory discovered the woman's clothes he wore during his first ventures into transvestism.

'This wing was added to the northern end of the building,' said Basil, picking up a sun-baked brick beside the only section of remaining wall. 'It was Olive's room. Digging around here I found pencil shards and a few pieces of slate stone, possibly used by Olive or the Fouché children during her classes.'

He flipped open his folder of photocopies. One image of a simple lean-to structure, taken in 1893, was captioned in Cron's tiny handwriting: 'The room in which *The Story of an African Farm* was written.' Schreiner described it as having a leaky corrugated-iron roof and no ceiling. When it rained hard, she would sit under an umbrella and make a furrow in the floor to lead the water out the doorway. There was a bedstead, a box to hold her clothes, and Mill's *Logic* at arm's reach. In later life, she recalled this leaky room with great affection: 'I have been thinking just now with such longing of my little bedroom at Ganna Hoek with its hole in the roof and the stars shining through.'

Basil wandered off and I positioned myself in the most likely place Schreiner would have sat writing. I pictured a small sash window offering uninterrupted views of Van Heerdenskloof and the peaks beyond. As it faced north, sunlight would have streamed in throughout the day, and by night the moonlight. It was in this very spot, give or take a metre or two, that the famous story of an Eastern Cape farm took shape. Here she read and wrote by candlelight, or even by the glow of the full moon (Mrs Fouché was reluctant to grant more than a candle stub for her room, as 'nobody was any good who wanted a candle except to go to bed').

I tried to summon Schreiner's spirit, imagined her moving about this space, now exposed to the wild. She would no doubt approve of how the house had returned to nature. Standing in that enchanted place I wondered, too, about Schreiner's isolation, far from family and friends her own age. The unchanging rhythms of farm life would have constituted her entire world. Then again, this isolated setting provided the ideal incubator for an artist of Schreiner's temperament and served to concentrate her creativity. Her imagination could play out the loves, fears and dreams of a young girl on a farm in the Karoo wilderness without distraction or interruption.

I walked up the slope and climbed onto the remains of the dam wall. Doves trilled in the stillness, sunbirds chirruped in the bushes, the valley was filled with that soporific peacefulness so characteristic of a Karoo afternoon. I looked across the valley at the encircling hills whose colour and texture changed continually with the movement of the sun and passing clouds. In the distance lay the crumbling wall of a kraal, last vestige of the adjoining farm where Schreiner used to spend her free time, the home of the Cawoods before they moved to their grand Gannahoek manor house further up the valley.

We climbed back in the 4x4 and drove down the hill to the site of the former Cawood cottage. Not even the foundations remained. 'Erilda Cawood became a close friend and mother figure to Olive, who grew to depend on the older woman's support and approval,' said Basil. 'On Friday afternoons after her teaching was done, Olive would walk down from the Fouchés and spend the weekends here. The Cawood children adored Olive and would watch the path for a first sighting of her.'

Basil explained that the Cawood cottage had been a simple, flat-roofed structure with three rooms and a kitchen. Living was cramped and Schreiner had to sleep in a cot. Nevertheless, weekends were full of games and laughter, with the young governess reading humorous stories and fairy tales to the children, some of them in German, which she translated. There were hours of conversation and needlework with Erilda, and Olive took the opportunity to test some of her own writing on the older woman.

In 1879, Erilda asked Olive to become governess to her children and she moved from the Fouchés to the grand, new Gannahoek homestead where she continued working on *African Farm*. By this stage, the manuscript was probably far advanced and one might assume she was busy with revision and editing.

Basil and I headed up the valley to Gannahoek, a home-from-home Schreiner was to continue visiting throughout her life. In a letter to socialist/philosopher Edward Carpenter in 1892, she describes the farm as a

> beautiful place, one of the most beautiful in the world … The wild bush of mimosa thorns comes right down to the house and it's full of wild animals … I like to feel this wild, untamed life with 'the will to live' still strong and untamed in it, seething about one. It makes the old strength come back into one's heart. It's beautifully hot here. *You* know how lovely that is, the fierce clear sunlight shining full on you. Yesterday I went alone on the top of a kopje and took off all my clothes and wandered about for hours in the hot dry sand and thorn bushes.

Basil drew up at Gannahoek, a Cape Dutch-inspired house with squat rounded gables and bay windows set in a garden of sloping lawns and mature, shady trees. Christopher Cawood – tall, safari outfit, boots with gaiters –

invited us for coffee beneath stuffed kudu heads staring glassy eyed at us from the wall (these days, Gannahoek is primarily a game farm catering to wealthy international hunters). Pointing at a faded photo of three women in Victorian dress, Christopher said, 'Schreiner was governess to those gracious ladies, my ancestral Cawood aunts.'

It was in this house that Olive met Cron in 1892. 'I shall never forget the quick glance and the strangeness of her presence,' he wrote, recalling how she spoke with a vibrant ringing tone that entranced him, her face animated so that 'the compelling force of her genius, the rapidity and brilliance of her intellect, simply blazed through it.'

---※---

Driving back to Cradock later that afternoon, I was thinking about the landscape of Gannahoek and how its beauty had so captivated and inspired Schreiner. Landscape in the form of a farm – a domesticated landscape or 'nurtured nature' – occupies a powerful place in the South African psyche. The plaasroman (farm novel) is an important genre in Afrikaans literature and Schreiner's great book offers a sophisticated, English alternative to it. During the late Nineteenth and early Twentieth Centuries, the 'boereplaas' acquired a number of myths that were fundamental to white notions of belonging: taming the land, oneness with the soil, harvesting the bounty of nature for the greater good and, ultimately, a sense of identity that became a foundation of nationalism. These ideas were all given expression in the plaasroman.

In post-apartheid South Africa, the place of the farm in white culture has undergone a radical shift. As farm attacks and demands for land restitution increase, a clash of ideologies has been inevitable. The formerly dispossessed have begun to assert their claims, sometimes using violence as reinforcement, and government's ham-fisted attempts at various forms of redistribution, redress and policing have only added to the problem.

The realm of timeless harmony that the farm was once thought to represent has become a site of struggle. What farmers used to see as the benefits of a rural existence – isolation, living in nature, cheap labour, being master of all you surveyed – have become the very elements that threaten them. As Malvern van Wyk Smith points out in a paper entitled 'From

"Boereplaas" to Metamyth', where the farm was once the epitome of freedom, it is now a trap and a prison, in both a personal and an ideological sense.

In *White Writing*, JM Coetzee notes how the plaasroman has its roots in the pastoral literature of the American West, asserting the virtues of the garden – simplicity, peace, immemorial usage – against the vices of industrialisation and the city. Such literature presents a nostalgic, backward look at the tranquillity and stability of farm life, located at a still point between the wilderness of lawless nature and the wilderness of the city. For a settler nation, and particularly the Afrikaner, the retrospective gaze was always more reassuring than looking too closely at the present or future of a farming existence.

The feudal farm, safe in its fastness and worked by loyal native serfs, is a familiar colonial trope, as can be seen in similar writing from elsewhere in Africa. The initial dispossession of the land by whites is forgotten and the farmer becomes a benign patriarch ruling his subjects in a kingdom outside time and history. Coetzee claims (writing before the publication of Marlene van Niekerk's *Agaat*) that Schreiner is the great anti-pastoral South African novelist. Elements of the farm life in Schreiner's novel mimic the ignorance, idleness and greed of colonial society. Far from sitting outside history, the farm embodies all the complex relationships and tensions of Nineteenth-Century frontier living and colonial society. As such, Schreiner's novel is an anti-plaasroman, prefiguring by more than a century the kind of farm novel that has emerged in post-apartheid South Africa, where farm murders are the haunting spectre and 'ownership' becomes increasingly tenuous.

In contrast to the farm of traditional plaasromans, Schreiner's is set in a wild, barren plain that is more a product of nature than of labour. The personal, Calvinistic god of the Afrikaner farmer has been replaced by a great absence, which the protagonists try to fill with a veneration of nature. The novel's emphasis on the vast trajectories of time that take in palaeontology, dinosaur fossils and millennia of San habitation, undercuts the plaasroman's delusions of permanence and ownership.

The society of Schreiner's farm also mimics the hierarchies of frontier society, with servants who wash the feet of their masters, mute labourers and tensions between Boer and Brit. She shows us all the bigotry, closed mindedness and ennui of farm existence. In this place of contradictions, there is little space to conduct an honest, fulfilling life: you either remain naively ignorant (like farm manager Otto), you leave (as Lyndall does), you put yourself at the mercy of Nature (like Waldo) or you surrender to the inequality and brutality of rural society (as most other farm dwellers do).

In *African Farm*, then, the landscape serves as both backdrop and mirror to the society that tries to impose itself. In the end, humans never manage to tame the land and Schreiner implies that the best one can do is to follow its lead and submit to its will, its spiritual order. Redemption from the ideology of the plaasroman is to be found, then, in forging a spiritual connection with the land.

---—✷—---

One crisp autumn day in 1894, soon after their wedding, Olive and Cron climbed Buffelskop, the imposing peak to the west of Krantz Plaats. Due to her asthmatic condition, Olive found the going strenuous, but once on top she was spellbound. She had a deep love for the Cape's mountains and it's no wonder that she wished to be buried on the summit of this exposed mount adjoining Klein Gannahoek, Gannahoek and Krantz Plaats, all of them sites of great personal happiness. In *The Life of Olive Schreiner*, Cronwright describes the moment of her decision: 'Before we went down she said: "We must be buried here, you and I, Cron. I shall buy one morgen of this top and we must be buried up here." It jumped with my own desire, and so it came to be decided.' Later in life, Schreiner often recalled their ascent, the sublime panorama and her spontaneous decision to make Buffelskop their final resting place. After the death of her baby daughter in 1895, she found comfort in the idea that the tiny coffin would one day lie beside hers on the summit.

A narrow jeep track climbs the mountain behind Gannahoek. The views grew more spectacular at every switchback as Basil's 4x4 clawed up the slope, whining in low range. Tarn-like dams and ochre sandstone outcrops lined the route; grey rhebuck took flight at the sound of our engine. When the 4x4 could go no further, we continued on foot. Ironstone boulders clinked at our footfall and the way was lined with aloes flaming scarlet in their autumnal bloom.

Reaching the summit, we came to the igloo-like sarcophagus. This ascent to visit Schreiner's grave has become something of a pilgrimage for South African writers, with the likes of Guy Butler, Athol Fugard, Richard Rive and

Don Maclennan having scaled these heights to pay their respects. Basil and I stood gazing at a vista that had changed little since Schreiner's day. To the northwest lay the sweeping plains and dolerite koppies of the Great Karoo; in every other direction were peaks of the Winterberg and Elandsberg ranges – tall, dappled and beguiling. The valley below was home to Klein Gannahoek, site of Schreiner's greatest creation: in death, she had returned to her African farm. The Karoo landscape of her mind, her life story and her immortality, the interment of her body and her symbolic merging with nature had all come together in this place.

In 1921, on the eve of her burial, Cron wrote:

> Tomorrow she will be carried on the shoulders of the natives (which would have pleased her) and once more she'll be on the beloved kop: then the ironstone grave will be closed on all that is left of her and her child and her dog, and we shall leave her alone on that wonderful peak; no, not alone, but with the 'wild nature' she loved so intensely, with the immense vault of the Karroo sky, with her 'African stars' above her...

Basil pointed out the route followed by the funeral party from the dam far below, up the side of a koppie, through a gap in the cliff line and along an ironstone ridge towards the summit. It took the bearers of the three coffins two days to reach the top. At one point during the climb, there was an impromptu salute as a large white bird, probably a Cape vulture, soared over the party. Cron invoked the novel's 'Allegory of the Hunter', imagining Olive's soul hovering above Buffelskop 'in endless delight, like her "vast white bird with silver wings outstretched sailing in the everlasting blue."'

'Look!' said Basil. As if on cue, a Verreaux's eagle cruised by at eye level, its black-and-white wings beating slowly, before taking up station on a thermal above us. I was reminded of Roy Campbell's famous poem, 'Buffels Kop', in memory of Schreiner:

> In after times when strength or courage fail,
> May I recall this lonely hour: the gloom
> Moving one way: all heaven in the pale
> Roaring: and high above the insulated tomb

An eagle anchored on full spread of sail
That from its wings let fall a silver plume.

Basil cut into my thoughts: 'When Cron died a few years later, they couldn't find the map to the keystone – it was actually in the Cawood family Bible – so the undertakers simply lopped off the top of the sarcophagus and lowered his coffin in. They didn't do such a great job closing it again, which is why I wanted to reseal it properly.'

'You opened the grave!' I exclaimed.

'Ja, I came up here for a few days with my chaps. The superstitious buggers stood a good distance back when I pulled away the keystone.' He chuckled. 'The setting sun reflected off the brass of the coffins and bathed me in light. My guys thought it was Olive's ghost – petrified, they were – but we had a good laugh about it around the braai that night.'

The sun was melting on the horizon as we returned to the car. On the way down the mountain, I asked Basil to stop at the lip of a cliff above Klein Gannahoek, got out and walked to the edge. Although the western sky still held wisps of orange, the valley was already sunk in deep shadow. I imagined a flicker of light coming from a window far below …

It's almost suppertime in the Fouché household. A tallow candle burns on the table in the voorkamer. Mother is seated in her elbow chair; Father stands at the half-open door smoking his pipe. The children and their young

English governess troop in and take their places in the high-backed chairs. When the eldest daughter announces that the food is ready, they pull their chairs around the table where thick slices of bread and a large dish filled with hunks of boiled mutton is served.

Schreiner is completely immersed in this world, this farm, this corner of Africa she has grown to love. She is exactly where she needs to be for her genius to unfold. In later life she will never truly regain her creative centre. Her energy will dissipate itself in political pursuits and intense activity; her asthma and ill health will debilitate her, and personal tragedies, especially the death of her baby and further miscarriages, will drain her. This is Olive's time; this is Olive's place.

Basil starts the engine. We must be off the mountain before dark, but my mind wants to play out this last scene. I glance back into the valley: the eldest daughter is pouring coffee for everyone. Olive downs a cup, makes her excuses and says goodnight. She enters a little room off the stoep, lights a precious candle and settles herself on the bed. Taking out a notebook, she begins to write: 'The full African moon poured down its light from the blue sky into the wide, lonely plain …'

The vision of a young woman alone in a cold room at the foot of this brooding mountain has affected me more than I might have imagined. Basil sounds the hooter. I walk slowly back to the car.

---※---

JOCK BEFOK
Sir Percy FitzPatrick's Lowveld

A heavy object lands on my bed with a thud. Reluctantly I open my eyes. It's still early and a beam of soft light angles from the bedroom window. Our new Staffordshire bull terrier puppy has climbed the stairs to my attic room, seeking attention. I glance at the alarm clock on the bedside table beside a worn copy of *Jock of the Bushveld*. Soon I'll have to get up and get ready for school. Astie begins creeping along the side of my body, nosing against the blankets. He's khaki in colour, with a black snout and amber eyes; there's a guilty smile on his podgy face and a pink tongue lolling from his mouth. I reach out a hand to stroke his head as he nuzzles the pillow with a whimper of delight. I start to doze again with my dog beside me, his moist eyes watching my face. The last thing I remember before nodding off is the gentle thump of his wagging tail against my hip.

When I awake, four decades have passed. The child is now a middle-aged man and Astie has long been roaming the Elysian Fields of hound heaven, but I still vividly recall his joyful bounding across the lawn, his whining indignation at being given a bath, the yelps and twitches of his animated dreams, his droopy-eyed sadness at being left alone, the way he tickled his own back by creeping through the bougainvillea in a trance of pleasure. Sometimes, I still catch myself feeling a sharp ache for my boyhood companion.

Jock of the Bushveld is the true story of a man and his bull terrier during the early days of the Transvaal gold rush. As a young man, Percy 'Fitz' FitzPatrick (1862–1931) found employment as a transport rider ferrying goods between the port of Lourenço Marques and the gold fields. In those pioneering days before the advent of the railway, provisions of every kind were in high demand and stood at famine prices in mining towns such as Lydenburg, Pilgrim's Rest and Barberton.

FitzPatrick joined a colourful band of wagon drivers, bootleggers, diggers and remittance men trekking back and forth between the coast and the gold fields. Fitz and his indomitable bull terrier, Jock, crisscrossed the Lowveld for four years, sleeping under the stars, shooting for sport and for the pot and getting themselves into all manner of scrapes. *Jock of the Bushveld* recounts their tales of adventure and derring-do, and although there is much gratuitous hunting and cruelty, unacceptable today but the norm for the period, *Jock* is also the story of a man and his hound exploring and growing to love their wilderness environment.

As historian Saul Dubow has pointed out, *Jock* embodies the kind of 'South Africanism', under the umbrella of empire, that the state was trying to awaken after the disastrous and divisive Anglo-Boer War. The book has a cast of characters – Boer, British and black – whose identities are more genuinely South African than the stereotypes of imperial writers such as John Buchan and Rider Haggard. The Lowveld setting, too, is authentically evoked and *Jock* is bathed in nostalgia for frontier days when the bush was as yet untamed and the pioneering venture still in full swing.

FitzPatrick creates the impression that the opening up of the Drakensberg escarpment and Lowveld was an almost exclusively British endeavour and presents the frontier as a tabula rasa, for the most part forgetting the presence of centuries of black, and more recent Afrikaner, habitation. Jock is an imperial dog with all the privileges of his master, full of individuality, swagger and enterprise. Critic Stephen Gray goes so far as to suggest that rather than mere frontier adventurism, FitzPatrick's story is about 'annexation, pacification, conquest and subjugation' and abounds with snobbery and racism (much of it tempered or excised in recent versions edited by Linda Rosenberg). '*Jock* is designed to inculcate empire building ideals, and inculcate them young,' argues Gray. 'It is hardly an innocent tale about a man and his quadruped.'

My own interest in *Jock*, however, concerns FitzPatrick's powerful evocation of the bushveld wilderness. The idea for this, my second, literary journey was to retrace the old Lowveld wagon route that forms the spine of the book. But on rereading my battered copy in preparation for the journey, I realised there were a number of threads that needed further research. Which of the many wagon routes had FitzPatrick followed? Was it still possible to locate the settings of major incidents in the tale? And could Jock's grave still be found?

JOCK BEFOK

Fruitful visits to the Centre for African Studies at the University of Cape Town (UCT) provided me with a pile of articles, pamphlets and almost a dozen old maps of the region. Photocopies of the latter became scored with jottings and routes marked with pink highlighter as the prospective journey took shape. I was pleased to find that an intrepid Lowveld historian, the late Brian Simmons, had produced (with the help of Derek Coetzee and other local Jock enthusiasts) a number of publications about the wagon trails and erected roadside markers along the route of some of FitzPatrick's treks.

And so it came to pass, one grey-green, greasy, early summer's afternoon, that I found myself coasting up the main street of Lydenburg, the gold-mining town that had once been the main terminus of the wagon routes. I parked my hired car beside the gabled Cape Dutch church and adjacent schoolhouse: the Nineteenth-Century heart of the dorp. It was here on the commonage – effectively a Victorian truckers' stop – that transport riders outspanned after their arduous, 350-kilometre trek from Lourenço Marques. Inbound goods were unpacked and material destined for the coast loaded onto the wagons.

I'd been given the address of a bookshop called Wizards that might stock '*Jock* material' and found it at the back of the parking lot of a scruffy face-brick shopping centre appropriately named 'Jock'. Inebriated men in overalls reclined on the pavement, kwaito throbbed from a line of minibus taxis, and garish signage adorned a row of boarded-up stores. Wizards' interior – dark, musty and crammed to the ceiling with books and assorted bric-a-brac – provided a startling contrast. Cobwebs hung from bookcases; layers of dust had settled over everything. The shop was a time capsule lagging a century behind the scene outside and I wondered if I was the first customer of the day. An Afrikaans tannie behind the counter offered assistance and I told her about my quest.

'Ag, not another Jock junkie,' she chuckled. Pushing her spectacles to the top of her head, she stood up creakily, straightened her dress and led me to the shop's Lowveld section, where she pulled out a FitzPatrick biography and a copy of *Lost Trails in the Makhonjwa Mountains*, dusted them off and handed them to me.

'De Souza's book of trails will help you, I think, but also have a look at this,' she said, extracting a rolled sheet from a box. It was the rare Simmons and Coetzee map, 'Jock of the Bushveld Roads', depicting the old transport routes and marked with many of the places I'd been trying to locate in my research. This find was bound to make my quest a lot easier and was the first of a string of lucky breaks.

Heading north with the map spread out on the passenger seat, I was now on the *Jock* route proper. I drove slowly, taking in the middleveld scenery and imagining FitzPatrick coming this way on his first trek to Delagoa Bay at the start of the winter trading season. Clad in flannel shirt, moleskin trousers and broad-brimmed felt hat, he sat atop his wagon, self-consciously easing himself into his new pioneer persona. Was that the creak of wooden wheels, moaning of oxen and crack of a whip I could hear? I recalled FitzPatrick's trepidation at the start of his first trek: 'Many hundreds of miles – perhaps a thousand or two; many, many months – maybe a year or two; wild country, wild tribes, and wild beasts; floods and fever; accident, hunger, and disease.'

The road crossed the Potloodspruit and followed a wide green valley enlivened by the occasional violet brushstroke of jacarandas. At Kruger's Post, a popular outspan spot, the wagon route swung east over Robber's Pass and down the escarpment. There was once a trading store hereabouts and a few wattle-and-daub houses, one of which belonged to Seedling, the field cornet and only public official in the district. Although Seedling was ostensibly the local justice, he was a drunkard and a bully and stories of his cruelty and corruption abounded. He also owned a vicious baboon and took sadistic delight in enticing dogs to attack it. The big primate would grab them by the head and, using his feet, tear the dogs to shreds.

During one stopover at Kruger's Post, Fitz was in the trading store when a driver burst in to warn him that the baboon had been coaxed by Seedling into attacking Jock. Luckily, the primate was tethered to a long chain and the bull terrier had got the measure of when to lunge and when to feint or dodge, tactics he'd acquired in skirmishes with antelope in which he'd learnt to avoid flailing horns and hooves. But the baboon was a canny adversary with well-honed tactics of his own and the fight was evenly matched.

Using his sjambok, Seedling was preventing Jim Makokela, FitzPatrick's faithful Zulu driver, from intervening to save the dog. At one point, the baboon made a thrust and was yanked off its feet by the chain, at which point Jock darted in and went for the primate's belly. It was at this moment that a breathless Fitz arrived on the scene to find Jim and Seedling in a tussle, and Jock ripping open the baboon's stomach. Fitz managed to call his dog off, but by evening the primate was dead and the young transport rider had made a vindictive enemy.

A brown 'Jock of the Bushveld' signboard directed me down a farm road that led through a peach orchard to a derelict store with 'Krugerspos Kontant Winkel' painted on the roof. Beyond the sandstone building stood a modern farmhouse and I parked in the shade of a willow tree. From behind a wall came the thwack of a well-struck cricket ball.

'Hello!' I called.

An elderly gent with silver hair, naked save for a pair of grey shorts, appeared at the gate, followed by his barefoot grandson.

'Kan ek help?' he asked warily.

I told him my business in Afrikaans and the little blond boy's face lit up. 'Ja, oom, hierdie's die plek … this is exactly where Jock fought the baboon.'

The pair led me across the lawn to a boulder inlaid with a circular bronze plaque that depicted a bounding bull terrier and was engraved with the words 'Jock Trek – 1885'. These waymarks – some donated by Brian Simmons and his team, others by FitzPatrick's daughter, Cecily Niven, and erected by the Transvaal Administration in 1951 – would be my co-ordinates for the coming week.

'This is also where Jock was shot and killed in the hen coop,' said the boy, aiming an imaginary rifle and making the sound of a shot. 'I've read the book lots and lots of times.'

'Ja, the baboon was actually stealing chickens,' said the grandfather. 'That's why Jock went for him.'

'Nee, Oupa, you've got it wrong!' cried the lad. 'It was a jackal stealing the chickens.'

'Luister, Jannie, I've read that book too, although it was sixty years ago, I'll admit—'

Thanking the pair, I left them to their colourful interpretations of the story. It didn't matter that they'd got the place and details of Jock's death wrong, I thought as I drove away; at least the hound was alive in the minds of old and young in these parts.

The book presents a sequel to the baboon episode. Two weeks after the fatal fight, Fitz returned to Kruger's Post from a delivery run to Lydenburg and discovered that Seedling had taken revenge on Jim Makokela. The driver had been brutally flogged for some minor infraction and Seedling had also imposed an exorbitant fine on Jim, ransacked his kraal and confiscated his cattle.

Fitz immediately rode back to Lydenburg to lay a charge against the field cornet, but by the time he returned to Kruger's Post, Seedling had fled east into Portuguese territory. As Fitz and Jim were heading that way, they resolved to track down the fugitive and teach him a lesson he wouldn't forget. They were only a few days behind Seedling as they descended the escarpment and heard from other drivers that the man was in a state of terror, assuming his pursuers wanted to kill him. Both Fitz and I would cross Seedling's path again in Mozambique.

From Kruger's Post I traced the wagon trail across Rietvallei and Doornhoek farms, following the R533 over Robber's Pass. Zigzagging down the escarpment on the lovely, protea-lined road, I was thinking about the long-suffering oxen and how they would have struggled with the gradient as they made the descent to the next outspan at Pilgrim's Rest. Today it's a quaint heritage village, the peaceful streets lined with restored, corrugated-iron houses and giant jacarandas, but in the late Nineteenth Century it was a chaotic mining camp.

When twenty-one-year-old FitzPatrick left his Cape Town home to seek his fortune in the spring of 1884, Pilgrim's Rest was the first place he came looking for work, but by that time, many gold diggers had already abandoned the valley for richer finds elsewhere and opportunities were scarce. After a few weeks of pick-and-shovel drudgery, he decided to press on over the pass to Mac-Mac South where the diggings held better prospects. Setting off on foot, he was caught in a violent hailstorm on Stanley Bush Kop Ridge and sought shelter under an overhang beside the road I was now following.

By sundown, the storm had passed and he continued on his way. Up ahead, he spotted an ox wagon trapped in a flooded drift and in danger of being swept over a waterfall. Fitz ran to help, plunging into the torrent and pulling the lead oxen away from their downstream heading. His brave deed earned him the gratitude of the transport rider, who subsequently helped him get a job as a shop assistant at the local store.

I pulled off the R532 at the bushy may hedge I'd been looking out for, a stone's throw from the stream of Fitz's heroics. Behind the hedge, I found the Mac-Mac Memorial, which pays tribute to the diggers and transport riders of the gold-rush era. Designed by Brian Simmons and Derek Coetzee, it's a circular monument with a wagon wheel as centrepiece and a floor paved with ceramic tiles depicting the old routes. There's also a toposcope indicating the direction of nearby towns and mining camps, as well as a roll of honour listing the most prominent diggers and transport riders, with Jock's name taking pride of place on a bronze plaque mounted on a cairn.

The R532 continued south towards Sabie, a lovely road winding through pine forests and grasslands dotted with tree ferns, watsonias, red-hot pokers, nerinas and ericas, all in luxuriant profusion. I passed gushing streams and waterfalls, and snatched glimpses over the escarpment's edge to the Lowveld below, reminding me of FitzPatrick's description of these heights in his article, 'Jock of the Bushveld and Those Who Knew Him':

> The everlasting mountains – just the same – stare out eastwards across the hazy bushveld towards the sea, like colossal watchdogs – with the foothills for forepaws. We walked and waded up the Mac-Mac gorge to the falls, sheer three hundred feet, and saw the great walls, as of old, clothed and draped with staghorn moss like exquisite green lace, fold upon fold and tier upon tier, overlapping away up and up until pattern and plan were lost to the eye, and all bespangled with countless millions of glistening drops from the wafted spray – beautiful beyond description when the sun towards midday drove his shafts of light down into the depths of the gorge.

Lost somewhere in the forest to my left lay the ruins of the store in which FitzPatrick was first employed. It was during this period that he befriended local transport riders and decided to try his luck with them. Borrowing money from his mother, he purchased a wagon and oxen and, on 8 May 1885, set off for Delagoa Bay in the company of a handful of riders to buy supplies for resale on the Lydenburg gold fields. One member of the party was Ted Sievewright, owner of a pregnant bull terrier called Jess. Among the litter born on that first trek was a red-hued puppy destined to become South Africa's most famous dog.

Late in the afternoon, I reached the forestry town and former outspan spot of Sabie where I checked in to the appropriately named Jock-Sabie Lodge. Evidence of the dog was everywhere: a Jock conference centre, framed Edmond Caldwell illustrations from the 1907 edition on the walls, rooms named after incidents in the book and a Jock Dining Hall, where I was the only guest that night, discreetly serenaded by uniformed Sotho waitresses who sang along to cheesy Californian rock as SuperSport cricket cast a flickering blue glow from a muted television. The waiter offered steak that came medium, well or extra-well done: I chose medium and got extra-well – transport-rider style, one assumes.

The next morning, I met the first of my contacts, John Theunissen, a FitzPatrick fundi who runs the Sabie tourist office and was more than happy to take the day off and show me the local wagon-route sights. John is a large, affable fellow in his sixties with a passion for history and the double bass. Bespectacled and balding, he looks not dissimilar to PW Botha and wore loose-fitting trousers held up by polka-dot suspenders. Like his double, he was comfortable with the lengthy monologue, which suited me just fine as most of his tales turned around pioneer history.

We took the R537 past Spitskop, an important waypoint for transport riders, and John pointed out the distant, claw-like peak of Legogote Mountain, another vital co-ordinate on the wagon route. My guide explained that, like navigators at sea, pioneers used mountains and other prominent geographical features as bearings when crossing the bushveld in their terrestrial ships.

The road followed a steep decline across what had once been the farm Kruisfontein. The slope would have been daunting enough for a lightly loaded descending wagon, but a lot worse for a heavily laden ascending one. In preparation for the climb, riders halted on a flat-topped spur at the base of the hill where they halved their loads and double-spanned their oxen. To the uninitiated, one group of draft animals might seem like any other, but FitzPatrick soon learnt that training, skill and courage of man and beast were required for the difficult stretches.

'It was on this pass that Fitz witnessed the masterful handling of a wagon by one Charlie Roberts,' said John. 'All the other riders had either got bogged down in thick mud or abandoned the ascent. Loads had been dumped, spans blocked the way and fragments of yokes, skeys, strops and riems were strewn everywhere. But Charlie – an elderly transport rider in poor health – skilfully avoided the obstacles by following the precipitous verge and led a single span steadily up the slope with hardly a pause. Charlie loved his oxen and knew each one by name, offering encouragement to them and using his whip only sparingly. It was a lesson in the art of driving that Fitz never forgot. At the top of the pass stood Lekkerlag Hotel, so named because the guys who made it up had a lekker lag, a damn good laugh, that they'd done it. But also a lag at those who were still stuck on the incline.'

We left the tar and threaded our way through eucalyptus plantations. 'The wagon route led down this valley and forded the Sand River tributary, then crossed Zwartfontein and Peebles farms till it reached the Sanderson brothers' trading store, where the wagons usually outspanned for a good, long rest,' said John, directing me onto a side track and motioning me to slow down. 'The turnoff is somewhere along here. We're actually on the old Peebles farm at the moment. It's just that nowadays the land has been divided into smallholdings and some of it's been handed over to the locals. Land-claim stuff, you know … There, take a left at that gate.'

We entered the farm of Kobus Kok and drove past fields filled with blesbok, neat banana groves and an awkwardly angled grass runway with tall trees at one end, electricity pylons at the other and a Cessna parked beside a barn. Beyond the strip stood a face-brick house set high on the slope overlooking rolling farmlands and the granitic tooth of Legogote in the distance.

Kobus and his pack of garrulous white Alsatians met us on the lawn. Forty-something with pale-green eyes and a friendly, open face, he was happy to forego farm work for a few hours and give us a Jock tour. We piled into his 4x4 and headed uphill until we reached an ochre house with a green, corrugated-iron roof.

'This used to be the Sanderson store, but it was also a helluva popular outspan spot,' said Kobus. 'Exhausted oxen were exchanged and left here to rest and fatten up – the store had a mielie field for the purpose. The oxen were collected again by their owners when the wagons made the return journey later in the season. The old house has changed quite a bit, but the wide veranda running right round it is original.' Kobus let us in through a side door. 'This long room was used for repairs and the men would pull the wagons in by hand through big doors at the end.'

When Fitz visited the store on his first trek, Bill Sanderson showed him a lion skin he was drying on the lawn. The young man's imagination was fired by the idea of big-game hunting and he couldn't stop asking questions. In fact, he embarked on his first tentative, unsuccessful hunts at Peebles. From his fellow transport riders he began, over time, to learn the lore of tracking, how to read spoor and tune his mind to the sounds, scents and moods of the bush.

On the lawn, I found a Jock plaque set in a small stone pyramid beside a water trough dating from Sanderson's time. Kobus said he knew of another plaque nearby and suggested we go and have a look for it. However, he confided that the neighbouring farm had been subject to a land claim and access might be tricky. Its new black owner had 'taken the package' and abandoned the farm, which was now settled by squatters who frequently raided Kobus's land. He'd recently tried to prosecute some of them for trespassing, without success. 'We need to be careful,' he said. 'Wouldn't they just love to nail me for trespassing on *their* land? I'll give the head guy a ring, just to be on the safe side.'

There was no answer from the man's cell phone, but Kobus was game to risk it. 'In just four years, the new owner has let a productive and affluent farm go to rot,' he explained as we drove down the hill. 'The ou sits in Joburg collecting R15 000 a month from government for farm improvement and maybe he gets a bit of rent now and then from the squatters. He doesn't give a damn what happens to the land.'

The entrance gate was off its hinges, the electric fence peeling from its posts and the farm road deteriorated to a web of dongas requiring four-wheel-drive. The sky had grown dark and threatened rain; the air was oppressively muggy and our clothes stuck to our bodies. This little jaunt was starting to feel like not such a good idea. 'Maybe we should drop it,' I suggested. 'I mean, we've seen one plaque already.'

'No man, don't be put off,' said Kobus as we passed a vandalised electricity transformer. 'This is Africa, this is our future, we just need to get used to it. There were dangers for FitzPatrick and there are dangers for us today. Things don't change that much. Hey, just look at how this section of the road has cut deep into the earth over time: this bit *was* the original wagon route!'

Kobus drew up at what would once have been a grand homestead, now in disrepair. Scrawny dogs barked from the stoep; Kobus pressed the hooter. A surly man carrying a bucket on his way to collect water at the stream ambled over. Kobus explained in Shangaan that he'd tried to phone the headman and that we weren't trespassing … and did he by any chance know where we could find the Jock monument? The man scratched his temple. The famous little dog? No, he'd never seen it.

We crisscrossed the farm in search of the cairn. Most of the banana trees had been felled and, as the irrigation pipes had been ripped out, the macadamia-nut trees were dying of thirst. Around the fringes of the fields, the bush had already begun to reclaim once profitable farmland. Back and forth we drove until Kobus came to a halt and said, 'Mmm, those boulders look bloody familiar.' So we got out and did a systematic search, working our way across the hill's contours.

'Over here!' came a shout. Deep inside a thicket, Kobus had found the block of dressed sandstone inlaid with a green ceramic Jock plaque. 'Lucky it wasn't made of brass, or the thing would have been stolen ages ago,' he said. 'Funny that the guy at the farmhouse didn't know where the plaque was. It's just a hundred metres from his home. Maybe they just don't see these irrelevant colonial things?'

'Not his history,' said John.

'Ja, you've got a point,' said Kobus.

Given the encroaching bush, I wondered whether we might be the last Jock enthusiasts to see this particular plaque.

'All the white farms around here are up for land claims,' said Kobus as we drove away. 'Mine too. We're fighting to stay, but I don't know how long we can hold out. Maybe my farm will look like this in a couple of years? Ag man, it's a rearguard action, just like Zimbabwe.'

We said our goodbyes and drove back up the escarpment, via Hazyview and the sweeping bends of Kowyn's Pass, to the attractive town of Graskop. To its west lies a spectacular promontory, site of Paradise Camp, where Fitz and a friend retreated during the hot months when Lowveld trekking was impossible. To earn some money while camped at their 'summer quarters', the men felled timber and delivered it to nearby gold fields, but for the most part it was a happy interlude of relaxation, exploration and hunting.

The time at Paradise Camp produced some of the most memorable landscape descriptions in *Jock*:

> From the broken battlements of the Berg we looked down three thousand feet, and eastward to the sea a hundred and fifty miles away, across the vast panorama. Black densely-timbered kloofs broke the edge of the plateau into a long series of projecting turrets, in some places cutting far in, deep crevices into which the bigger waterfalls plunged and were lost. But the top of the Berg itself was bare of trees: the breeze blew cool and fresh there. The waters trickled and splashed in every little break or tumbled with steady roar down the greater gorges. Deep pools, fringed with masses of ferns, smooth as mirrors or flecked with dancing sunlight, were set like brilliants in the silver chain of each little stream; and rocks and pebbles, wonderful in their colours, were magnified and glorified into polished gems by the sparkling water.

FitzPatrick goes on to describe the contorted sandstone formations at Camp Paradise, comprising 'a thousand grey sentinels', and a bathing pool with crystal-clear water, natural diving boards and enveloping tree ferns. He recalls the dramatic thunderstorms that swept through the valleys, rending the air with celestial cannonades. Afternoon showers would swell the streams, transforming them into roaring torrents. When the rain passed, Fitz and Jock would venture into the kloofs to see what they could shoot for the pot. The forest floor squelched underfoot as they padded across staghorn moss, monkeys peering down at them, green pigeons and purple-crested louries gorging on figs in the high branches. Man and dog were in their element.

For Simmons and his fellow historians of the Lowveld Diggers' and Transport Riders' Society, finding the site of Paradise Camp had not been easy. Simmons and two researchers scoured the area around Graskop on and off for years. All they had to go on were the references in *Jock* and the account by FitzPatrick's daughter, Cecily, of a visit to the site with her father in 1906. Then one afternoon the historians found faint tracks leading to the edge of the escarpment and deduced that these must have been made by sleds dragging firewood and water to Paradise Camp. Further exploration revealed the 'thousand sentinels' and the rocks in the shape of animals, mentioned in the book.

'It's a long and very muddy walk from Graskop to Paradise Camp,' said John. 'The exact spot is almost impossible to find these days, but you can get a great view of the site from just across the gorge.' So we drove round the lip of Driekopkloof on a fabulously scenic road, past the quartzite finger of The Pinnacle, in the direction of God's Window viewing site, until John told me to pull off. We climbed out and waded through long grass to the escarpment's rim.

'Right there, on the opposite ridge, that's Paradise Camp,' said an out-of-breath John, pointing across the gorge. The promontory lay a few hundred metres away, separated by a kloof dense with yellowwood, Cape beech and other hardwoods. Columns of godly sunlight shafted between the clouds, lighting aspects of the vista. A single ray played across the emerald crown of Paradise while the red sandstone buttresses, forested kloof and Lowveld bush below remained in deep shadow.

'In the book, you'll remember that this gorge is where a troop of baboons managed to fight off the leopard that was finally shot by Fitz – with the help of good old Jock, of course,' said John.

I looked east across the steamy plains. Down there in the milky, pale-blue haze lay the threat of tsetse fly, malaria, debilitating heat and roads made impassable by summer rain. My route led that way.

---*---

I woke to persistent rain and crossed the lawn for an early breakfast in the lodge where German tourists at the next table were ordering a 'joke' breakfast. 'Jock, not joke; it's a dog's breakfast,' I corrected them under my breath. The ambient music had 'progressed' to Italian pop and a waitress named Pinky sang along with a delightful interpretation of the lyrics.

Thick mist slowed my progress to a crawl on the road to White River and it was still raining cats and jocks when I settled myself at a corner table in the Nelspruit News Café. Moments later, my next contact, Marius Bakkes, burst through the door carrying a framed map, pile of books and a folder stuffed with papers.

'Ag, man, jammer ek's laat – I just had to go collect this stuff to show you,' he said, shaking my hand with an enormous paw. Tall, brusque, no-nonsense, bespectacled and with a greying goatie, Marius was editor of the *Lowvelder* newspaper and another Jock aficionado. I was friends with his larger-than-life, author brother, the one-armed Chris Bakkes (a crocodile bit off the other arm – long story), but had never met Marius. It was immediately apparent that he was as genial and magnetic as his younger sibling. The blood of trekkers and pioneers courses strongly in the Bakkes veins: men-of-the-veld, gentle and strong, artistic and talented.

'A lot of people around here are a bit Jock befok,' he said.

'Ja, I've noticed,' I replied.

'Jislaaik, man, I wish I could sommer take a week off and join you on this adventure of yours. By the way, this is for you.' He handed me a map, titled 'Ou Transport- en Wapaaie, Suidelike Laeveld en Platorand: 1844–1902'. Gold dust, I thought. We pushed the coffee cups aside and unfolded it across the table. The map was marked with mines, diggings, alternative wagon routes, tsetse-fly belts, outspan spots and the safest drifts for ox wagon crossing. Using this map, and the various Simmons publications, I was pretty sure I'd be able to follow FitzPatrick's exact footsteps for the rest of my trek.

'You can see the trajectory of beacon mountains: Spitskop, Legogote and here,' he jabbed his finger, 'this is Skipberg or Ship Mountain, the most important waypoint for transport riders in the Kruger Park. That's where Jock was born – you must go and pay your respects.'

Marius also gave me a sheaf of pamphlets produced by the Lowveld Diggers' and Transport Riders' Society – all out of print and vital research material. We chatted animatedly for a couple of hours and I scribbled pencil notes on the maps, until Marius's cell phone started bleating – his office and deadlines were calling – and I had a plane to meet.

I'd invited my actress sister to join me for the rest of the *Jock* quest and she was due to land at Nelspruit Airport that morning. The last trip we'd done together had been a washout, with incessant rain confining us for days in a B&B in the eastern Free State. This journey, I'd hoped, would make up for the previous debacle, but torrential rain on the way to the airport boded ill. I arrived half an hour late to find that Grethe's flight had been delayed. In fact, her plane was circling above the airport, unable to land due to the thick mist. Eventually, a brief patch of blue offered deliverance and my sister emerged from arrivals, blonde and glamorous in full bush regalia with cowboy hat and safari jacket.

'A bit Meryl Streep,' I said.

'You did say you wanted me in some of your photos, so I went for khaki chic with a hint of camo.'

'Yes, but it's not *Out of Africa* and we don't have a stylist or wardrobe team. You won't be able to keep this up.'

'Watch me.'

'By the way, sorry about the weather. Again.'

'Don't worry, probably not your fault, I'm sure it'll clear up. It simply has to. I only brought summer garb.'

We drove through the bleak, semi-urban sprawl of eManzini to Numbi Gate, where we signed in to Kruger for a few days of Jock tracking in the park. Once through the gate, I felt a familiar thrill that had hardly mellowed since childhood, once again entering this primordial landscape crisscrossed by sand rivers, teeming with big game and lorded over by magnificent leadwood, jackalberry and knobthorn trees. Early rains had already turned the bushveld from drab khaki to shades of viridian and emerald. However, the drizzle meant little chance of good animal sightings, so we headed straight for the appropriately named Jock Safari Lodge on the H2-2, a modern road that closely follows the wagon trail past the old outspan spot at Pretoriuskop, now a Kruger rest camp.

'So, what's with you and the dog?' asked Grethe.

'I suppose it's partly to do with Astie – you know how attached we all were to Staffies as kids. Also Mom reading *Jock* to me at bedtime – it's such an iconic South African tale, and vaguely democratic too, with no interracial strife: Afrikaner and Brit, Zulu and Shangaan, all getting along fine together. In those years straight after the Boer War, this kind of story was unifying. The Afrikaners adopted Jock as much as the English and FitzPatrick was an early patriot. Someone even called him the first true South African.'

'That's very rose-tinted of you, Justie. The way I remember it, the book is a catalogue of bloodthirsty hunts – hardly great literature.'

'I guess not, but it *is* a classic South African story, as embedded in our culture as biltong, Mrs Ball's and AK-47s. *Jock* hasn't been out of print in more than a century.'

'Popular fiction for children, just like *Spud* – not much of a recommendation and you know it.'

Grethe had the map open on her lap as we followed the wagon route towards the pink granite tooth of Ship Mountain. A turn-off marked 'historical site' led us down a rutted track to the banks of the dry Samarhole River where a plaque announced the birthplace of Jock in May 1885. There was a spruit on our left and grasslands beyond dotted with red termite mounds. Visitors aren't allowed out of their cars in Kruger, so we sat for a few minutes and paid our respects. Well, at least I doffed my metaphorical bush hat while Grethe made calls to the crew of *Isidingo*, the soap opera she was acting in at the time.

None of the transport riders were aware that Ted Sievewright's feisty bitch, Jess, had given birth to a litter of puppies at the very moment the wagons were being inspanned for the next leg of the trek. The men couldn't understand why Jess wouldn't let them approach a pile of goods that needed loading, until one of them heard the faint yelp of a puppy.

Jess had given birth to a litter of six: five fat yellow beauties and one scrawny, half-brindled runt, variously dubbed 'the odd puppy', 'the rat' or 'the specimen'. The five healthy pups soon found owners, but the runt looked destined to be put down. However, baby Jock was a fighter and began winning skirmishes with his bigger siblings. Although intrigued by the runt, FitzPatrick nevertheless described him in unflattering terms: 'Besides the balloon-like tummy he had stick-out bandy legs, and a neck so thin that it made the head look enormous. But what made him so supremely ridiculous was that he evidently did not know he was ugly.'

Despite reservations, Fitz asked Ted if he could have the runt and a bond between man and dog was quickly formed. Fitz was a good teacher and Jock a quick learner, especially when it came to things the puppy loved, such as practice hunts on mice and field rats, but slower when it came to things he didn't, such as being left to guard a rifle. Both pup and master were Lowveld rookies and acquired their bush lore together. Jock learnt that it wasn't necessary to nose a snake to discover what it really was and found out the hard way that it wasn't a good idea to turn a scorpion over with your paw.

Jock was obedient and faithful, and in time became an accomplished hunter. As Fitz wrote: 'Good hunting dogs were rare; as rare as good men, good horses, and good front oxen. A lot of qualities are needed in the make-up of a good hunting dog: size, strength, quickness, scent, sense and speed – and plenty of courage.' Jock had all of these.

We continued down the H2-2 as far as Afsaal, formerly a popular outspan spot, then turned north onto a private road that led to Jock Safari Lodge. This luxurious camp was originally developed by the FitzPatrick family and his descendants still have exclusive use of parts of the lodge for a few weeks a year. We were greeted at the gate by manager Louis Strauss, a gregarious Afrikaner whom I'd first met in the Okavango Delta a decade earlier. While our bags were being delivered to the rooms, Louis showed us around the lodge, pointing out Jock memorabilia: reproductions of the book's Caldwell drawings, FitzPatrick quotations and Jock sculptures, including an almost life-size bronze of the bull terrier fighting a sable.

Our host asked whether we'd had any good sightings on the way in and Grethe mentioned we'd passed a few skittish rhinos and a herd of elephants. 'It's interesting that FitzPatrick never mentions those large mammals in *Jock*,' said Louis. 'Already by the 1880s, most had been shot out by the big-game hunters who preceded the transport riders. Thank goodness for the founding of Kruger, or else this would all be farmland today.'

Louis had arranged for us to meet Mike English, a Jock aficionado and former section-ranger of the southern Kruger, who joined us the next morning for breakfast. Mike is in his eighties – tall and soft-spoken in green anorak and khakis, his mottled skin deeply weathered from too much time in the bushveld sun. He is of the loyal, hardy, straight-shooting type, a gentleman ranger from a Kruger Park that is no more. Over bacon and eggs, he told us about his years of trying to trace the exact routes of the various wagon trails, often spending days at a time on foot in Big Five country.

'The old Transvaal government tasked a Hungarian immigrant, Alois Nellmapius, with building and maintaining the road to Lourenço Marques,' he said. 'It was also his job to set up refreshment stations for the ox wagons. To this end he was granted eight farms, about twenty-four kilometres apart. You'll have passed a couple of them on your way here.'

'Such as Peebles and Pretoriuskop,' I said.

'Exactly. Long years ago, a couple of rangers, Thys Mostert and Charlie Nkuna, began looking for the wagon routes and I took over where they left off. Charlie's uncle had worked for the famous Wolhuter family and knew the old roads like the back of his hand. I actually flew the route in a helicopter a while back. From the air you can just make out the trail – very faint, but it's still there. Here, take a look.'

He opened a folder of aerial photographs and showed me how the wagon route was vaguely discernible as a pale hairline in the veld, often only a few metres from the modern road. Once the breakfast plates had been cleared, he rolled out a set of 1:50 000 maps marked with codes that referenced handwritten notes in the margin. Every kind of detail was recorded in Mike's neat cursive, from trading stores and the site of murders to the boundaries of the Nellmapius farms and springs for watering oxen.

He pointed to a spot southwest of Jock Lodge where a leadwood tree still bears bullet scars from target practice by transport riders. 'I removed the heads so that tourist types wouldn't go digging in the trunk for souvenirs with their pocket knives,' he said. 'My theory is that this is where the chapter about Fitz getting lost in the veld took place.'

Mike reached into his bag and brought out an old shoebox, carefully laying out its contents on the table: ceramic gin bottles, Martini-Henry rifle rounds, the ring from a trek chain, nails from a wagon and parts of an ammunition box.

'I found these at the outspan spots in Kruger, but I haven't a clue what to do with them and no one is interested in this sort of stuff any more, not even the local museums. Very few folk still care about this part of our past,' he said quietly, almost to himself.

That afternoon, I left Grethe under an umbrella beside the pool (thankfully the rain had stopped) and drove a route Mike had suggested. Pulling off beside the leadwood used for target practice, perhaps by Fitz himself, I opened my copy of *Jock* to reread the scene of him getting lost. Man and dog had left the wagons for a short mid-afternoon hunt, during which Fitz took a long-range shot at a kudu bull, managing only to wound it. The hunting pair set off in pursuit and although Fitz lost the spoor, Jock 'would sniff about quietly, and, by his contented looks back at me, and brisk wagging of that stumpy tail, show that he was on it again.'

But the spoor led them far from camp and when they finally gave up the chase, Fitz searched in vain for the wagons. He started to come upon his own tracks and realised he'd been walking in circles. By sunset, there was nothing for it but to gather firewood, settle down and try to make himself comfortable for the night. Fitz describes the scene:

> I was lying on my side chewing a grass stem, and Jock lay down in front of me a couple of feet away. It was a habit of his. He liked to watch my face, and often when I rolled over to ease one side and lie on the other he would get up and come round deliberately to the other side and sling himself down in front of me again … I felt very friendly to the comrade who was little more than a puppy still; and he seemed to feel something too; for as I lay there chewing the straw and looking at him, he stirred his stump of a tail in

the dust an inch or so from time to time to let me know that he understood all about it and that it was all right as long as we were together.

Suddenly, Jock stood up and directed Fitz's gaze to a herd of cattle a few hundred metres away. They had, in fact, settled down for an uncomfortable night a stone's throw from their wagons.

Sitting in the car thinking about Fitz getting lost, I recalled my own moment of being alone on foot in Kruger … The rumble of the 4x4 receded into the distance and I was left all on my own – no rifle, no map, no knife; only instinct and (patchy) common sense to guide me. My heart was thumping. Don't run. Listen. Breathe. After getting my bearings, I thought: 'Find a tree.' So I headed off the track in search of one that was easy to climb with branches high enough to keep me clear of predators – we'd seen lions in the vicinity the previous day.

Time drifted as I sat in the crook of my jackalberry. A bushbuck browsed by, not noticing the human fruit dangling above; then a pod of warthogs all asnuffle. After half an hour, I began to feel more in tune with my surroundings and found the courage to descend the tree and venture into my domain …

I'd come to northern Kruger for a field-guiding course in a remote corner of the park not accessible to ordinary visitors. The week of training culminated in each participant being dropped in the veld for a period of contemplation. Given the possible presence of lions, my 'contemplation' was more of the 'heightened vigilance' variety. But before long, I began to let myself be seduced by the environment, allowing Kruger to work its enchantment. After a few hours, I heard an engine: the 4x4 returning to fetch me, but some entranced, captivated part of me wanted to linger in the wilderness.

Driving southeast of Afsaal, I followed the H2-2 in search of another Jock plaque, passing the hidden perennial spring of Fihlamanzi, often a lifesaver for parched oxen back in transport-riding days. This section of the modern road lay precisely in the ruts of the wagon trail, until a T-junction forced me south, then east, following two sides of a triangle whose third was the transport riders' route to Nellmapius Drift, the main crossing point on the Crocodile River.

On the north bank of the fording spot, I found a memorial that marked the location of Alf Roberts's trading store, Tengamanzi, which provided a welcome stop to rest and re-provision before braving the drift. A pod of hippos watched me from the river, described by FitzPatrick as at times 'silent and oily like a huge gorged snake', at others 'foaming and turbulent as an angry monster'.

Tengamanzi is the site of the famous duel between Jock and the crocodile. The encounter played out on a Sunday morning after a long night's trek when the wagons were outspanned near the river. Fitz needed a change of clothes and a wash after days of travelling in clouds of dust kicked up by the oxen. He found a suitable pool and an exposed rock on which to stand and wash, a loaded rifle close at hand. Returning to the wagons, he heard a commotion among the drivers and an assegai-wielding Jim shouting, 'Ingwenye Umkulu! Big Crocodile!'

Jim hastily explained that this particular croc had already taken four itinerant miners as well as a woman and baby from a nearby kraal. It had to be killed and Fitz agreed to help. Local herdsmen showed him where he might get a good shot and he crawled to the river bank on his hands and knees, only to find the enormous crocodile lying in exactly the spot he'd been soaping himself only minutes before.

Fitz took careful aim and gently squeezed the trigger. The reptile reared up like a horse and plunged into the stream, still very much alive, as drivers and herdsmen swarmed along the banks, shouting and pointing. Just then, a rush of blood to the head saw Jim letting out a fierce yell and leaping into the stream, bent on spearing the monster. 'Come on, Baas!' he shouted. Knowing it was utter lunacy to enter a river with a wounded crocodile, but fearful for and goaded by Jim, Fitz followed him in. With considerable irony, he writes: 'I cannot say that there was much enjoyment in it for the first few moments.'

With water up to his neck, he realised that his rifle was now of little use. Unable to contain himself, Jock now dived into the stream and swam past the men to lead the chase, whimpering with excitement. Jim threw his assegai and got a lucky hit. Spraying blood-stained foam, the crocodile turned and lunged, missing Jock but managing to flick him into the air with its tail. More assegais rained down from the bank and the monster was done for, turning belly up and floating past Fitz, followed by Jock, trying to hang onto its scaly tail, and then Jim, swimming doggy paddle and snorting like a hippo. Fitz had ruined his Sunday outfit, but the trio had bagged their first croc.

Our days at Jock Lodge followed the traditional safari rhythm of early-morning and late-afternoon game drives, with the heat of the day devoted to reading and relaxing. I passed the time in lazy lodge lounging, recumbent in the heavy shade of a jackalberry, a procession of impala grazing across my gaze line and the odd kudu bull with regal headdress striding by. Our bend in the Biyamiti River was loud with the trilling of Cape turtle doves, the beak-clapping of red-crested korhaans and squabbling of arrow-marked babblers. The mugginess grew intense through the day, enforcing frequent swims. After lunch came the booming of celestial artillery from the direction of the Drakensberg escarpment and the occasional shower. Transport riders followed a similar routine (without the cocktails, loungers and pool) and most of the trekking was done in the cool of evening or before dawn, which also avoided the tsetse flies.

We encountered abundant wildlife on our game drives, many of the mammals with bandy-legged young. In place of the transport riders' favoured Martini-Henrys, I shot with my trusty Nikon. Our ranger would switch off the engine and allow big game to approach the vehicle. During these encounters, I thought of FitzPatrick's keen observation of animals. Despite being an enthusiastic hunter, and as is often the apparent contradiction among his breed, the descriptions of animals in *Jock* speak of a deep love of nature. For instance, he tells of his awe at the sight of impalas cantering through the bush:

> Suddenly you see one animal take off away back behind the others, shoot up, and sail high above the arch of all the rest, and with head erect and feet comfortably gathered, land far beyond them … Something is wrung from you – a word, a gasp – and you stand breathless with wonder and admiration until the last one is gone.

The veld's smaller fry also captivated Fitz and he describes in detail the antics of mongooses, water monitors and otters, as well as the spiky armour of caterpillars, leaf-shaped stick insects and the industry of ants.

On our last night in Kruger, I was woken by the roaring of lions. Unable to get back to sleep, I let the sounds of the bushveld wash over me: the baritone hooting of a spotted eagle owl, the quavering call of a fiery-necked nightjar and the Biyamiti's chorus of frogs. I imagined Fitz, snug beside a fire under his blanket, with Jock curled against him for warmth, twitching every now and then as he pursued an impala through the tall grass of his dreamland.

Long before dawn, the transport riders would wake and I pictured Fitz placing a billycan on the fire to make tea while Jim loaded the wagon. Jock remained curled beside the coals, reluctant to start the day. Eventually he got up stiffly, blinking his eyes and stretching his stocky body. A whip crack rent the cold, fragrant air and the voorloper brought in the oxen at a trot. The inspanning would not take long and, with a second crack of the whip, the driver would bellow that age-old cry of the bushveld: 'Trek!' Wheels creaked as the beasts took the strain and heaved their wagons into motion, aiming the convoy at a horizon turned to gold by the rising sun.

Clouds of dust kicked up by the wagon train enveloped man and beast alike, soon colouring them the same shade of khaki. If the road was good, riders could doze atop their wagons, but driving a span was seldom easy and you needed to watch that each ox pulled its weight and traction remained equal. Late morning, the riders would usually call a halt. During the resting hours, there were invariably repairs to be done, oxen to be doctored, water to be sourced. When the heat became oppressive, men and dogs found shade or dozed under the wagons, and afternoons drifted by to the soothing call of laughing doves and the shrill monotone of cicadas. Then came the second 'scoff' in the late afternoon which lasted until nightfall, when camp would be made.

On a good day, they might have covered as much as thirty-five kilometres. The animals stood around exhausted, lines of brown streaking from nostrils, eyes and mouth where the dust had turned to mud. If there were predators about, the oxen remain picketed to the trek chain for the night.

Lanterns were lit and the smell of woodsmoke drifted through camp as men relaxed around the fire. The hunters' pot, a driebeenpotjie that was continually replenished with game meat, would be placed on the flames and doughboys shoved into the ashes for baking. A mug of gin would make the rounds and someone might strike up a tune on the harmonica, its mournful voice accompanied by the rumination of oxen. Slowly men and dogs would start turning in, lanterns would be doused and the stars would sizzle in their brilliance as the trekkers drifted off to sleep.

---—✷———

We left Kruger via Malelane Gate and made for the border post at Komatipoort. The Crocodile River meandered in lazy bends on our left; the land remained flat, decked with plantations of banana and sugar cane. Approaching the frontier, the road bisected low hills near Oorsprong Siding and I recalled that it was in these parts that Jock almost lost his life. The plucky hound had already experienced a few narrow escapes with antelope, such as getting himself entangled in the horns of an enraged kudu bull. On this occasion, man and dog were hunting mixed game around a series of waterholes when Fitz managed to wound a kudu cow and Jock duly took up the chase. Closing with the antelope, he leapt for one of her hind legs just as she lashed out with a flying kick. The hoof connected with the dog's jaw and sent him somersaulting through the air.

Jock lay motionless, blood oozing from his mouth, nostrils and eyes. Fitz ran to a nearby spruit and collected water in his hat, which he poured over Jock's body and cupped into his mouth, but to no avail. Returning with a second hatful of water, his heart leapt as Jock sat up and shook his head groggily: he was going to be all right. Fitz was only later to realise that the kick had left his companion stone deaf.

Arriving at the Komati River, we pulled off and got out to stretch our legs. I strolled to the middle of the Julius Furley Bridge and looked upstream to where a sheet of white water poured over a weir. In FitzPatrick's day, this was Furley's Drift, an important crossing point for the wagons. The Komati is wide here and flows strongly, and it's no wonder transport riders made the crossing in the winter months when the water was low. Rumour had it that sly old Julius Furley fed the local crocodiles to further 'encourage' travellers to use his fording spot, where he'd erected a makeshift hotel.

From here, the wagon route led southeast through the Matibaskom gap in the Lebombo Mountains, then followed a straight line across the Mozambican lowlands to Lourenço Marques. Today, the N4 pierces the border further north at Komatipoort. Within half an hour, our passports were stamped and we were descending into the sticky heat of the coastal plain, bound for Maputo.

We spent the night in the Art Deco wedding cake that is the Cardoso Hotel on a bluff overlooking the estuary where sailing ships used to unload cargo destined for the interior. Grethe and I whiled away the afternoon in a lovely tropical garden, gazing down on the waterfront as the sun set over Maputo. I imagined a bustling Nineteenth-Century scene below: sailors from countless nations spilling ashore off square riggers, coasters and steamers, Portuguese officials making life difficult and, beyond the port, the lure of the taverns and brothels of Baixa. More at home in the bush, Fitz preferred not to linger long in this city where the 'liquor was cheap and bad, and there was very little in the way of law and order.'

It was while outspanned with a group of transport riders near the harbour that Fitz first crossed paths with the giant Zulu, Jim Makokela, who was to become his right-hand man. Jim had been working for a cruel wagon driver who used to beat him with a sjambok. The Zulu gladly annexed Fitz as his new boss and was never to let him down.

Our Maputo interlude was brief and the next morning we drove back along the EN4 towards the border. I'd read that Jock's grave lay close to the main road beside the Chambanjovo River near Old Pessene. When Fitz gave up transport riding and made a home in Barberton after the disaster of his final trek, Jock failed to settle in to town living. Due to his deafness, he kept having close shaves and on one occasion was nearly run over by a wagon while dozing in a busy street, so Fitz decided to send his dog to a rural setting where he'd be safer. His friend Tom Barnett ran a store at Old Pessene and agreed to take Jock in.

Tom's shop is the setting for two episodes in the book. The first concerns the fugitive field-cornet Seedling who, after a desperate time alone and on the run in the Mozambican bush, decided to find sanctuary at Tom's store. But his horse succumbed and the ailing man got within a kilometre of the shop before he too collapsed and died of thirst. Fitz and Jim arrived at the trading store a few days later and learnt of Seedling's fate.

The second episode concerns Jock, who met his end while valiantly defending Tom's chickens, and was buried beside Seedling under a large fig tree. More than half a century later, FitzPatrick's daughter, Cecily, tried to find the grave during an expedition to Mozambique, recounted in her book *Jock and Fitz*. After an exhaustive search, her party came upon the site of what they assumed to be Tom's place. There was nothing left of the store, but digging in the dirt they found pieces of broken china, glass and bricks. Nearby stood a clump of trees which an elderly local assured them was the site of Seedling's, and hence Jock's, grave. Members of the search party suggested they do some digging to see if they could find remains, but Niven thought it would be 'a pity to disturb the dear old dog's bones'.

About twenty minutes west of Maputo, we pulled off the EN4 onto a sandy track, parked and walked into an open stretch of nondescript bush. Niven's book provided the co-ordinates – 32º 20' 4"E and 25º 46' 5"S – but reaching the spot using my GPS, we found no tree bearing Jock's name carved in the bark and no sign of the ruins of Tom's store. It would have been futile to start scratching around for a few old bricks and broken china, but I did feel Jock's presence as we stood in the baking sun, sweat pouring from our bodies.

'There should be a memorial or something to commemorate the passing of such a famous dog,' I said.

'Let's build a cairn of stones for Jock,' suggested Grethe. 'Then I'll take a picture of you next to it.'

'Mmm, it's a bit hot, don't you think? And where are we going to find stones?'

'We can look around,' she said. The terrain was unrelentingly sandy.

'Really?'

'I suppose not.'

'We can build a pile of stones in our heads,' I said. 'There, it's done.'

We trudged back to the car and its merciful air-conditioning.

From Old Pessene I wanted to follow one of the wagon trails to the Barberton gold mines. Transport riders could opt for a safe route on high ground to avoid the tsetse fly or a lower road that was shorter but riskier. On FitzPatrick's last trek he chose the latter, known as Pettigrew's Route, and paid a heavy price. He'd given in to the temptation to squeeze in one extra trip at the tail end of the season. The idea was to do the journey on his own, spend all his savings on a large load for four wagons, and reap rich rewards in Barberton.

Re-crossing the border back into South Africa, the N4 more or less follows Pettigrew's Route, thus tracing the trajectory of FitzPatrick's demise. I thought of his weakened oxen – already bitten by tsetse on the way down to the coast – now struggling in the spring heat. The big pool at Matolla Poort was dry and Fitz had to make a long detour, trekking through the night, to find water, but the alternative pools were infested with tsetse and the oxen were bitten again.

At Furley's Drift, he had to use three spans – more than forty cattle – to get each wagon through the ford. Distances formerly covered in one trek now took as many as five. Then lions attacked the outspan at night and Jock had to be fastened in the tent wagon lest he try something foolish. One lion approached from upwind, using its scent to induce a stampede in the direction of the waiting pride. Two terrified oxen broke free and thundered into the darkness, never to be seen again.

At Thankerton farm on the Crocodile River, Fitz could no longer bear to watch the valiant but futile efforts of his most trustworthy ox, Swartland, and had to shoot it. As if things weren't bad enough, the drought broke suddenly and dramatically. At first, Fitz marvelled at the transformation wrought by the rain:

> The smell of the baked drought-bound earth; the faint clearing and purifying by the first few drops; the mingled dust and damp; the rinsed air; the clean sense of water, water everywhere; and in the end the bracing sensation in nostrils and head of, not wind exactly, but of swirling air thrust out to make room for the falling rain; and, when it was all over, the sense of glorious clarified air and scoured earth – the smell of a new-washed world!

But the rain also brought flash flooding, rendered by FitzPatrick in sublime terms: 'the rumbling thunder of big boulders loosed and tumbled, rolled like marbles on the rocks below; whole trees brought down, and turning helplessly in the flood.' The roads became muddy furrows and some oxen simply gave up while others drowned. The first wagon had to be abandoned near Malelane, but there were soon not enough oxen to pull the remaining three and another wagon, plus its load, was left by the wayside.

Near Kaapmuiden, the trail swung southwest and followed the Kaap River to Barberton. A large farm called Excelsior lay in the gap between the Crocodile and the Kaap, and it was here that Jock and his master had their last hunt, immortalised in elegiac terms in the book. Fitz had decided to give the oxen a day's rest before the last push to Barberton and the pair set out to see what they could bag for the pot.

We turned off the R38 onto a farm track and parked beside a sugar-cane field. To the west lay the rounded hills of Excelsior Nek and, in the distance, the blue peaks of Krokodilpoort. Our imaginations had to replace cane with bush, but the landscape was otherwise unchanged. I pictured Jock and Fitz stalking a sable bull, heard the crack of a rifle and, when the gun smoke cleared, saw man and dog hurtling through the grass after the wounded animal. Fitz knew all too well the danger of the antelope's scythe-like horns, but his cries for Jock to back off went unheard. Finally, the hunter caught up and witnessed the sable making a stand. 'The beautiful black and white bull stood facing his little red enemy and the fence and play of feint and thrust, guard and dodge, was wonderful to see.'

Jock penetrated the antelope's defences, fastened onto a hind leg above the hock and somehow kept his grip as he was flung furiously about. A desperate lunge to get at the dog brought the bull to its knees, allowing Fitz a clean shot. The sable felled, Jock stood over his conquest with a wide grin and lolling tongue, puffing like a steam engine. Fitz's congratulations were answered with 'the friendly wagging of that stumpy tail, a splashy lick, a soft upward look, and a wider split of the mouth that was a laugh as plain as if one heard it.'

We followed the Kaap upstream as far as Louw's Creek, a tea-coloured trickle wending its way beneath a thick riparian canopy. This spot symbolically marked the end of the tsetse and malaria zone: from here, the route climbed into cooler, healthier airs. For transport riders, the last stretch was notorious for its interminable ascent and its eight drifts – just when the grail of Barberton seemed within their grasp. But for Fitz, it was too late: by the time he reached the ford at Fig Tree Creek only twenty oxen remained and his third wagon got stuck in the stream, unable to be moved. The last wagon followed suit and Fitz reached Barberton on foot leading his three remaining oxen, all of which died within a week. Jim was paid off and returned to his kraal. Fitz was ruined.

Back in the 1880s, Barberton was a hardbitten mining camp frequented by diggers and all manner of conmen, cardsharps and women of the night, bent on relieving the miners of their gold. It was a place of saloons, dance halls and dosshouses where fortunes could be made and lost overnight. Today, it's a quaint and sleepy Victorian town set in lush hill country, its rough edges having long since been knocked off.

In Barberton, FitzPatrick began a new life that would lead him to fame and fortune via journalism, the corporate mining world and national politics, but it took him a while to adjust. Both he and Jock continued to feel an almost unbearable 'trek fever', days of 'restless, sleepless, longing for the old life; of "home-sickness" for the veld, the freedom, the roaming, the nights by the fire, and the days in the bush!'

To make matters worse, Jock's deafness was a constant worry, hence his move to Tom Barnett in Pessene where he was tasked with guarding the store against mongrel dogs that used to sneak into the compound and make off with anything they could lay their claws on. Jock became a murderously efficient watchdog and Tom enjoyed greater peace than ever before. There was, however, a chicken house in the backyard that continued to be plundered at night and, being deaf, the sleeping Jock was often unable to prevent these attacks.

One bright moonlit night, Tom was roused by the screams of his chickens. Opening a back window, he aimed his rifle at the fowl house, hoping to get a shot at one of the marauding dogs as it emerged from the coop. There was the sound of a scuffle within and Tom fired just as a dog appeared in the doorway. Tragically, it was Jock. The mortified storekeeper found the body of the thieving mongrel inside the fowl house: Jock had done his duty to the end.

On Barberton's high street, you'll find a stocky bronze statue of Jock beside a steam locomotive. Their proximity is emblematic: by the 1890s, steam engines had largely replaced ox wagons and the interior of our country, especially around the mines, underwent a rapid process of industrialisation. Fitz's last trek symbolically marks the end of an era in South Africa. *Jock of the Bushveld* is thus a temporal journey in the grandest sense: from the realm of ox wagons and frontiersmen living off the land to the complicated business of industrialised modernity. Fitz and Jock saunter off into the pages of fiction to become myth, representatives of a period of pioneering history that was about to fade.

Standing beside the statue, our journey complete, I was thinking about my own bull terrier, Astie. Initially, we were inseparable chums and would play together for hours in our suburban garden, but things began to change. With puberty came other interests – sports, hobbies, girls – that deflected my attention from Astie. I'd return from rugby practice or jaunts with friends and find him lying at the door, head between his paws, watching me with those loving, hurt eyes. My parents took over walking, feeding and caring duties while I got on with the important business of being a selfish teenager.

Then came national service and I was stationed at naval bases for long periods. I heard of Astie's death in a letter from my mother. He'd become gravely ill – his kidneys – and had to be put down. I grieved, but only briefly, and was far from home, so his passing had a degree of unreality to it. Three decades later, standing beside a memorial to another loyal bull terrier, I felt unaccountably bereft. Guilt and sorrow welled up as though his death were yesterday.

'Bastard,' I muttered, walking away from my sister and back to the car, angrily trying to fend off feelings that were too little and much too late.

FitzPatrick wrote *Jock* more than two decades after his own dog was killed while guarding a henhouse far from his master's side. I have a hunch that the book is partly about guilt. No matter the reasons – between master and hound the reasons, however logical, are meaningless – Fitz abandoned Jock. The book was, I think, about making amends. In this light, *Jock of the Bushveld* is a very personal apology from a man to his dog.

———✳———

From left: Astie, Hector (Astie's uncle) and the author

BAND OF BROERS

The Long Ride of Deneys Reitz

'Opsaal! Saddle up, we're going to cross!' comes the cry in the pre-dawn darkness as excitement courses through the men and their horses. After days of searching, scouts have finally found a drift across the Orange River not guarded by the enemy.

Although General Smuts – or Oom Jannie as his men call him – still looks neat in his grey riding breeches with a blond beard trimmed to a point in the French manner, the rest of the Boers wear mostly rags. Deneys Reitz, the nineteen-year-old son of President Kruger's state secretary, has recently joined the commando and belongs to a scouting group calling itself, ironically, the Rijk (dandy) Section. They are anything but dandy: Reitz has no underwear and no shirt under his threadbare coat, his trousers are full of holes and his rawhide sandals are being held together with patches.

The Anglo-Boer War is deep into its second year and the British have gained the upper hand, seizing both Boer republics, burning farms and herding Afrikaner women and children into concentration camps. Great drives comprising tens of thousands of soldiers have swept across the veld, destroying everything in their path and pushing the defenders into ever tightening corners. The Boers have resorted to guerrilla warfare and occasional commando raids into the Cape and Natal to harass the enemy.

Now a single file of horses descends into the canyon in the dark, moving silently and scanning the opposite side of the river for sentries. At first light, they splash through the stream, climb the south bank and fan out. They've made it at last. This band of brothers – some 250 horsemen – has arrived on Cape soil to take the fight into the enemy's backyard. The date is 4 September 1901.

After months of bitter, winter fighting on the Highveld, the Smuts raid holds much promise. Even if the commando fails to inspire the Cape Afrikaners into open revolt, it will divert thousands of troops away from the beleaguered republics, test the possibility of a future large-scale invasion, or at least force a stalemate that will help to bring about favourable peace terms. The men are full of hope, but little do they know their movements have already been spotted, an ambush is being prepared and their first battle is only hours away ...

———*———

One of the finest books about the Anglo-Boer War was written by Deneys Reitz (1882–1944) a year after the cessation of hostilities during his self-imposed exile in Madagascar. Only published in 1929, *Commando: A Boer Journal of the Boer War* received immediate acclaim as an outstanding depiction of one of the greatest commando raids in history, the daring tale of a group of unsupported men on horseback against the might of the British Empire. Indeed, the story had the makings of an epic, reminiscent of the 300 Spartans of Thermopylae, and the literary achievement is all the more remarkable when one considers that the original manuscript (written in Cape Dutch) was crafted by a young man who'd just turned twenty-one. However, the text was much altered in the intervening twenty-six years, and most of the bitterness in defeat and anti-British sentiment was removed to contribute to the political project of imperial reconciliation and post-war nation-building in South Africa.

Commando is the spirited account of life on the open veld, of running skirmishes and narrow escapes, recounted with an optimism and joie de vivre that contrasts sharply with most similar accounts of only a decade later during the First World War, such as those of Robert Graves, Erich Remarque and Siegfried Sassoon. Reitz's story is also implicitly a praise song to the South African landscape and the romance of roaming its wide-open spaces. In a sense, it's our nation's greatest 'travelogue': a tale of hardship, patriotism, honour and camaraderie set against a sublime backdrop that becomes as much a character as its participants.

The story begins with an exuberant, seventeen-year-old Reitz contemplating 'the prospect of war and adventure with the eyes of youth, seeing only the glamour, but knowing nothing of the horror and the misery.' The ensuing narrative traces his war journey to all corners of South Africa. It was my intention to follow his entire route, but upon studying the yellowing map that accompanied my 1932 edition, I realised the folly of such a plan. His circuitous meanderings through KwaZulu-Natal, Mpumalanga, North

West, Free State and even into Botswana would have kept me on the road for months, and I had other authors to chase. However, the climax and most famous part of his odyssey was the 'invasion' of the Cape with General Smuts. That journey alone would keep me crisscrossing the veld for weeks.

I arrived at sunrise on the south bank of the Orange River at Kiba Drift, starting point of my 5 000-kilometre pursuit across the length and breadth of the old Cape Colony. The river's ruffled, brown waters muscled between low hills. The Free State banks opposite were steep, tree-lined and rocky, but the fordable stretch below me provided Smuts with the break he needed. I pictured the Boers coaxing their horses through the turbulent current with Reitz among them, leading his roan and the little Basotho pony that carried his supplies.

'It was the finest commando with which I ever served,' he writes. 'The rank and file were mostly keen young farmers from the Western Transvaal, the pick of De la Rey's fighting men, and in command of them was perhaps the one man in South Africa who could have led us through the perilous days to come.' Smuts had already proved himself an inspirational leader able to make lightning decisions in the heat of battle. Beside him rode Tottie Krige, his brother-in-law and right-hand man. Tottie was a cousin of my grandfather, Japie Krige, and his sister Isie (Smuts's wife) was to nurse Reitz back to health over a period of three years when he returned from Madagascar in 1906 with severe malaria. Enhanced by these connections, versions of the Reitz story – some factual, some fanciful – have always circulated in our family.

After fording the stream, the Boers let their steeds graze the luxuriant grass on the Cape side of the river before making for nearby Wittenberg Mission Station. Armed Basotho horsemen of the Herschel Native Police appeared on the horizon and approached cautiously, but neither side seemed ready for a fight just yet. However, as the commando neared the mission, they noticed riflemen lining a low koppie and peering from windows of the church. Realising that they were being funnelled into a trap, the Boers broke into a gallop and when the first volley rang out, most of the shots went high. Reitz and his group had been lagging behind and had to run the gauntlet through a defile that led past the church.

'As we sped past, more natives rose from behind the fence lining the road. Fortunately these last were armed only with assagais [sic] and knobkerries, which came whirring about our ears.' Nineteen-year-old Johannes

Bodenstein of Klerksdorp took a bullet in the chest and tumbled from his horse. Somehow, the rest made it through and joined the commando further down the track.

I stepped from my Suzuki 4x4 and traced the trajectory of shots fired from the church windows. Today, Wittenberg is a peaceful hamlet, its sandstone church with red tin roof and stained-glass windows a thing of austere beauty. Chickens clucked contentedly, cattle ambled by and a woman swept the stoep of the parsonage as morning light bathed the low ridges all around. Among the rocks, I found the bullet holes of the hot exchange, and climbed the koppie to see the place where the Basotho had aimed their rifles at the fleeing Boers. For Reitz, it had been a very close shave.

Shaving it close was the order of the day. Trying to avoid more trouble, the commando swung west, away from the garrisoned town of Lady Grey, and headed for the mountainous country southwest of the Witteberge. Major General Kitchener had sent six bodies of troops to block their escape routes: every koppie, poort and pass provided the British with opportunities to attack. The Boers desperately needed to break out into open country where they could range more freely, but scouting ahead of the commando on a farm ominously called Moordenaarspoort, Smuts nearly met his end.

I knocked on the door of the old farmhouse. Oom Daantjie Schoeman – white moustache, large spectacles, checked shirt, very short shorts – gripped my hand firmly, recognising another war-history enthusiast. Over coffee, he told me how his grandfather, Daniel Schoeman, warned the Boers that the British were close by. 'My oupa told them it would be terribly dangerous to go snooping along the poort road, and that scouts of the local volunteer guard were probably watching the farmhouse at that very moment. But stubborn old Smuts wouldn't listen. Come, Justin, let me show you the place it happened.'

A quarter of an hour later, we stood at the spot where a patrol had lain in wait beneath a rocky overhang that forms a waterfall after rain. Smuts and three of his scouts came riding by at point-blank range. Oom Daantjie showed me the four metal stakes he'd hammered in the ground to mark the approximate position of each rider at the moment of ambush. The third stake, sporting a white flag, represented Smuts.

'A volley of shots rang out and the Khakis were dead sure they'd bagged all four Boers, but Smuts was still alive: his horse had been shot from under him,' said Oom Daantjie. 'He tumbled into a donga and crawled away, then sprinted back down the valley, arriving at our house without his hat and covered in mud. Before rejoining the commando he had a proper wash and my oupa gave him a hat that belonged to my oupagrootjie.'

Smuts later described the Moordenaarspoort ambush as 'the one snare from which, under the circumstances, I had no right to escape'. Reitz believed that if Smuts had been killed, their Cape raid would have been over there and then.

The winter and spring of 1901 were among the coldest in living memory, punctuated by sleet, snow, gales and thick mist. The Boers suffered terribly in their threadbare clothing and the horses died of exposure, but the adverse conditions also worked in their favour, never more so than at the battle of Boshoffskraal. After Smuts's lucky escape, the commando turned west, but Major General French had them in his sights and the noose was tightening. The Boers spent three days looking for a way through the chain of mountains in their path but each route was blocked. Nightfall on 11 September found them in a shallow depression on a plateau atop the Stormberg, surrounded by British soldiers. The exhausted commando was low on ammunition, half-starved and at the end of its tether. Skirmishing parties held the enemy at bay, but in the morning there would be no escape as the Khakis moved in to mow them down with machine guns and pom-poms. Surrender appeared the only option.

Then a genie in the shape of a hunchback bywoner (tenant-farmer) emerged from a cottage in the middle of the depression they were defending. Hans Kleynhans, a pitiful sight on diminutive crutches, told the Boers he knew a secret way down the mountain, and without hesitation Smuts placed his trust in the cripple. Kleynhans was helped onto a horse and led the procession into the night on a daring last roll of the dice.

A cold, blustery evening found me on top of that mountain with local farmer and historian Sandy Stretton. 'Lucky for the Boers, thick mist had settled over the plateau,' he said. 'The marshy ground on your left is where the commando made its escape and you can just see the remains of the Kleynhans cottage over there.' My eye traced the line of the Boer retreat, threading in single file through the bog, the voices of British troops echoing in the murk all around them. Even the horses seemed to understand that silence meant survival.

At the edge of the Stormberg escarpment lies a stone memorial and two flagpoles commemorating the spot where Kleynhans showed the Boers the way over the lip and down into the abyss. 'There was a gap of about 250 yards in the Khaki line where the pickets didn't patrol,' said Sandy. 'They never imagined the Boers would be crazy enough to take their horses over a cliff, not realising that there was a section of mountainside free of rock.'

I peered over the edge at the steep, grassy slope and pictured the Boers and their horses struggling down the escarpment, often glissading into one another. Within a few perilous hours, they had negotiated the descent and broken out into open country. When the Khakis advanced on Boshoffskraal the next morning, they found only a hunchback in a smoky hovel where the commando should have been. 'Yes, sir, the Boers were here. No, sir, I didn't see which way they went.'

That night, the legend of the Smuts commando was born. A fortunate Houdini act it certainly was, but they couldn't keep running without fresh mounts and provisions, and the shortage of ammunition had become critical. By now, many Boers were emaciated figures clad in animal skins and grain bags; some were forced to walk carrying their saddles as so many horses had died. But Smuts spurred on his men, trying to put as much distance as possible between the commando and its pursuers.

They came to a railway line and considered piling boulders on the tracks to stop a train that came chugging past, but Smuts thought better of it. Reitz wistfully watched the windows stream by and caught a glimpse of officers drinking wine and smoking in the brightly lit dining car. He later discovered that General French and his staff officers were on that train, rushing to the Stormberg to close the trap from which the Boers had just escaped.

Famished and half asleep in the saddle, the commando pressed south. Whenever they were delayed by a ditch or stopped to cut a fence, men tumbled from their mounts and fell asleep on their hands and knees, but the unshakeable will of Smuts drove them on. The night of 15 September was the most terrible of all, forever after remembered by the men as the Groot Reën (Great Rain). Their guide lost his way and they stumbled about in the dark, ankle deep in mud and icy water. Reitz recalls: 'Towards midnight it began to sleet. The grain-bag which I wore froze solid on my body, like a coat of mail, and I believe that if we had not kept moving every one of us would have died. We had known two years of war, but we came nearer to despair that night than I can remember.' Fourteen men vanished into the darkness and were not seen again; more than fifty horses succumbed.

I followed a farm road shrouded in mist until I reached the Stagger Inn, a famed Eastern Cape establishment set in undulating, forested country dotted with dams. Ann Bryan brought me a glass of sherry in the lounge where a log fire crackled and the heads of eland and fallow deer eyed me from the walls. 'Our family settled here in 1853, but with all the current land claims, things are getting too difficult,' she said. 'I fear for the future. We're thinking of selling off most of the farm.'

'Your family must have been here when Smuts rode past,' I said.

'Yes, my granddad told me how he watched the commando coming over Penhoek Pass. Smuts always cut the fence wires right at the posts, which Grandpa thought was rather considerate to local farmers as it was easier to repair. The Boers were, of course, farmers themselves.'

Two days after their Great Escape, the commando attacked a camp of the 17th Lancers – a crack cavalry regiment whose badge featured the Death's Head and the words 'Or Glory'. Colonel Haig had ordered the Lancers to hold fourteen kilometres of the Eland's River, and its C Squadron, comprising about 125 men under Captain Sandeman, had taken up position on the farm Modderfontein, near Tarkastad. Their camp consisted of the homestead, stone kraals and tents pitched in a field below a dolerite dyke upon which they placed a pair of guns for defence.

The Boers were advancing down the Eland's River Valley when they received a tip-off from a farmer that there were English cavalry up ahead. Smuts had to make a hasty decision. His commando was so low on provisions, horses and ammunition that this was perhaps the last chance to re-equip itself and fight another day. Smuts chose to attack at once with what weapons and fit horses he had at his disposal.

The Rijk Section was in the vanguard as they charged down the road, catching an enemy patrol by surprise and opening fire. A wild steeplechase ensued. Reitz shot a trooper from his horse with his last two bullets, threw away his own rifle and dismounted to grab the dead soldier's Lee-Metford and bandolier. One group of attackers made for the farmhouse, where a guard at the door shot a Boer through the head. Then he was killed, the front door was broken down and the house overrun.

I pulled up under the trees at Modderfontein's large homestead. Farmer Willie du Plessis met me on the stoep and ushered me inside. 'The attack was so sudden, it caught the Lancers completely by surprise,' he said, leading me down the hallway. 'The officers were just sitting down to lunch here in the dining room. It was chaos. During the battle my great-grandparents, Hendrik and Elizabeth van Heerden, were locked in the bedroom. It's just as well: one soldier was killed right here in the hall. Do you see that mark?' Willie pointed at the ceiling.

'Looks like a bullet hole,' I said.

'Exactly. A Mauser bullet.'

While the homestead was under attack, Reitz and his party were skirmishing along the ironstone dyke behind the house. They ducked and dived around boulders as bullets whipped overhead. When the mountain gun redirected its fire on the main body of the commando that had come galloping into view, Reitz grabbed his chance. Asking Muller to use his binoculars to help with aiming, he brought his sights to bear on the artillery men, slowly breathed out, and squeezed the trigger.

Willie led me round the side of the homestead and up onto the dyke. 'The Lancers had pitched about thirty bell tents down there near the family cemetery,' he said. 'The mountain gun and machine gun were up here, so they could cover the camp, farmhouse and road.' Willie pointed out two circles of red stones that marked the emplacements. 'Reitz and his group were just over there. They managed to kill three of the artillery soldiers and silence the gun.'

The Boers began to overrun the camp, but the Lancers didn't lack for courage and there were plenty of ongoing skirmishes. Lieutenant Sheridan, cousin of Winston Churchill, fired twice at Reitz but missed. Reitz returned fire and grazed his temple. Staggering to his feet, Sheridan was killed by Jack Borrius with a bullet through the head. Captain Sandeman rallied a group for a last stand at the kraals where a sharp fight at close quarters ensued. Reitz was lucky to survive as a shot grazed his face and he was to spend the coming days picking cordite out of his cheek and neck with a penknife.

Further resistance was hopeless and a white flag now appeared. Among the wounded was Lord Vivian, propped against a rock wearing a tunic over his pyjamas. The officer got talking to Reitz and suggested that the young man take a look in his bivouac tent as he had no further need for its contents. Having started the morning with a grain-bag for a coat, a lame horse and two cartridges, Reitz now became the proud owner of a fine cavalry tunic, riding breeches, a sporting Lee-Metford rifle, full bandoliers and Lieutenant Sheridan's mount, a grey Arab, as well as a sturdy riding mule for his equipment.

The commando had suffered six wounded and one killed to the Lancers' sixty-three men dead or wounded – more casualties than on any other day in the regiment's long history, including the Charge of the Light Brigade in 1854. Plundering concluded, the Boers rode out feeling like 'giants refreshed', refitted from head to hoof and handsomely provisioned. 'Moreover, we had renewed confidence in our leader and in ourselves, a factor of considerable importance to a body of men in a hostile country,' writes Reitz. But there were dire consequences to this victory too: some of their number would pay dearly for looting British uniforms, as Kitchener ordered all Boers captured in khaki to be summarily executed.

Willie and I stood beside the graves of the fallen, a row of white crosses etched against the koppie's skyline. It was a melancholy spot, the wind moaning through the thorn trees and the dead seeming to haunt their old defensive positions. I read the inscription on one of gravestones, 'In loving memory of Richard Brinsley Sheridan, of Frampton Court. Lieutenant 17th Lancers, born 22nd May 1874, killed in action 17th September 1901. Faithful unto death.'

I thought of all the British and Commonwealth soldiers who had found a final resting place on the South African veld, the words of Thomas Hardy's iconic Anglo-Boer War poem echoing in my head:

> They throw in Drummer Hodge, to rest
> Uncoffined – just as found:
> His landmark is a kopje-crest
> That breaks the veldt around
> ...
> Yet portion of that unknown plain
> Will Hodge for ever be;
> His homely Northern breast and brain
> Grow to some Southern tree

The weather was at last improving and sunny days put more heart into the men as they advanced across open country once more. For a week they trekked south, making a night-time crossing of the railway line near Kommadagga Station, where an armoured train with powerful searchlights loosed a few shells in their direction but caused no injuries. As they approached the Zuurberg mountains, comprising a series of rugged ridges running east–west with deep valleys in between, the enemy's noose was again closing. Troops were being detrained ahead of and behind them – up to 3 000 at Kommadagga alone – to plug their escape routes and food supplies were running critically low once more. Smuts had no option but to lead his men straight up and over the first ridge of the Zuurberg.

I followed in hot pursuit, pausing at Kommadagga Station to photograph its vandalised buildings and rusty signs, then onward up Zuurberg Pass in pelting rain, dodging the wrack of rock falls, water streaming in torrents across the road. The valleys were lush with Afromontane forest – spekboom and boerboom, acacia and aloe. I crossed the first ridge, imagining the commando occupying these heights as they held the British back with accurate fire.

After a scouting mission in the mountains, Reitz returned to the Boers' new defensive line on the second ridge to find most of the men prostrate or unconscious. Many were vomiting repeatedly and only a few of the able bodied managed to keep the advancing Khakis at bay. It transpired that the half-starved commando had thought a local cycad, deceptively named 'Hottentot's bread', was edible, but when consumed raw, the kernels of this pineapple-like fruit are highly toxic. The Boers were in a bad way and Smuts was practically comatose. The ensuing rear-guard action across the folds of the Zuurberg, with the British constantly trying to outflank them, was going to be a close-run thing.

I reached my overnight stop at Camp Figtree, a colonial-style lodge adjacent to Addo Elephant National Park, with corrugated-iron buildings set on a ridge overlooking the Zuurberg's wooded valleys. The main lodge lies in the shadow of enormous fig trees and is all Victorian elegance with Persian carpets, dark-wood antiques, log fires and four-poster beds hung with mosquito nets. I felt a bit like a British general indulging in a spot of R&R between bouts of Boer baiting. Sunset found me on the stoep surveying wild mountain country, a set of maps laid out before me as I plotted my next historical ambush, G&T in hand and a Narina trogon's husky hooting for accompaniment.

The following morning, I was up early and in the saddle, riding a handsome chestnut called Flip with game guide Vusi leading me along bridle paths and over bald-crowned hills in a section of Addo that offers horse trails. Although I rode a far fresher steed than any the Boers possessed, I nevertheless got an inkling of their difficulties: the kloofs were deep and thickly wooded, the ridges exposed to rifle fire. My eyes scanned the hills behind us, alive to pursuing Khakis. It was good to be out of the car, enjoying the creak of leather, the clopping of hooves and the warm breeze that ruffled Flip's dark-root mane. A herd of hartebeest cantered by and I thought what good biltong they would make if we'd been hungry men on commando.

The Anglo-Boer War was the world's last great horseback conflict. By the start of the First World War, just twelve years later, everything about modern conflict had changed. Armoured cars, tanks, aircraft and massed artillery fire would have decimated the Boers, but at the turn of the last century, free-ranging horseback warfare was still possible and it suited the republicans perfectly. As long as they had water and grazing for their mounts, and biltong in their saddlebags, they were not constrained by roads, fences or supply lines and the country was theirs to roam. The Boers were superb horsemen who took great care of their steeds, often feeding their animals before themselves, and they learnt ways to keep horses fresh, frequently resting and rotating them. Indeed, the endurance of the Boer mounts astounded the British, who had no tradition of long-distance horsemanship.

The Boers were also able to live off the land, requisitioning or raiding farms, eating wild plants, plundering ostrich eggs and shooting game. This mode of warfare bred tough, resourceful, ruthless fighters who were highly mobile and developed guerrilla techniques adapted to the topography: usually a short, sharp fight followed by flight, using the terrain to ambush, escape and hide.

For the most part, the Khakis lumbered after their quarry with cumbersome wagons and artillery. A commando of 250-odd men was too large for a British scouting party to tackle and too mobile for an army column. Reitz noted that when the enemy tried to emulate the Boers, their heavy troop horses were no match for the commandos' hardier and lighter mounts. The British shifted tactics, building chains of blockhouses and using armoured trains to patrol, but when outnumbered or outgunned, the Boers simply vanished in a cloud of dust and clatter of hooves.

Watching the back of Flip's head, I was easing my way into a slow and steady rhythm that grew more comfortable with each ridge, each kloof. I felt a degree of trust was developing between us, man and steed becoming one, just like my Boer ancestors, that is until I tried to take a photograph while on the move. At the sound of my camera's autofocus beeping, docile Flip turned true to his name and tried to eject me from his back. After a few further attempts, and near dismountings, I gave up and let him have his way.

Vusi brought us to a halt for a closer perusal of the cycad that had caused all the trouble. It looked like a mini palm tree with stunted fronds. 'This is *Encephalartos altensteinii*, better known as the broodboom, and it nearly brought your commando to its knees,' he said. 'The outside pith can be eaten. Local people used to bury it and let it rot, then knead it into a cake and bake it in the embers of a fire. But the red, inner kernels are helluva poisonous. Wanna try one?'

'For historical authenticity?'

'Ja.'

'You first.'

Some of the Boers were so sick they had to be tied to their saddles during the retreat and were cruelly jounced along, barely conscious. I imagined Armstrong shells bursting around us, the terrifying thud of pom-poms and clatter of Maxim rounds. The situation did not improve when they approached the southern side of the Zuurberg, where the British were busy detraining more troops. There was nothing for it but to trek back over the mountains and try to reach the open country of the Karoo to the northwest.

Bedrogsfontein Trail in the Zuurberg section of Addo retraces the commando's escape path. I joined ranger Michael Kepe, who offered to show me the route and explain the intricacies of the fight. The spectacular 4x4 trail climbs from Kabouga to Darlington through riverine thicket and Afromontane forest, ascending to fynbos uplands and onward into arid Nama-Karoo. We ground our way up a steep, rocky track – site of a battle that turned into a rout – our progress watched by kudus and warthogs.

The Boers had halted near the top of the pass to slaughter a pair of oxen for a meal and rest up for a few hours in the shade of two ancient milkwoods. Michael directed me to park beside one of the enormous trees and we stepped out. 'These slabs of stone mark some of the graves of the fallen,' he said. 'They've been knocked over by grazing cattle, probably descendants of the two that were braaied here by the Boers.'

After their feast, the men were dozing under the trees when suddenly the alarm was sounded: Khakis were coming up the road. The Boers scrambled to ambush the strong column of 1 000 horsemen, packed tightly together on the narrow pass. When the commando opened fire, they wreaked havoc in the ranks with many terrified horses leaping off the cliff, some with their riders still mounted. Writes Reitz, 'The road became obstructed with dead and wounded horses, for we were firing into the brown, and we could hear angry shouts, as those behind tried to pass. Only a few men reached the bottom.' It's estimated the British suffered 200 casualties and more than 700 horses were killed at Bedrogsfontein that afternoon.

The ensuing days saw the commando ranging northwest across Karoo plains, thankful to be in roomy country once more, and I was on their tail, sniffing out backroads that closely followed their route. My Suzuki's tank was full, maps were spread out on the passenger seat and the road unravelled before me. I was mid trek, my feet were loose and I was fancy free. With pen and camera in place of rifle, padkos in a Kwikspar saddlebag and my imagination adrift on the open veld, I rode commando in my head.

Driving across Aberdeen Flats with the Camdeboo's jagged blue mountains adorning the northern horizon, I was thinking about warfare, landscape and climate. The Anglo-Boer conflict was played out across the great South African stage on terrain designed for epic. Geography was everything in this struggle and a horseman spending months traversing the land couldn't help but develop an intimate relationship with his environment. Throughout *Commando*, Reitz offers moments of appreciation for the landscape, its moods and seasons. He describes the wild Sabi Lowveld as 'a strange and remote region … full of fascination'; Zululand is 'lovely mountain country everywhere dotted with picturesque native kraals'; the Mpumalanga escarpment has 'mountains and forests and gorges more beautiful than any I know of in South Africa'; the Free State has 'great game-covered plains' grazed by vast 'herds of antelope and troops of wildebeest'; the Eastern Cape's Winterberg has lush farmland, 'gorgeous forest-covered steeps' and 'primeval' vegetation.

At times, Reitz describes battle scenes in elegiac terms – a Victorian set piece with landscape as majestic backdrop: 'Far below on the plain the Tugela wound shining in the sun, and the bank beyond was alive with English foot and horse. From the wooded hills further back came the flash of the British guns.' Elsewhere, the land is rendered in apocalyptic terms, such as when he witnesses the destruction wrought upon Free State farms by the enemy's scorched-earth drives.

For the Boers, landscape was also experienced in strategic terms: mountains and koppies for spying out the enemy, while rivers, ridges and dongas offered defensive positions, and all the while guarding against getting hemmed in by kloofs or trapped on mountaintops. Open plains were preferred, as enemy dust clouds could be spied a long way off and evasive action taken. Climate and weather played their part too. Icy nights, snow and swollen rivers exacted great hardship, but rain and mist disguised their spoor and movements, while the waterless wastes of the Karoo and Namaqualand proved excellent terrain for small, mobile forces.

---※---

I stopped in Aberdeen to pay my respects at the grave of Jack Baxter, a young member of the Smuts commando shot by firing squad for wearing khaki. The words 'Vir vryheid en vaderland' (for freedom and fatherland) were engraved on his obelisk-shaped tombstone. Colonel Scobell, who carried out the execution, recounts in his diary how Baxter

> never even changed colour when I told him his sentence, just asked for paper and pencil and wrote letters all the time. I saw the job through, and as he sat on a box to be shot, I could not help shaking hands with him, telling him how sorry I was and how much I admired his bravery. He said: I am all right. Don't bother about me. We are soldiers and have to die sooner or later. I am not afraid to die. Thirty seconds later he was dead.

When Reitz heard about Kitchener's order, he got rid of his Khaki uniform and thenceforth made sure he always wore civilian clothes. But it wasn't only wearing khaki that could get you executed; Cape rebels were viewed as traitors by the British and threatened with a similar fate if captured. It was a terrible predicament for Cape Afrikaners, who had great sympathy for the republican cause. Despite the risk of imprisonment or banishment, they often aided the commandos, supplying food and provisions, offering hiding places and tending to the wounded. When I was a child, my grandmother, Sannie Uys, used to tell me stories of the war and how she and her relatives had helped the commandos.

'The Anglo-Boer War struck deep into almost every Afrikaans family in the Cape Colony, shocking them by its sudden violence and jolting them into an awareness of their racial identity,' Ouma Sannie recalled during a talk on the radio in 1963. 'And it struck particularly deeply in our family, living out its, up to that moment, slow, peaceful life on our farm Bontebokskloof near the beautiful old village of Swellendam.'

Our family had many relatives in both Republican armies. Indeed, Sannie's eldest brother, Petrus Arnoldus (Nolsie), had moved to the Orange Free State to take up a teaching post and joined the Free State Boers as soon as war broke out. 'Our hearts were very much involved and our sympathies on only one side, although we as a family had many English-speaking friends,' said Sannie. There was the constant fear that Nolsie would be killed in the fierce fighting at the beginning of the war. And if he were captured, would he be shot as a Cape rebel, or had he taken out naturalisation papers in time? There was considerable relief when Nolsie was captured and banished to St Helena Island as a prisoner of war.

Sannie also told me the story of hiding an escaped POW in the milkwood forest on their farm, and of the time her sister, Anna, helped a wounded Boer left behind by a passing commando in 1901. Anna was staying with their grandparents, Oupa and Ouma Lourens, in Heidelberg, a village occupied by British troops to counter guerrilla activity in the area. One morning just before dawn, Anna woke to the crackle of rifle fire coming from the main street. A small commando galloped through town, trying to break north into the Karoo. The skirmish didn't last long and soon the Boers had vanished, but one of them had been shot from his horse and lay bleeding in the street.

The English colonel in charge of the garrison asked if our family could tend to the lad. 'Of course, bring the poor boy,' said Ouma Lourens. And that was how a mortally wounded Boer ended up spending the last days of his life in the voorkamer of my great-great-grandparents' home. Before he died, the youth told Anna in a faint whisper to look in his Bible where she would find his address, and would she be so kind as to write to his family? The little veld-Bible told Anna that his surname was Bellingham and that he came from Graaff-Reinet, making him a Cape rebel and thus liable to be executed if he recovered. And that is how a long friendship was initiated between our family and the Bellinghams of Graaff-Reinet, united by the death of a son.

From Aberdeen, I veered southwest towards Willowmore and passed Vlaklaagte, where Reitz and a small group became separated from the commando during a skirmish. Over the ensuing weeks, they tried to catch up with Smuts, and their acts of daring and high adventure during that quest make for some of the liveliest reading in *Commando*. 'Like sailors adrift in a boat, we anxiously scanned the horizon for a sign of the commando, but the country to the south lay open before us,' writes Reitz. The chase was on.

I, too, split from Smuts's route and followed the peregrinations of Reitz. His tiny party could not afford to get involved in any skirmishes until it had rejoined the main body, so the men tried to stay out of sight. Crossing the Swartberg proved the biggest obstacle. Reitz knew that Smuts was making for Oudtshoorn, but Meiringspoort was garrisoned and had blockhouses at both ends, so his band would have to struggle up and over the mountain instead. 'Before us rose the Swartbergen, steep as a house, but we climbed it all day, dragging our leg-weary horses, until we reached the top at dusk. From here we could look south over more mountains and deep valleys, and far beyond lay a grey haze, which we took to be the sea.'

Once south of the berg, they discovered to their dismay that Smuts had headed north again … and so they would have to re-cross the mountains, this time in the region of Seweweekspoort. After a series of narrow escapes, they reached the Swartberg foothills west of Oudtshoorn.

Farmer Hermanus Potgieter of Red Stone Hills guest farm, where I spent the night, showed me the Jewish shop at Kruisrivier where Reitz's party 'requisitioned' provisions, especially condensed milk, and 'acquired' a new horse for the ascent. As Seweweekspoort was guarded, they chose a little-known track over Wyenek. Reaching the top of the mountain, they gazed down on Gamkaskloof, otherwise known as Die Hel. This hamlet, deep in the Swartberg's rugged folds, had no access roads and was to provide a safe haven for the weary Boers.

'On the floor of the chasm, a thousand feet below, we made out a cluster of huts,' writes Reitz. 'We climbed through a fissure in the crags, and reached the bottom soon after sunset. As we approached the huts, a shaggy giant in goatskins appeared and spoke to us in a strange outlandish Dutch. He was a white man named Cordier, who lived here with his wife and a brood of half-wild children, in complete isolation from the outside world.'

As my Suzuki traversed Swartberg Pass, I admired the sandstone cliffs, red in colour, lichen-stained and warped into outlandish shapes. A steep descent on the breathtaking switchbacks of Elands Pass, threading my way between rain squalls and rainbows, brought me to Gamkaskloof. The tiny settlement of Die Hel could not have changed much in the intervening century. I thought of Cordier's Swiss Family Robinson existence and how this kloof appeared to Reitz as an island outside time.

In the hamlet, I asked around for Annetjie Joubert, great-granddaughter of Cordier, but she was on holiday at the coast. A crackly telephone line got me through to her. 'My oupagrootjie was good to Reitz: gave him honey beer and slaughtered a goat,' she said. 'The two men got on well. In gratitude, Reitz gave Cordier a memento: a little silver boot that serves as a snuff box. I've still got it. You must come kuier again when I'm there and I'll show you the ruins of my oupagrootjie's cottage.'

Cordier guided them north along secret paths over the mountain and down onto the plains west of Prince Albert. A few good leads as to the whereabouts of Smuts now sent them in the direction of Sutherland. They crossed the railway line, avoiding the pair of blockhouses guarding the Dwyka River bridge, which they spotted in the distance. An armoured train puffed by without molesting them.

I pulled off the road at Dwyka to take a closer look at one of the square, three-storey structures, built of dressed stone with concrete lintels, steel loophole plates and a (caved-in) corrugated-iron roof – it looked more derelict performance-art piece than menacing fort. For the soldiers sent to guard these lonely outposts – Britain's last castles – it was a painfully boring existence, occasionally enlivened by moments of terror. There was something vaguely absurd about these blockhouses that appeared so medieval, built as they were for an enemy that no longer possessed artillery, rather than the product of Twentieth-Century warfare. Spotting the Boers riding by on the veld, far out of range, the soldiers must have felt as though they were trapped aboard anchored ships while the enemy sailed about at will. Nevertheless, blockhouses were not all 'folly' and did help to hasten the end of the war by restricting commando movement and preventing bridges from being blown.

On I drove, pursuing Reitz across the Karoo plains. A few kilometres further west, I came to the Ketting blockhouse, almost identical to the ones at Dwyka, and immortalised in Rudyard Kipling's poem 'Bridge-Guard in the Karoo':

> Sudden the desert changes,
> The raw glare softens and clings,
> Till the aching Oudtshoorn ranges
> Stand up like the thrones of Kings –
> …
> More than a little lonely
> Where the lessening tail-lights shine.
> No – not combatants – only
> Details guarding the line!

Further down the defensive chain towards Laingsburg, I stopped to look at a much larger blockhouse guarding the railway bridge over the dry bed of the Geelbek River. It was a concrete affair with pitched roof and two steel turrets projecting at opposite corners of the top floor to provide covering cross-fire – no doubt an oven in summer and an ice box in winter. There was a steel door set high above the ground and accessed by a retractable ladder; the walls were scrawled with incoherent modern graffiti. During the war, the area around the blockhouse would have been thick with barbed wire hung with tin cans and other devices to alert the sentries if Boers tried to cross in the dark. I thought of how such fortifications were a symbol of British dominion over the land and of their determination to crush the Boers. Today, such ruins are hardly noticed by drivers speeding up and down a route that was once a vital artery of Empire and is now simply known as the N1.

Reitz's band moved fast over these plains, all the while scanning the horizon for any sign of the commando. Coming over a rise near Zeekoeigat on the Tankwa River, they could hardly believe their eyes. 'There, on the banks of the river below, was the welcome sight of many horses at graze and smoke rising from among the trees to show that our long quest was at an end.' A sentry rode out to identify the intruders and then galloped back to spread the glad tidings. There was wild celebration in camp that night. Even the usually taciturn Smuts was overjoyed, congratulating them on remaining adrift in enemy territory for three weeks and coming through without losing a single man. Reitz described his pleasure at being back with his 'old mother commando as she enclosed her stray children in her arms once more.'

I turned north on the road to Sutherland, heading into the parched, desolate Moordenaars Karoo. My abode that night was not far from Zeekoeigat in a cottage called Isle of Sky on a farm adjacent to Tankwa Karoo National Park. It was a simple, whitewashed stone building whose rustic interior had solid wooden furniture, an Aga stove, zebra skins for carpets and the heads and horns of antelope adorning the walls. The date on my cell phone told me it was Valentine's Day.

Sunset was a mess of bloody reds and a stiff southerly wind had sprung up, lashing the thorn trees and twirling dust devils towards a bleak horizon. Daniel, the farmhand, and his wife, a petite woman with meerkat eyes, arrived to prepare the fire. He mumbled apologies about the lack of hot water in the shower; she scurried about lighting paraffin lanterns. Then they disappeared into the dusk. There wasn't enough light to read the pile of old magazines in the corner, no cell phone reception to call home and my laptop was drained of battery power.

I sat beside the fire, braaing a coil of wors and sipping a mug of acidic wine. The sky was oppressively big, splattered with too many stars. 'Happy Valentine's Day, ou maat,' I toasted my inner romantic. Retreating from the wind, I ate my supper indoors, but the wors tasted off and the provocatively named Lay's chips, bought earlier in Prince Albert, were stale. Meal over, I looked around the cottage. It was 8 p.m.: what now?

Reeking of meat and wood smoke, I climbed into bed as sand filtered down from the ceiling and the corrugated-iron roof banged in the wind. On the bedside table lay a copy of *Rooi Rose* from the last century, brittle as parchment and looking like an archaeologist's lucky find. The fashionable blondes in swimsuits would have to be my Valentines. Somewhere in the distance a jackal whined, its thin voice eddying across the plain – looking for a mate, ou maat? In the wee hours, the dodgy wors proved my suspicions correct in dramatic fashion. I ushered in the dawn, not in the arms of a bikini-clad blonde, but embracing the toilet bowl with almost as much passion.

Feeling like I'd eaten *Encephalartos altensteinii*, I was uncomfortably back in the saddle heading west along the dry Tankwa River, its course marked by dark-green karee trees and the lighter green of wild willows. For the men of the commando, the going grew easier now. There were no more railways or blockhouses and the arid environment could not sustain extensive grazing and was thus unsuitable for large enemy columns. The British, in turn, felt that the Smuts commando and other rebel bands roaming the region did not pose a serious threat to Cape Town or the Boland and were content to keep nudging them north.

The barren terrain suited the Boers and they had plenty of support from local farmers. The Northern Cape was the last place the Boers could conduct a proper Nineteenth-Century campaign, far from the great drives of the industrial war machine that ploughed across the republics. However, although free to range the north, Smuts had not yet achieved any of his larger goals: striking a blow at the heart of imperial authority at the Cape, bringing meaningful relief to the republics and fomenting rebellion among the Cape Afrikaners.

The commando followed the Tankwa to Elandsvlei, an oasis of pear trees and palms where they camped for a couple of days, allowing the Boers to recuperate. It was the first time since they'd crossed the Orange River that they remained in one place for more than twenty-four hours, and the men relished the chance to relax. I stopped to shake hands with farmer Karsten and take a few photos of his Cape Dutch homestead with its elegant gable, vine pergola and two tall palm trees standing sentinel over the house and werf – a lovely place indeed for the Boers to encamp.

The well-rested commando then threaded its way through the Cederberg and along the Koebee River. I followed them through these majestic mountains, overnighting in a thatched sandstone cottage built into the side of a kraal on Papkuilsfontein farm, whose homestead dates back to the Eighteenth Century. As I was still feeling the wors for wear, farmer's wife Mariëtte van Wyk brought me a home-cooked supper in the cottage. 'My grandfather, Philip Strauss, fought alongside Smuts back in the day,' she said as she unpacked the bobotie and malva pudding from a cooler box. 'This area was very important because Vanrhyns Pass gives access to the interior. Any British column trying to come through here was looking for trouble. There were Boers behind every rock and my oupa was one of them.'

'Did he tell you stories about his time with Oom Jannie?' I asked.

'Oh ja, lots of stories. The one that affected me most was about Lemeul Colyn. He was a bywoner who joined the commando, but they found out he was actually an informant for the English. His treachery helped the enemy attack a Boer camp on the Olifants River and many men were killed. My oupa was present at his trial on the farm Onder-Aties and told me when Oom Jannie gave the verdict that Colyn must be shot by firing squad, the poor man fell on his knees, begging to be spared as he had eight children. What would become of them and what would become of his wife? Smuts then asked Colyn whether he'd thought about all the children of the Boers who'd been killed because of his treason. I'm pretty sure he said it was thirty-eight children, and this was the part that gripped my heart. Next morning at 5 a.m. Colyn was shot.'

'In *Commando*, Reitz says he helped organise the firing squad,' I said.

'Ag man, Justin, the horrors of war,' said Mariëtte.

———*———

The commando reached Vanrhynsdorp, a pro-Boer town recaptured from the British by Commandant Manie Maritz. For the first time, the men could conduct themselves normally: stroll the high street, visit friends and do a bit of courting. Smuts set up his headquarters in a house on Van Zyl Street and directed the summer's operations from there. Reitz was promoted to Smuts's staff and was sent on a number of long rides to places as far afield as Kakamas on the Orange River, delivering dispatches to rebel groups and rallying support.

I visited the tourist information centre on Voortrekker Street, which had served as the Boer hospital, and then the cemetery to view the graves of the fallen. An inscription on one headstone read: 'Wie voor zyn land het leven laat, diens roem en glorie nooit vergaat' (Whoever dies for his country, his fame and glory never perish). I also paid a visit to 17 Van Zyl Street to view Smuts's headquarters. The elegant house dates from 1751 and is said to be the oldest building in the district, having served down the years as an inn, school, church, magistrate's court and private home. The building was flat-roofed and fronted by a long, narrow veranda lined with chairs and benches under an afdak of green corrugated iron. During the war, when visitors came to enquire about Oom Jannie, they'd be greeted by a group of taciturn Boers lounging on the stoep and given vague answers that boiled down to no one being quite sure where exactly the general could be found. At the time, Smuts was certainly the most famous, and most elusive, resident of Vanrhynsdorp. From this HQ, he pulled the strings that saw a number of strategic attacks

– notably at Middelpos, Tontelbos and the farm Windhoek – to counter the British, who continued sending columns north to try to dislodge the Boers and resupply their garrisoned towns.

There was also a light-hearted episode during the Vanrhynsdorp period, recounted in *Commando*. Many republican Boers had never seen the ocean, so one morning Smuts led a party of about eighty down to Vischwater (Papendorp today) at the mouth of the Olifants River. I took a detour to the coast and parked beside the saltpans to survey the turquoise tendrils of the Olifants leaking into marshland, the murmur of surf echoing over the dunes to my left. I pictured the Boers shouting, 'The sea! The sea!' as they threw off their clothes and galloped bareback into the waves, whooping with excitement. Reitz got talking to an old fisherman on the beach and asked him the way to England, explaining that the commando wanted to cross over and capture the city of London. The horrified man exclaimed, 'My God, baas, don't do it; the water is over your head here and you will all be drowned!'

That night, they camped in the dunes, sitting around fires of driftwood and sharing the stories they would tell their families when they one day returned home. The Boers spent two more days at Vischwater, boating on the estuary and helping fishermen pull in their nets, before returning to their various units, happy to have ridden their horses into the sea and enjoyed an eddy of pleasure in the tide of war.

Smuts still hoped to attack the Boland, but his generals persuaded him that taking the copper mines in the Northern Cape would be strategically more prudent. The commando duly split up and headed into drought-stricken Namaqualand, crushing resistance at Garies and Leliefontein, before laying siege to Springbokfontein (today's Springbok).

I followed in their wake, up the N7 across stony plains covered with low scrub and succulents, a ridge of mountains my constant companion on the eastern horizon. It was furnace hot and the road ahead dissolved into milky heat mirages. Turning right near Garies, my Suzuki nosed its way into the Kamiesberg, a realm of dome-shaped granite whalebacks of monstrous proportion. I stopped at Leliefontein Mission Station to visit the site of a notorious skirmish in which Maritz's commando massacred the local Nama inhabitants. When Reitz later came upon the scene of carnage, he was deeply affected and considered Maritz's actions ruthless and unjustifiable: 'We found the place sacked and gutted, and, among the rocks beyond the burned houses lay twenty or thirty dead Hottentots, still clutching their antiquated muzzleloaders … General Smuts said nothing, but I saw him walk past the boulders where the dead lay, and on his return he was moody and curt, as was his custom when he was displeased.'

There was no time to linger: Springbok had to be taken. *Commando* offers a detailed account of the attacks on the town's three stone forts. During one dawn assault, Reitz slithered forward to within forty metres of a roundhouse fort and hid behind a boulder. As the sun rose, he began sniping at the loopholes until he'd all but emptied his bandolier. The soldiers returned fire but, blinded by the sun, were unable to locate his hiding place. When the fort eventually fell, Reitz discovered that his aim had been deadly accurate, having killed or wounded several soldiers and peppered the water cistern, forcing the defenders to abandon their position due to thirst. What's more, he realised it was 2 April – his twentieth birthday and the third he'd spent at war – but celebrations would have to wait as the next fort beckoned.

'From what we had seen of No. 3 in daylight, we judged it to be the most difficult of all, for it stood on a high rock, like a castle on the Rhine.' I parked in the centre of town and climbed the small, pyramid-shaped koppie to look at the site of the third fort. The hillock was studded with granite boulders and mature kokerbooms and commanded a fine defensive position, but by now the Boers were skilled at taking lone blockhouses, particularly given their recently acquired stock of miners' dynamite, and they made short work of No. 3.

With the fall of Springbok, and much booty taken, the commando turned its attention to the nearby towns of Concordia and O'okiep (today's Okiep). First, though, Reitz needed rest. He had not slept for three days and, collapsing on a bed without removing his boots, he was out like a lantern for a full twenty-four hours.

Concordia surrendered without a fight, but the larger mining settlement of Okiep was a much harder nut to crack. Driving around the town today, you can see why the Boers struggled. The surrounding koppies created natural fortresses and more than a dozen were topped with blockhouses. I spotted the remains of one of them – the Crow's Nest, which fell to the Boers during the siege – on an outcrop northeast of town. But energetic Lieutenant Colonel Shelton's force was sizeable, well supplied and properly armed, and neither side gained the upper hand in the fighting that ensued.

I spent the last night of my trek in the Okiep Country Hotel. Sitting at a table for one with a glass of lukewarm Merlot, I tried to imagine Okiep in the autumn of 1902. There is no mining in this sleepy town today, but in the late Nineteenth Century this was the world's richest copper mine. During the war, it was a bustling settlement whose community included many Cornish miners and their families, as well as a large coloured population that helped defend the town. Shelton had more than a thousand men at his disposal and there were another 2 000 non-combatants. Rationing had to be introduced and civilians weren't allowed to move about during daylight for fear of snipers. The climax of the siege, and one that could have ended in disaster, was the Great Train Raid. This involved a 'Spaghetti Western'-style attempt by the Boers to drive a steam train packed with dynamite into the heart of the defences. Fortunately, it failed, as a great many civilians may have lost their lives.

Smuts was content to lay siege to Okiep, knowing that this would surely lure a powerful relieving force from Cape Town. It was during this period of relative stalemate that a message arrived announcing that peace talks were to be held in the Transvaal. Although Smuts and the other commandos still had control of large swathes of the Northern Cape, Kitchener's scorched-earth policy, concentration camps and blockhouse tactics had finally taken their toll.

Smuts chose Reitz and Tottie Krige to accompany him to the negotiating table. A ship was waiting in Port Nolloth to take them to Simon's Town and from there by train to Vereeniging. The combatants of the Smuts commando could hold their heads high: they were undefeated, on the offensive and remained a fit and confident fighting force after eight months in the saddle.

The three emissaries rode through their own ranks to the British line, where the Boer escort took their horses and they all sang the commando hymn. Firing a farewell volley into the air, the escorts wheeled around and galloped away cheering, confident that Oom Jannie would return with an honourable settlement. It was an emotional farewell for Reitz. He knew that unconditional surrender would be the most likely outcome of the talks, but what he did not know was that he and Smuts were riding into the pages of history and that their story would become the stuff of legend.

That evening, the three Boers stood silently on the quay in Port Nolloth, waiting to board the steamship *Lake Eyrie* where luxurious cabins and soft beds awaited. 'I do not know what was in the minds of my companions, but perhaps they too were thinking of the long road we had travelled, of campfires on mountains and plains, and of the good men and splendid horses that were dead.'

My journey, too, was done. I left Okiep at sunrise, bound for my Cape Town home. Over to my left, caught in the spokes of the rising sun, I saw a commando approaching across the plain and pulled off to watch them. Scouting groups passed ahead and behind me, Reitz no doubt among them. Then came the main body, riding with an easy gait, stirrups long, raising a tall cloud of dust. Now the drumming of hooves grew louder and I could make out the men more clearly, bandoliers strung across their chests, cowboy hats pushed back on their foreheads and grim determination on their faces. By some unseen signal, the commando changed direction and wheeled away to the north.

I started the engine and drove on, watching the shroud of dust receding in my rear-view mirror as the long, straight N7 spooled out before me.

———✷———

THE SOUL OF THE WHITE BABOON
Eugène Marais's Waterberg

I left Johannesburg one bright winter's morning and headed north on the N1 through veld that was dry and brittle, the sky bleached white. I was bound for Modimolle, Limpopo, in the footsteps of South Africa's unofficial poet laureate whose soul, or perhaps a ghostly vestige thereof, I hoped to find lurking in some hidden kloof of the Waterberg.

Poet, lawyer and naturalist, Eugène Marais (1871–1936) is considered one of our nation's foremost intellects and one of its greatest poets. He began his professional life as a journalist in Pretoria, then studied in London (law and, for a short time, medicine) before returning to South Africa and immersing himself in the natural world. Marais was one of the first people to undertake a close examination of the life of wild primates and, due to his groundbreaking research on chacma baboons, is widely acknowledged as the father of ethology, the scientific study of animal behaviour. In the introduction to Marais's *The Soul of the Ape*, American anthropologist Robert Ardrey makes grand claims about his contribution to science: 'As no gallery of modern art can fail to be haunted by the burning eyes of Vincent van Gogh, so the pages of no future science can fail to be haunted by the brooding, solitary, less definable presence of Eugène Marais.'

The poet-naturalist led a tragic life: his wife died soon after their marriage and he began taking opiates, resulting in a morphine addiction that cast a shadow over his tormented, brilliant career. Perhaps the happiest years of his adult life were spent in the Waterberg, mountains to which he retreated from the world and where he was able to find periods of relative peace.

Situated some 180 kilometres north of Pretoria, the Waterberg straddles an area of 15 000 square kilometres, its southern escarpment presenting a line of crags dominated by the Seven Sisters, while the central plateau comprises wide-open grasslands and its northeastern ramparts rise out of the Bushveld in a series of dramatic formations. With plentiful ground water, these mountains were for millennia home to hunter-gathering San and, before them, early hominids stretching back more than two million years. In Marais's day, the Waterberg was the realm of gunrunners and big-game hunters, its fringes loosely settled by hardy pioneer families and mining prospectors.

Since childhood, Marais had dreamt of visiting these highlands. In *The Road to Waterberg*, he writes about how, as a boy growing up in Pretoria, this region had

> always been associated with all the wonders of unpeopled veld, and to us who were born and grew up on the outskirts of the wilderness it represented the ideal theatre of manly adventure, of great endeavours and the possibility of princely wealth. Ivory was then what gold and diamonds became afterwards, and stories were told of bold and lucky hunters killing twenty tuskers in one morning – the value of a principality of land in a few hours ... Even now, with invading civilization marching across the hills in seven-league boots, Waterberg still holds its charm.

From 1907 to 1916, Marais lived in these mountains and wrote extensively about the fauna he observed and studied there. His experiences provided material for his two most important non-fiction works, *The Soul of the Ape* and *The Soul of the White Ant*, as well as a number of poems, short stories and anecdotes about the natural world that appeared in magazines and books. His seminal study of termites led him to the conclusion that each colony should be considered a single organism, a prescient insight that had to wait more than half a century before it was popularised by Richard Dawkins.

Most significantly, he lived among a troop of baboons for long periods, making revolutionary discoveries for science. I wanted to track his life in the Waterberg, particularly events that led to the genesis of *The Soul of the Ape*, a work that had captivated me as a student writing a doctoral thesis on the influence of Darwinism on literature. I hoped to visit parts of the berg that were still in the kind of wild condition Marais encountered a century ago, perhaps even meet the descendants of the baboons he once studied, and explore the haunts of his great book.

———*———

THE SOUL OF THE WHITE BABOON

Mid-morning, I turned off the N1 near Modimolle (formerly Nylstroom) and headed east in search of the farm of my prospective guide. Peet Rossouw is a filmmaker (in 1979 he directed an SABC documentary series about Marais), amateur historian, farmer and Marais fundi who grew up and has spent most of his life in the Waterberg. I was put in touch with him by my sister's friend, Katinka Heyns, who'd recently made a movie, *Die Wonderwerker*, about Marais's time in the mountains. Rossouw had been Heyns's location scout and researcher for the production and, in our brief email correspondence, indicated that he'd be happy to share his knowledge with me.

The rambling stone house lay at the end of an overgrown driveway. I parked beneath a leafless tree, passed through a cactus garden and stepped onto an enclosed veranda hung with strips of biltong pegged in lines like meaty washing. I knocked on the front door and a gentle voice within called out: 'Kom binne, ek's nou-nou by jou.'

The door opened into a large-volume living space with chunky, darkwood furniture, African artefacts, a painting of a farm gate, butterflies pinned in a frame and a pile of *Weg!* magazines on the coffee table. Peet emerged from a bedroom – a tall man in his seventies with thick spectacles, thinning white hair and a slight stoop. He had a craggy, handsome face, big hands and a sad smile. Despite his wife's ill health (Katinka had told me she was suffering from cancer), he would give up a day to help with my quest.

'Come, let's go find you Marais,' said Peet, his hand on my shoulder and calling to his wife to lock all the doors and windows. These farms of the South African north have become fortresses once again, I thought.

As I nosed the hired car down the driveway, Peet told me how his garden was frequently raided by nyalas and kudus, come to plunder his prize blooms and drink the water in his birdbath. 'The Waterberg is still a pretty wild place, but when I was a kid, it was pure wilderness,' he said. 'I remember enormous herds of game, as far as the eye could see, coming down from Botswana and ranging across the veld, but not any more.'

Beyond Modimolle, we joined the old coach road and drove north until we reached a low concrete bridge between red cliffs where Peet told me to pull over. 'This drift is called Hessie-se-Water,' he said. 'You might recall from your research that it's where Hessie van Deventer climbed off the ox wagon ...'

I'd read Marais's story of Hessie and her husband Jossie, returning to their farm after Nagmaal in Nylstroom. She was a feisty woman, he a conservative Dopper, and the pair had a tempestuous relationship. The homeward journey saw yet another one of their heated quarrels. Things came to a head as they passed through the drift and, losing his temper, Jossie shouted: 'If you want to behave like a she-devil, why don't you get off?'

In a fit of pique, Hessie climbed down and Jossie pulled away, leaving his wife to trudge back to the farm through the night. Arriving home, Hessie sank into a chair and proclaimed that she could no longer walk.

For the next seventeen years, Hessie suffered from paralysis. Jossie consulted all manner of doctor and herbalist, but his wife remained steadfastly immobile in a pushcart. When Jossie heard there was a new 'doctor' (Marais had no formal qualifications) in the district, he hoisted Hessie onto a wagon and drove her to Rietfontein farm, where Marais had taken up lodgings. An examination revealed that her legs still exhibited reflex movement and the young 'doctor' surmised she could be cured by hypnosis. To the onlookers' astonishment, after a few hours of his ministrations, Hessie van Deventer stood up and walked. Marais's fame quickly spread throughout the region: here was a man who could make the lame walk by 'mesmerising' them, and from then on he was known as the 'miracle doctor'.

Standing on the bridge, Peet cut into my musing: 'I interviewed Tannie van Heerden before she died and she told me that the business of Hessie being sick and unable to use her legs was all just nonsense. She was simply "die bliksem in" with her husband. After she was forced to walk all the way back to the farm that night she said to herself, "Ek gaan sit waar ek sit," and that was that, but when everyone was out the house, Hessie got up and went about as normal. It was her revenge on Jossie. Many years later, when she was getting gatvol with all that sitting around, she heard about Marais and cooked up a plan to be "healed". You see, the revealing part is that the day after being cured, she climbed on a horse and went riding, which would have been impossible if she'd really had no movement in her legs for all those years.'

We got back in the car and continued north on the old coach road. 'This is exactly the route Marais followed on his first visit, when the district made such a deep impression on him, a journey he immortalised in *The Road to Waterberg*,' said Peet. Marais had been met at Nylstroom station by an old acquaintance, Dolf Erasmus, and they set off in a cart and four horses, travelling through the night. 'For the first time in my life, I was to enter the Waterberg, the mystery region of my boyhood,' he writes. 'It was an intensely dark night and when we drove down to the drifts it seemed as if we were sinking into a gulf of impenetrable darkness.'

The cart ascended a pass lined with syringa and boekenhout trees, and onto the straight white road that Peet and I were following, built by Transvaal Republic artillery engineers and unchanged in more than a century. As they made their way slowly north, the mountains rose out of the land and somewhere in the dark hours, Dolf's team turned off the road onto the soft grass of the first outspan.

'Stop here,' said Peet, holding up his hand. I pulled off and we got out. 'This is where they halted to rest the horses and that is Marais's Utopia,' he said, sweeping an arm across the Waterberg foothills. An icy wind teased the dry grass, grey thorn trees hugged the earth, the light was midday harsh and the distant hills pale and nondescript – a far cry from Utopia, I thought.

Marais climbed down from the cart and stared at the vista, marvelling at the intensity of the stars:

> I was caught by a sense of the vastness which held me breathless for a moment. It seemed as if we stood on some mighty projection thrust out into the heavens ... I felt like a wanderer visiting his homeland after many years, troubled and puzzled by that sense of strangeness which speeding time forever brings ... A sense of peace and quietness, such as nought else within the circle of human experience can evoke, came from the velvet night in which the stars had their setting.

Marais lay down on the dewy grass and looked up at the Milky Way feeling 'indescribably happy'. In that moment, it seemed that nothing – not even the gnawing disquietude of his addiction – could 'touch that sense of peaceful exaltation which had obliterated all the troubles and fears and sordid hopes that constitute civilised life.' On this, his first night in the Waterberg, his heart had stumbled upon exactly what he'd come looking for.

Yet even in his euphoria, oblivion offered itself as a shadowy alternative as he morbidly noted, in almost the same breath, that the sudden destruction of our solar system would mean 'less to the visible whole than the withdrawal of a single atom of oxygen from the Seven Seas.'

Peet came and stood beside me, saying in his refined Afrikaans: 'You must remember that Marais arrived at the end of a very bad time in the Waterberg. The inhabitants had come through a long period of drought, the decimation of their cattle by the rinderpest and three years of war. Our people were poverty stricken and traumatised. Marais had also been through trauma with the death of his wife and then the drugs. He thought he could break his addiction here, far from the city. He thought he could escape. With their typical hospitality, the Waterbergers gave him warmth and love and a roof over his head, and he in turn saw things through rose-coloured spectacles and experienced, or chose to experience, a kind of paradise. At least in the beginning.'

The pair climbed back on the cart and rode through the night until they reached the farm Doornhoek. Erasmus was a tin and platinum prospector and, along with a number of other miners, had set up camp on the farm. Marais was so enchanted by his stay at Doornhoek that he returned a year later, in 1907, bent on settling in the area and buying prospecting rights. He was appointed as mine doctor and took permanent lodgings on nearby Rietfontein farm.

Marais became fascinated by a troop of baboons that frequented a kloof on Doornhoek and conducted three years of intensive research among them. He also purchased a newborn baboon which he raised as a pet, intent on learning as much as he could from the primate's behaviour. Marais named him Piet and the pair went everywhere together. When he arrived at work in his Cape cart, the little baboon would leap down and take the horse's reins like a well-trained touleier (span leader). Piet drank from a cup, befriended other domestic animals and carried kittens and puppies about with him. He was fond of waking Marais by gently drawing apart his master's eyelids with his fingers. The baboon also fell in love with a human baby, wouldn't allow anyone near the infant and became a devoted and reliable babysitter.

Further up the old coach road, we came to the entrance of Doornhoek, where warning signs adorned the gate: *enter at own risk, no firearms, beware heavy moving vehicles, strictly private*. The farm had been a prosperous tin mine in Marais's day and is still the (decidedly rundown) Union mining concession. Peet tried phoning the farmer to let us in, but there was no answer from Boet.

Just then, a bakkie drew up with a group of Zimbabwean labourers hanging on precariously in a wire cage on the back. Its driver was the farm manager, Thys, who greeted Peet warmly and let us in. We followed the bakkie up a hill strewn with derelict cars, trucks, farm implements and a pair of eviscerated bulldozers. 'As you can see, Boet farms with scrap metal,' said Peet. 'He's a bit, um, hoe sal ek nou sê … eccentric.'

'Boet who?' I asked.

'Nee man, we don't know each other's surnames in the Waterberg; it's sommer Boet or Peet or Thys. Everyone knows who you're talking about.'

We parked beside the dilapidated homestead in a garden where moth-eaten emus pecked at the lawn. I noted an enormous swimming pool under construction (abandoned?) beside a half-built, double-storey face-brick building. Boet was clearly an obsessive collector, for the garden and stoep were piled with junk of every kind, from broken furniture to fridges, car engines and a rusted shipping container. I even spotted a 1920s sedan and a Nineteenth-Century Cape cart just like the one Marais used. Perhaps it *had* belonged to the poet.

We were led into the house by Thys. Thirty-something and sporting a wobbling beer boep, he wore tight rugby shorts, veldskoens without socks and a floppy felt hat. Marais might well have claimed that Thys's ancestors had kept their gene pool intimate and familial.

'Boet is baie siek,' said Thys.

'What's wrong with him?' asked Peet.

'I don't know, but tomorrow I'm sure as hell taking him to hospital.'

We waited in the living room while Thys went to check on Boet. Doornhoek's interiors were even more interesting than the exterior. High-backed chairs with protruding stuffing lined the walls as though in preparation for a dance and loose parquet flooring clacked underfoot, eliciting a strident response from two African grey parrots. The walls were hung with old South African flags and Transvaal Republic vierkleurs, rows of cowboy hats and a few Mausers, while a large-calibre artillery shell stood on the dining-room table. Ashtrays overflowed with stompies and the room reeked of cigarette smoke and layers of dust.

Thys reappeared, saying Boet would like to see us, and we followed him down the corridor to a darkened bedroom. My eyes took a moment to adjust to the gloom and register the bloated figure on the bed, naked save for blue pyjama shorts. Boet's skin was so pale it appeared transparent, even luminous; hair sprouted in ginger and grey tufts from his scalp and was echoed in copses of beard. I was introduced as 'the writer from Cape Town', but Boet was too weak to raise his head from the sweat-stained pillow.

'Hummm,' he murmured.

We stood in the doorway while Peet conducted a stilted conversation about farming and the drought, to which Boet mumbled the occasional response. Given the strangeness of the encounter, I couldn't help thinking of our host as a human incarnation of a termite queen, so eloquently described by Marais in *The Soul of the White Ant*. Was this bedridden oom the master of all the farm's worker ants, radiating a mysterious influence and controlling their movements, however far they might roam? If these bedroom walls were the 'skull' of the nest, then Boet's bloated frame was its brain, a white blob pulsing in its darkened cavity, and the whole farm was its body. Just like a termite mound, Doornhoek was a single, giant, immobile organism.

I tried to recall the words of the soliloquy delivered by Nature to the termite queen in *The Soul of the White Ant*. It went something like: 'Beloved, you are going to suffer a great loss. Instead of living in glowing sunlight, you will spend your days in darkness; instead of the citizenship of the wide veld and the freedom of the air, mountains, trees and plains, you will become a prisoner in a narrow room with drawn curtains. But by way of compensation, you will become a far more important and wonderful being. Although reduced to an immobile shapeless mass buried in a living grave and needing Thys to help you go to the toilet, you will become a sensitive mainspring. I guarantee you the protection you need, and not only from Armed Response and Farm Watch. The million dangers, the million enemies, the Julius Malemas and Andile Mngxitamas who threaten your safety and your land, will fling themselves in vain against your electric fences, your impenetrable armour.'

Boet's husky voice interrupted my musing to suggest that we take a look around the farm and visit the Marais sights, to which we readily agreed. We set off, all three of us seated up front in Thys's single-cab Ford. I sat in the middle, legs astride the gears with camera bag on my lap. Thys smelt of cigarettes and continued to light up throughout the tour, talked non-stop about the 'kaffir government', Blue Bulls rugby, lazy farm workers and how he'd ended up working for Boet after he could no longer cut it in the city ('the kaffirs get all the jobs').

'Such a lekker quality of life up here,' he said, as we drove through a blighted landscape, past more derelict vehicles and onto a ridge that overlooked the detritus of a century of mining: broken headgear, grey slag heaps, pink wounds in the mountainside and rusting machinery. We paused beside an abandoned building with smashed windows.

'This used to be the clinic where Marais treated the miners,' said Peet. 'He came by cart every day from Rietfontein. Boet still has the medicine case that Marais used.'

We drove down a bumpy gravel road and took a right turn into Baboon Kloof, following a track that meandered beside a stream as the gorge narrowed and rocky walls pressed in. Thys parked beneath a wild-pear tree, the Bushveld bride, its white flowers creating an Impressionist arch over the road.

'This is where Marais spent all those years studying the fokken' baboons,' said Thys. 'Come, I'll show you.'

We walked upstream, our boots crunching on pebbles worn smooth by the water's abrasion, until we came to two circular piles of stones. A yellow sign indicated that this was where Marais and fellow researcher Alec Austin resided off and on from 1906 to 1908.

'The stones are all that remain of the two rondavels,' said Thys.

Back then, an enormous troop of more than 300 baboons occupied the kloof, a rocky ledge and shallow cave in its eastern flank providing refuge from predators at night. After years of war and the destruction of many Waterberg farms by British soldiers, the baboons – normally hunted because of their crop-raiding habits – had enjoyed a long reprieve and were thriving. Using stale bread and mielies, the two researchers were able to accustom the troop to their presence. Marais writes in *My Friends the Baboons*: 'Mr Austin and I built our huts in the mountain valley a few hundred feet from the upper entrance of the kloof, and within a few months we were on such friendly terms with the baboons that we could walk through the troop as a farmer does among his sheep.'

Marais recalls that there had been good rains and the gorge was luxuriant with wild peaches, tree ferns, red milkwoods, wild plums and giant fig trees. 'The beauty and profusion of nature, which every day we had to admire anew, simply cannot be described,' he writes. 'Such a wealth of plants, so many birds of every kind, gathered within such limits I had never before seen equalled, not even in the tropics.'

The men began to learn the ways of the troop and took meticulous notes, recording what they believed to be rudimentary laws, some form of government and the first signs of culture. They recognised a 'council of eleven' – older baboons that led the troop – and paid particular attention to these males. Over time, Marais began making observations about their intellect, morality, even their 'soul'. The poet-naturalist was in his element: 'I do not think that I ever passed a happier time in my life than the three years we spent in the mountains of Doornhoek.'

The product of his baboon research was *The Soul of the Ape*, in which he postulates that the human psyche, like the human body, has evolved from lesser animals. Marais had the mind and the patience of a scientist, but the heart and intuition of a poet, which gave him the flexibility and empathy to make innovative discoveries. His interest in primates had begun as a child and was resumed in London where, as a student, he hand-reared a baby chimpanzee and a marmoset. Making animals part of one's family and studying them round the clock was not to become accepted practice until half a century later.

When deciding to settle in the Waterberg, it had been one of Marais's intentions to conduct a sustained investigation of nature, what he called 'an experiment in life'. Indeed, he was to turn Doornhoek and Rietfontein farms into zoological laboratories where he researched natural phenomena of many kinds and conducted all manner of experiments. His intellectual appetite was insatiable and his studies encompassed everything from the song of cicadas to the sex life of kudus and tortoises, from puffadder fangs to aristida-grass fertilization and the Morse code of toktokkies; he even trained a fox terrier to follow the scent of a termite queen.

It was through such experiments that he came to his theory of the phyletic and causal memory in various animals, as espoused in *The Soul of the Ape*. He postulated that 'lower' animals, such as birds, had retained their instincts (phyletic memory), whereas 'higher' animals such as baboons and humans had lost most of their instincts, replacing them with an ability to learn and to understand cause and effect (causal memory). The huge advantage of sublimating or submerging one's instincts was the ability to adapt quickly to new conditions and to learn new patterns of behaviour. It made the apes, and ultimately humans, eminently suited to rapid change.

Through his investigation into the psyche or 'soul' of baboons, Marais realised that humans under hypnosis displayed similar attributes, giving him an inkling into the evolution of mental processes in higher primates. He believed that hypnosis laid bare the 'subliminal soul', which is in reality the 'animal soul' still present in man's mentality, and induces a partial reawakening of the old animal mentality. According to this theory, the story of our psychic evolution has been the slow ascendency of causal memory over phyletic memory, but the latter has never been completely displaced. Latent in *Homo sapiens* are ancient sensory abilities which we sacrificed in exchange for developing our intellect. To prove this, Marais conducted numerous (dubious) experiments on two sisters, Jane and Mary Brayshaw. He found that under hypnosis their hearing was as much as eight times more acute than normal; so too their senses of sight, smell, taste and touch, which surpassed even that of baboons. Under hypnosis, humans became animal once more; the grey brain of their intellect was temporarily neutralised and the ancient, white matter took over.

Thys led us deeper into the kloof. The valley floor was now only a few metres wide, populated by large boulders, tall trees reaching for the light and pools of crystal water. A baboon's bark would be deafening in this narrow gorge, I thought, recalling Marais's description of how 'a big male would wake the echoes of the mountains with his tremendous voice.' Up ahead, the path was blocked by a jumble of red rocks: we could go no further. I stood in a shaft of sunlight beneath a giant fig tree, the boulders around us baking in the heat, the leaves flickering a sunlight semaphore, water splashing from a cleft in the rock and all the while laughing doves filling the air with their song. It felt like a womb, a pulsing hollow of warmth and diffused light. For Marais, this enchanted corner of the Waterberg was an incubator for ideas that were to change the way humans viewed their origins.

'I like to think of this kloof as Marais's spiritual home,' said Peet softly. 'You can feel his presence here; you can feel he was happy here.'

'Ja,' said Thys, 'it's a fokken lekker spot. We come here on weekends and camp, get vrot dronk, play music and have one helluva opskop.'

---※---

After dropping Peet at home, I took the road west to my overnight accommodation in Marakele National Park. As I drove into the softening light, I was thinking about Boet and his fiefdom. Scarred by a century of mining, Doornhoek had become a dump for scrap metal and old ideas. Boet lay in his bed, behind electric fences, surrounded by rifles and old South African flags, while antagonistic farm labourers camped on the land, awaiting their day. In a sense, it was a vision of a possible end of the line for white South African farmers, a snapshot of their eleventh hour.

By welcome contrast, Marakele is an efficiently run national park in an unspoilt corner of the Waterberg where I hoped to find the kind of untamed wilderness Marais encountered a century ago. I signed in at the entrance and crossed the Kwaggasvlakte grasslands passing large herds of wildebeest and zebra, then through an electric gate into the park's Big Five uplands. My accommodation at Tlopi rest camp in the heart of the reserve was a safari-style tent set beside a picturesque dam with no fences to keep predators at bay. The tent sat on a raised wooden deck among wild olive trees noisy with the chatter of weaver birds, while spurfowl scuffled beneath the deck and Egyptian geese kicked up a racket along the water's edge.

As I unpacked, a scarlet sun slipped below the horizon, bats closed the wounds of the day with their untidy stitching and a frog orchestra began tuning up. The camp was deserted and as the fingers of darkness crept out from under the trees, I found my spirits dipping. Alone again on another journey; another braai for one. Perhaps my mood was due to a lack of caffeine: I'd forgotten to buy coffee and had been craving a hit all day, which would account for the headache, but sunset held its own set of familiar melancholies too. In *The Soul of the Ape*, Marais presents his theory of 'Hesperian depression', described as the anxiety and gloom one often feels at the close of day. 'Normal mental pain in man, generally speaking, is tidal in character. With sunrise or during the early morning it is at its lowest ebb, to reach its highest flow in the evening about the time of the setting sun.'

At this hour, infant baboons grow silent and seek out their mothers, adults assume attitudes of dejection and the troop finds the protection of cliffs as predators begin to prowl. So too humans, who have traditionally feared the 'evil powers' of the night and sought the comfort of caves, shelter and fire. In evolutionary terms, this moment of anxiety has the beneficial effect of drawing the group together at a time of increased danger. I had no group to be drawn into and no cell phone reception to make contact with loved ones.

With the coming of darkness, the igniting of the stars and the need for industry – grilling the meat – my spirits lifted a notch. I lit my primordial flame with firelighters, adding wood and briquettes: much better. There was the splash of catfish, the insistent call of a fiery-necked nightjar and the stars humming softly, their celestial generator on low pulse. I stabbed the darkness with a torch beam, looking for eyes.

My braai flames licked a corner of the night, chops and wors sizzled on the grid and my Nederburg Baronne tasted of iron, as if squeezed not from grapes but from the berg's red rocks. I thought about how bushveld nights such as these could take you by the throat and hold you, how utterly beguiling these mountains were and how easily Marais must have fallen for them. His most famous poem, 'Winternag', evokes just such a night:

> O koud is die windjie
>   en skraal.
> En blink in die dof-lig
>   en kaal,
> so wyd as die Heer se genade,
> lê die velde in sterlig en skade.
>   En hoog in die rande,
>   versprei in die brande,
> is die grassaad aan roere
>   soos winkende hande.
>
> O cold is the thin wind,
>   and keen.

> Bare and bright in the dim light
>   is seen,
> as vast as the mercy of God,
> lie the plains in starlight and shade.
>   And high on the ridges,
>   among the burnt patches,
> the seed-grass is stirring
>   like beckoning hands.

Long after lights-out, I was woken by the wind banging my tent canvas like a lesser god wanting in. I got up, rolled down and secured the outer flaps, then tried to find sleep again. Deeper in the night I woke once more, this time to the barking of baboons on the krans. Perhaps a leopard was among them, sowing terror. The first light of dawn was rent by the roaring of lions, their baritone voices bouncing off the crags above my tent and rolling west towards the Kalahari, announcing their ownership of the land.

I was up before the sun and drove to Lenong View Point along a lovely winding road, embowered in places, that led up the side of a mountain whose slopes were covered with yellowwoods, euphorbias and five-metre cycads. The heathland below was dotted with *Drosera* carnivorous plants, or sundew, able to catch insects in a manner similar to Venus flytraps.

A troop of baboons had gathered on the summit and I stopped to watch their antics. Pink-faced babies rode on their mothers' backs, jockey style, young'uns cavorted in the bushes, playing tag and tumbling about in mock combat, a few adults stood sentry around the fringes watching for danger, and one large male yawned ostentatiously, baring a set of fearsome yellow teeth at me. And was that a spot of covert copulation I spied behind the rocks, undertaken by some beta male and cheating female? If I were Marais, I'd be taking careful note of the troop's behaviour: how the group was structured, how leaders kept order, perhaps even recording signs of the rudimentary morality which had somehow found a slightly more complex form in the shape of the primate watching them through his binoculars from the white sedan.

I looked out over their shaggy heads at the blue folds and soaring cliffs beyond. From somewhere nearby came the sound of tinkling water, for these are truly water mountains, their peaks and valleys soaking up the summer showers, then leaking from every pore for the rest of the year, creating an Eden for plant and animal alike. Springs and spruits, thermal pools and creeks gurgle from every nook, testament to the sponge-like quality of the berg.

Returning to camp for breakfast, I found bulbuls pecking at the remains of last night's meat stuck to my braai grid. A family of bushbuck – delicate white spots, stockinged legs, big ears, Bambi eyes – moseyed through camp, as tame as Labradors, nibbling on choice shoots. I approached one of them to take a photo and she let me get to within a metre, then waited patiently for me to adjust my camera settings and click a dozen shots before she ambled off. Below the deck, catfish swished through muddy water as black crakes strutted the bank on incandescent legs. A Natal spurfowl – its chest a maze of speckled feathers – waddled by, stabbing at the crumbs around my feet.

Next, a troop of vervets came to drink, the babies playing jungle gym in a nearby tree while the elders stood guard. From Marais, I knew that the phyletic memory in vervets is far stronger than in baboons. One of the monkeys attempted a raid, bent on stealing my yoghurt, but was deterred by a hurled box of matches and a string of curses. She retreated to the apex of my tent, watching attentively, head cocked, eyes greedily registering each mouthful of berry yoghurt, assessing the risks of another foray.

Marais would no doubt have analysed her doings to some significant end … perhaps assessing whether her instinctual, phyletic memory was stronger than her causal memory or were they were equally shared: a sort of 'dual control'? Was a stupid baboon with a strong phyletic memory the equal of a clever vervet with a strong causal memory? It was a bit too much for me: quiet marvelling and the odd photograph was all I was good for.

Later that morning, I booked a tour of the park with Sidney Mikosi, award-winning field guide and Marakele's resident bush guru. Sidney is a charming, handsome Venda in his thirties with many a gold tooth to light up a ready smile; his cell phone's ringtone was the song of the black-collared barbet. He picked me up in his open Land Cruiser and we headed into the hills along a road rouged by iron-rich dust. Sidney talked about Marakele's fauna and geology – the sedimentary nature of the rocks, the huge Cape vulture colony – and pointed out ruined farmhouses from Marais's day, recently incorporated into the ever-expanding park.

Sidney also spoke about the unique flora: 'Did you know that your guy discovered a rare, endemic cycad which was named after him. *Encephalartos eugene-maraisii* is as old as the dinosaurs, but unfortunately it's hot property with plant thieves and the Waterberg has been largely cleaned out. I know where you can still find a few, but we like to keep it secret. Some Zimbabwean guys were caught the other day with a bunch of them. They get paid R500 a plant by some rich businessman in Pretoria, but in America, they sell for millions.'

Sidney also told me how the Waterberg had such a high iron content that it attracted lightning, producing spectacular electric storms. Each year, fires are sparked just before the rains and the plants know this in their genetic sap, making provision for the annual forge. In fact, in a strange perversion of the kiss of rain as bringer of life, many species need fire for their seeds to germinate.

I asked Sidney whether Marakele suffered much rhino poaching and he confided that an adult had recently been killed, but for the most part his rangers had a handle on things with regular armed patrols.

'You want to see a rhino?' he asked.

'Absolutely,' I said.

'Okay, how about we try to bag one on foot?'

He pulled off the track into a clearing, loaded his rifle and set off at a brisk pace with me half jogging to keep up. Sidney's tracking skills were remarkable: in no time he'd found spoor and began following the faintest hoof prints through long grass. Within half an hour, we came upon a dominant male resting in the shade of a thorn tree – a handsome fellow, his body pale from a dust bath and his horns red from a recent duel with a termite mound. It appeared the mound had lost.

'This old boy has also been fighting with a young bull that keeps challenging him,' whispered Sidney as we edged forward at a crouch. No rest for the wicked, the rhino must have been thinking – first a cheeky termite mound, then an upstart whippersnapper, and now two humans trying to look like bushes. Sidney pressed on, unafraid, while I hung back to take photos … and to give myself a head-start if running was required. The bull allowed Sidney to get within ten metres before he stood up in a billow of dust, snorted gruffly and trotted off with the daintiness of a two-ton ballerina.

I spent the rest of the afternoon on my deck. Tlopi's peacefulness felt like a benediction, the mountains holding the camp in a close embrace. Marakele presented the bushveld in the vertical, not the soaring cragginess of the Drakensberg, but much older, worn and weathered mountains, already formed two billion years ago when Gondwanaland split. Its sedimentary ramparts are fortress-like, the squared-off sandstone blocks seemingly laid down by an ancient race. Some buttresses even look like outsize zimbabwes – a rounded architecture inspired by the shape of grass huts.

My time in Marakele was solitary and meditative. I spent the days reading Marais and watching the dam; each evening, I drove the loop road along a high contour through combretum country painted in russets and golds. Peeling plane trees with yellow leaves, mountain seringas in red livery, and stately, white-trunked sycamore figs. As I moved up the slope, the terrain grew more lovely. Proteas and cedar trees, yellow grasslands and rust-red ferns. The stillness of the kloofs was enhanced by the distant clatter of guineafowl and call of Cape turtle doves. Ethereal light bathed the slopes, the grey shapes of mountain reedbuck dotted the marshy ground of the valley below. As I came home one evening, an elephant bull blocked the road, shaking his dusty head at me. I waited for him to finish making his point, then passed slowly by.

Back in camp, I'd light a fire and sit watching the mirrored reflections in Tlopi dam until the star rivers began their ghostly streaming. Throughout the night, I'd be woken periodically by comforting, creature sounds: a mouse drinking from my basin, geckos hunting across the window mesh, something fiddling with the pots in the kitchen tent. Dawn brought a chorus of babblers, the pitter-patter of vervet feet across my canvas roof, and later the rasping of hadedas down by the water.

One icy, windless night, I left my flaps open. Somewhere in the early hours, I dreamt I heard a rifle shot and woke to an eerie light filling the tent as a shooting star, bright as a candle, arced across the opening. The mountains appeared lit by its greenish radiance. Perhaps I was still dreaming. In that dazzling moment, the crags morphed into a giant brain. Was it Marais's beautiful, convoluted, grey cortex lording it over the white brain of his phyletic memory? Muscular, brilliant, overbearing – pure intellect. The star trail left me feeling weak, emptied, my own grey matter shrinking as I slunk back into fitful sleep.

———*———

Next day, I contacted Peet to take up his offer of another tour of Marais sites. I set off from camp into a cold, windy dawn and, having run out of pilfered coffee sachets, was again suffering withdrawal symptoms. My head throbbed, I had the shakes and a dull listlessness had taken hold: my system needed a caffeine fix. Driving to Modimolle via the frontier town of Thabazimbi (Mountain of Iron), I passed the carnage of an Anglo American mining operation that had carved up the land in search of iron, reducing it to a mess of slices and dices no longer fit to be called a mountain.

Peet and his wife had spent the previous days in Pretoria consulting oncologists, but the news was not encouraging. However, putting on a brave face, Peet was all generosity and graciousness once more. We drove north to Mookgopong (Naboomspruit) and parked beside the station. 'This was Marais's nearest town, where he caught the train, purchased provisions and socialised,' said Peet.

We walked to a nearby face-brick building whose previous incarnation had been one of Marais's drinking holes. The old hotel has long since been modernised and is now the Dors Sports Bar and lodge. Inside, we found pool tables, a disco ball, the rancid smell of stale beer. I thought about how sensitive ghosts are to bad restoration and how they require that their haunts remain unchanged. Clearly, the spirit of this place had long since trekked.

Why was the bar open first thing on a Monday morning, I wondered? Probably for folks who needed an opkikker to start the week, or had no week to look forward to. The purple-haired woman behind the bar had never heard of Eugène Marais: 'I don't fink he comes here often, otherwise I'd know him,' she said.

I asked about coffee and, raising her eyebrows, she shook her head. By now, my headache had lowered like a veil and I needed to curl up in a darkened room to ride it out. Caffeine, my euphoric poison, I need thee now, but an impatient Peet said we had to hit the road. I remembered that Marais took Chlorodyne, an opium-based medicine, as substitute for the hard stuff. My own substitute, a Coca-Cola from the corner cafe, would have to do until I could find a proper fix. The effect of the gods' black nectar was almost instant and I was good to go.

We headed north, passing the Entabeni Conservancy and Resort where Peet had found an old homestead that became the principal location for *Die Wonderwerker*. 'Katinka shot the movie in a month, far less than we wanted, but budget constraints … ag, you know how it is. At least the film got produced.'

'A damn good movie,' I said.

'Ja, it was well made and we did things pretty authentically. The house was just right for the period, not modernised at all. For one of the scenes, we even learnt how to stretch riempies, twisting the leather on the branch of a tree.'

We drove into Bokpoort kloof, one of the berg's eastern portals, where stony slopes plunged to a stream shrouded by evergreen waterberry trees. In the early Twentieth Century, a footpath led this way to the farm Purekrans, home to Piet van Rooyen, brother of Gys, who was Marais's landlord at Rietfontein. Piet was a colourful character who had many brushes with the law and became a good friend to Marais.

Passing through Bokpoort on visits to Purekrans or on various hunting expeditions, Marais discovered that the kloof was a good place to study baboons. On one occasion, he and two friends stopped to watch a group of children from a nearby kraal at play, some of them cavorting in the stream, others fashioning oxen from clay they had dug in the river bank. At first glance, the group seemed to comprise only children, but upon closer inspection Marais noticed that a number of them were in fact young baboons. Mingling with the constant laughter and chatter in Sesotho came the jabber of the primates. The older children of the human group sat to one side, focused on their craft, the bigger baboons watching attentively and passing the occasional comment. When one of them picked up an artwork, a playful fight ensued with much slinging of clay and hilarity. 'My old friends laughed so much that they could scarcely remain on their horses,' recounts

Marais in *My Friends the Baboons*.

'Purekrans is up ahead, but the old homestead has fallen into ruin,' said Peet as we reached the top of the pass. 'According to my friend Oom Flippie, the Van Rooyens received a telegram from Marais in 1936 asking if he could come and stay and would they please fetch him at Naboomspruit Station. At the end of his life, Purekrans provided a sanctuary for Marais, even more so than Doornhoek or Rietfontein. He was in a very bad way with his addiction and the farm represented a sort of ideal he was grasping for, if you know what I mean – the Waterberg of his youthful happiness. One of the Van Rooyen sons, Hansie, went and waited for two days at the station. On the third day, they read in the newspaper that Marais had committed suicide.'

Peet pointed out the peak of Hanglip, rising out of the bushveld before us like the prow of a ship. While visiting a group of woodcutters in one of Hanglip's kloofs, Marais spotted an agitated baboon troop taking refuge on a cliff as a leopard crept along a ledge below them. Suddenly, two male baboons leapt from an outcrop and landed on the big cat. A short, ferocious struggle ensued resulting in the death of the leopard and one of its attackers, an incident that led Marais to ponder what drove baboons to risk their lives in this manner. Was it perhaps a form of altruism? Could it be that they weren't acting as individuals, but rather under orders from the group's 'soul'? Perhaps an individual was unimportant and only the survival of the species counted.

It was also near Hanglip that Marais apparently got to know a character he referred to in his writings as Oom Dirk, an elderly man who'd built his home beside a stream at the mouth of a remote kloof known as Geelhoutgrag (Yellowwood Moat). The thatched cottage had a wide, wraparound veranda and sat on a large slab of rock. 'Never have I seen anything more beautiful in my life than the lonely little house in its natural environment,' he wrote.

Visiting Geelhoutgrag in winter, he would sit beside a fire of blazing leadwood logs, drink plum brandy and listen to Oom Dirk talking about the veld, the Berg and the wonders of nature. Marais describes waking one morning and stepping outside to find the veranda, railings, window sills and chairs covered in chirruping birds, devouring the seed and worms laid out for them. On a couch amid the avian hubbub sat a smiling Oom Dirk, his body decked with tiny birds fighting for a perch.

Biographers have questioned the existence of Oom Dirk, as no one in the district knew of the man. Leon Rousseau has suggested that Geelhoutgrag is a fantasy – a synthesis of all that Marais longed for. Perhaps he viewed Oom Dirk as an idealised self and the house as a moated castle keeping the outside world at bay. Reminiscent of Yeats's Lake Isle of Innisfree, this corner of the Waterberg, lorded over by the towering peak of Hanglip, is Marais's ultimate sanctuary. Indeed, the hanging mountain became his mythical Thebes, symbolic of escape, and his famous poem 'Waar Tebes in die stil woestyn' almost certainly refers to Hanglip:

> Daar sal ek vrede weer besef
> Waar Tebes in die stil woestyn
> Sy magtig' rotswerk hoog verhef
> …
> O land van al ons liefde, daar
> Sou ek aanbiddend weer
> Die kloppe van u hart gewaar,
> U moederlike skoonheid eer.

> I shall know peace there once again
> where Thebes its mighty rampart rears
> silent above the desert plain
> …
> Oh land of all our love, oh there,
> while worshipping I would once more
> your soft maternal heartbeat hear,
> your beauty honour and adore.

North of Hanglip, bound for Marken, the land was dry, thorny and flat. During his visits to Purekrans, Marais would often venture this way, travelling alone in a donkey cart to explore the Palala plateau and wilderness beyond. Perhaps in these untamed, wide-open spaces he was able to hold his demons at bay and immerse himself in nature.

'Stop the car,' said Peet. I turned into a layby and we got out to survey a nondescript patch of veld. 'It was somewhere around here in 1915 that Marais ran out of morphine during his last hunting expedition. A rider from the party was hastily sent back to Rietfontein to get his "medicine", as he was burning up.'

Charlie Pienaar, leader of the hunting group, had tried to break his friend's addiction by each day reducing the dose of Chlorodyne, but Marais's notes from the journey track his deterioration and growing despair. Eventually, he could go no further and the party was forced to return to Rietfontein. Soon after, Marais decided to leave the Waterberg: his addiction had beaten him and he'd come to view his life as a complete failure.

However, by the following year, he'd rallied and felt strong enough to begin writing the book – daringly entitled *The Soul of the Ape* – he hoped would make him famous. Where Darwin's ground-breaking studies had focused on physiological evolution, Marais hoped to unlock the evolution of the human soul. The lost manuscript of his great work, for which he would indeed become world famous, was only rediscovered and published three decades after he'd walked out into a garden near Pretoria, placed the muzzle of a shotgun in his mouth and pulled the trigger.

By now, the sun was low in the sky and Peet suggested we turn for home, but before being dropped off, he wanted to show me one last Marais site. Ebrahim Ravat, an urbane Indian trader who owned a store in Nylstroom, was a close friend of the poet during his Waterberg sojourn. Marais often visited his home, enjoying Mrs Ravat's hot curries and talking long into the night with Ebrahim. The trader became Marais's source of opium (a substitute when his morphine supply ran out), which he imported from India.

Passing through Modimolle, Peet asked me to stop next to an Autozone spare-parts dealer emblazoned with garish red signage. The building had once been Ravat's store with the family home situated behind. Walking down a side lane, we came to a scruffy yard.

'The house has long since been demolished and this is all that remains,' said Peet, pointing to a patch of brick paving. 'I got to know Ravat's son quite well and he remembers how Marais used to sit in the lounge reading the Quran with his father, a snippet I included in my documentary. I thought it would be edited out by the SABC – racial mixing and all – but to my surprise the programme flighted without any cuts. The Nylstroom Indians expressed their gratitude to me as their story had seldom been told – erased from apartheid narratives as was so often the case back then. Lots of local farmers were deeply indebted to Ravat because he used to bail them out in times of drought and they took *many* years to pay him back. Later, apartheid laws alienated the Ravats from the farmers. Ag man, it's that old South African story ...'

On my last morning, I awoke to find a great wave of clouds pouring off the crags above Tlopi Camp. I packed my bags, zipped closed the tent and drove down the pass to the exit gate, nosing between zebras and wildebeests too lazy to move out of my way. Red road, peroxided grass, the ochre fingers of termite mounds protruding from the veld; in my rear-view mirror, the mountains were pale Pierneef cut-outs with attendant cloud stacks.

Leaving the park, I headed east towards Alma on a road that followed the foothills of the Sand River Mountains, southern bastions of the Waterberg, swelling and shrinking in a rounded blue calligraphy. Lonely farms, rusty gateposts, Afrikaner cattle. Following Peet's handwritten directions and cryptic map, I drove a dozen kilometres beyond Doornhoek on the Mookgopong road until I came to the tall flame tree he'd told me to look out for.

Finally, Rietfontein. I'd saved the farm for last, believing – hoping – I'd find Marais's ghost still in residence.

A chance encounter had initiated the poet's long association with this farm. One day, while riding to Naboomspruit in his Cape cart, Marais was suddenly laid low by a recurring bout of malaria and stopped at a local farm to ask for a glass of water. Looking handsome in his riding breeches and fashionable attire, he made a strong impression on the farmer's wife, Maria van Rooyen, known locally as Tamaria (Tant Maria). Concerned that the stranger was gravely ill, she invited him in, and so began a long friendship.

In 1908, Marais left Doornhoek and took up lodgings at Rietfontein. Tamaria and her husband, Gys, were a hardworking couple who had rebuilt Rietfontein after its partial destruction by British soldiers during the war, and turned it into a prosperous farm. The industrious Gys was also a wagon-builder, bricklayer and blacksmith, while Tamaria ran the domestic side of the farm in addition to being a competent nurse and midwife. For the better part of nine years, Marais lived in the stoepkamer, kept his cattle and horses on the farm, tended to the sick of the district and continued his prospecting and ethological research.

It's a warm winter's day as I step from the car. A derelict homestead sits among the trees to my right and a sign reads 'Private Property, No Trespassers'. I climb over a locked gate and approach the house down an overgrown lane, spurfowl scuffling in the long grass to my left. Up ahead, I spot a shaggy palm and the dying alhambra tree planted by Marais and painted by his artist friend Erich Mayer in 1913. Behind the house is the ridge where he studied termites, meticulously recording the life cycle of their nests.

Down the slope to my left lies the smithy where Gys and Marais used to work, now dwarfed by a rioting bougainvillea that threatens to engulf it in a purple tsunami. Pushing open a broken door, I find piles of farm junk – tyres, pipes, tin drums. Further down the slope I can see the thermal springs, now part of Die Oog Holiday Resort, where Marais use to bathe among the reeds. He fashioned a seat from an old barrel and would wallow for hours in the steaming water, trying to numb his pain.

I cross the werf and approach the abandoned homestead, stepping over an old irrigation pipe that looks like a black mamba in the yellow grass. I picture Marais conducting experiments on the lawn and on the stoep, consulting patients or courting the young women of the district, and the long nights he paced this werf, fighting his demons. He'd confided to Tamaria that he needed morphia as a medicine and entrusted her with his stash, instructing her to ration him to small daily amounts, an arrangement fraught with complication and, eventually, conflict.

The house is a squat affair with a rusty red roof – built on the foundations of an older structure and marred by ugly steel windows and a face-brick stoep. It's flanked by two Norfolk pines and a row of frangipani trees; round the back I come upon a bakoond that could be from Marais's time. Climbing through a smashed window at one end of the stoep, I find myself in a bedroom that might well have been where the poet slept. It's empty and the floor is caked with dirt, but I narrow my eyes and make out a wardrobe, a padlocked chest with wrought-iron handles and a beechwood bookcase crammed with hardbacks, among them Darwin, Freud and Yeats. Battered suitcases, a wooden bed, a table and two peasant chairs … or am I channelling Van Gogh?

Vagrants have been sleeping in some of the rooms and I come upon dirty blankets, bits of cardboard serving as mattresses; the stale smell of humans or animals, or both. Blackened walls indicate fires, like those of early hominids who have just woken from millennia of primate slumber.

I take a volume of Marais poems from my bag and read:

> Wanneer dit reën op Rietfontein
> En deur die stof 'n straal van groen verskyn,
> Wanneer die wolke, swart en swaar belaai,
> In voue oor die berge pak en swaai,
> Dan sit oom Gysbert op die stoep alleen;
> Hy asem sag die geur gemeng van stof en reën
> …
> Van agter uit die groot kombuis
> Kom daar aanhoudend die gesuis
> Van kole op die vuurherd aangeblaas
> Van pot en pan die klinkende geraas –
> Dis net so seker as die boek
> Tant Malie bak nou pannekoek!

> When it rains on Rietfontein
> And streaks of green gleam on the dusty plain,
> And when the swollen clouds, all black and grey
> In folds over the mountains clutch and sway,
> Oom Gysbert sits out on the stoep, quite calm
> Breathing the smell of dust and rain like balm …

> Sounds filter from the kitchen grand
> And when he hears the coals being fanned
> With constant hiss, and all the while
> The clink of pots and pans – he'll smile
> It's just as certain as the Book
> Tant Malie's baking 'pannekoek'!

For nearly a decade, Rietfontein provided a refuge and Marais took to calling it his ark, referring to the many animals he raised there. Standing on the dilapidated stoep where the poet once sat with Oom Gysbert, smelling the dust and rain, I find myself trying to place him, fix him in this site, hear his voice. My mind conjures a walking, talking, agitating, questing spirit, but the only 'voice' I hear is wind in the leaves. The house gives nothing back; not even reading his poems in situ seems to help. Rietfontein is a worn, depressing place. In 1916, after his demons had found him once more, he left the farm on unhappy terms, never to return.

I walked slowly back down the road, climbed over the gate and sat for a long time in the car, feeling at a loss. In truth, Peet had been right. I, too, had felt closest to Marais in the kloof on Doornhoek farm. My mind arced back to the green cleft with its sparkling brook, the happy splash of falling water, the bright stream of promise. Although Marais never returned to the Waterberg, he held it in his heart and yearned for it always. That Edenic kloof had symbolised – epitomised – a period of freedom and I heard its water now, like the high notes of a faraway piano.

But even in that cocooned paradise, the stream of pain ran dark, the shadow continued to follow him, biding its time. I remembered his account of death among the Doornhoek baboons. Late one night, he was woken by unusual sounds and lit his lantern, only to find a black hand pressed against the windowpane. Marais and Austin got out of bed and were astonished to see the council of baboon elders seated outside their huts. The two men decided to inspect the troop's sleeping place and were escorted to the site by the big males. In deeply affecting prose, Marais describes what happened next: 'I can still remember the impression the scene made on me. The wild rocks shadowed by dark rock-growth, the large uncertain black forms gathered around us, the flickering light of the lantern, and, above all, the unearthly silence – all combined to give an eerie sensation which was closely related to fear.'

Until that moment, the baboons had never allowed the men to enter their sleeping area, but on this occasion there were no warning barks. In the dim lamplight, they could see the troop clustered in a circle, males on the outside, females and babies in the centre. All were quiet, 'something so unusual that it strengthened the impression that we were in the presence of some great tragedy about which the males had tried to tell us but which we could not decipher.'

Marais and Austin failed to discover what was wrong and returned to bed, but just before daybreak, they were woken by strange sounds coming from the cliff. 'What we heard was the terrible blood-freezing cry of woe from the baboons – persistent and heart-rending … It sounded, to our ears, more moving than even the cry of mourning of human beings, just because the lamentation of the baboons is wordless.'

At the base of the cliff, they found the corpses of eight young ones that had died in the night, a line of black faces watching from above. Appearing to understand the meaning of death, the troop allowed the men to remove the bodies, but one young mother followed them back to the huts making begging sounds. The bodies were laid out on the ground and she touched her lips to her dead child, then sat down beside it and continued begging with outstretched arms. Marais thought she wanted something that, to her dim intelligence, only humans could give: the gift of life. It was the same thing the council of elders had asked for the night before. Anticipating the approaching deaths, they'd sought help from the magicians who'd come to live among them. The young mother waited outside the huts until all hope finally deserted her and then returned to the troop.

Marais was acutely aware of the living pain of consciousness bequeathed to all primates by their causal memory. It found its darkest expression in his morphine habit. In an article on addiction in *Die Huisgenoot*, Marais wrote candidly about the power of drugs over both humans and the higher mammals, noting that one way to relieve the pain of consciousness is through the 'euphoric poisoning' of alcohol, tobacco or drugs. As an example, he noted how Waterberg baboons had discovered that the fruit of a certain cycad produced intoxication. Marais knew, of course, that the ultimate stilling of pain was death. Like many thinkers before him, he came to the conclusion that 'the mere existence of the soul is based on stress and pain, and that there is only one perfect solution: to make an end to one's existence!' For him, death's surrogate was morphine, and in the poem 'Diep Rivier' he courts both his intoxicant and the end he both fears and craves:

> O, Diep Rivier, O, Donker Stroom,
> hoe lank het ek gewag, hoe lank gedroom,
> die lem van liefde wroegend in my hart?
> – in jou omhelsing eindig al my smart.
> Blus uit, O Diep Rivier, die vlam van haat –
> die groot verlange wat my nooit verlaat.
> Ek sien van ver die glans van staal en goud,
> ek hoor die sag gedruis van waters diep en koud;
> ek hoor jou stem as fluistering in 'n droom,
> Kom snel, O Diep Rivier, O Donker Stroom!

> Oh, Deep River, Oh, Dark Stream,
> how long have I waited, how long dreamed,
> the blade of love twisting in my heart?
> – in your embrace all my pain ends;
> Blow out, Oh Deep River, the flame of hate –
> the great longing that never leaves me.
> I see from afar the gleam of steel and gold,
> I hear the soft murmur of waters deep and cold;
> I hear your voice like whispers in a dream,
> Come quick, Oh Deep River, Oh Dark Stream!

The 'blade' of a morphine needle, the 'steel and gold' of the syringe, provide only temporary relief. Ultimately, the greater good of death is the embrace he most desires. Even in his enchanted Waterberg valley, the stream could grow dark, but during those few precious years his soul had experienced moments of freedom and his genius had found the space, and the place, to blossom. All it had needed was a troop of amiable baboons, untrammelled nature in the raw and that bright, living stream.

The whip-crack of a shotgun punctures the silence, echoing down the kloof, through the Waterberg's convoluted crags and out across the Bushveld plains, echoing and echoing …

———✶———

FIRESIDE ENGLIKAANS

Herman Charles Bosman's Marico

In 1926, Herman Charles Bosman (1905–1951) was posted as a novice teacher to a school in the Marico district of the Western Transvaal. He remained there for less than six months, but the imprint made on him by the region and its people was to leave an indelible mark on the landscape of South African literature. Memories of his time in the Bushveld haunted Bosman for the rest of his life and he was to transform them into the stuff of narrative brilliance. 'The farmers there were real Boers,' he later wrote. 'I am told that I have a deep insight into the character of the Afrikaner who lives his life on the platteland. I acquired this knowledge in the Marico, where I was sent when my mind was most open to impressions.'

The farming folk he met were natural raconteurs, spinning yarns of the five Boer republics, the Victorian diamond rush and the two Boer Wars. Bosman's stories are filled with versions of the Bushveld characters he came to know: cattle rustlers and charlatans, war veterans and veld maidens, predikants and tribal chiefs. They are tales of compassion and violence, young love and betrayal, but they are also powerful evocations of place that bring the Bushveld to life: its red earth cut by lonely mule tracks, thorn veld stretching to the horizon, sunsets scarlet with Kalahari dust and the full, capricious Marico moon. Like Thomas Hardy conjuring his mythical Wessex, Bosman tried to capture what he called 'the soul of the veld' in his creation of a fictional Marico.

Almost all of Bosman's 150-odd short stories are set in the Marico and more than a third of them are narrated by his famous storyteller, Oom Schalk Lourens. The rest, known as the Voorkamer sketches, deal with a later period and involve a group of farmers who regularly gather to wait for the government lorry to deliver their post. These stories are set in Jurie Steyn's voorkamer, which also served as the Drogevlei post office. The men sit around discussing the goings-on of the district, the latest news from the outside world, and lament the pitfalls of 'progress'. In many of these sketches, the upstart know-it-all schoolmaster (a thinly disguised Bosman) is the butt of their jokes.

However, it is Oom Schalk Lourens who looms large and has, over the course of a century, become one of South Africa's most famous literary characters. The details about Oom Schalk's background are sketchy, but we can deduce that his stories play out during the period soon after Union in 1910. Hailing from the Free State, Oom Schalk was granted a concession north of the Dwarsberge near the Botswana border. He has memories of both Boer Wars and earlier skirmishes with local tribes. However, as many biographers have noted, we shouldn't look too closely at the facts – it's not for nothing that Oom Schalk has become known as the greatest liar who ever trekked.

In Oom Schalk, Bosman created a delightfully entertaining bosvelder who presents himself as slow witted but hides a shrewd understanding of human nature and the ways of the heart. Over a lifetime of fireside conversation, Oom Schalk has honed the art of storytelling, becoming a master of pointless digressions, biting throwaway lines and twists in the tail. Occasionally, he lets slip some of the tricks of his trade. 'It is not the story that counts,' he confides in 'Mafeking Road'. 'What matters is the way you tell it. The important thing is to know just at what moment you must knock out your pipe on your veldskoen, and at what stage of the story you must start talking about the School Committee at Drogevlei. Another necessary thing is to know what part of the story to leave out … And you can never learn these things.'

The stories sketch an evocative picture of the hardships endured by bushveld farmers and the cycles of life. It's a world where drought, cattle raiders and rinderpest threaten; where God-fearing Boers still consider loading their wagons and trekking as a solution to their problems; where wild game is shot for the pot, coffee is brewed from the roots of the witgat (shepherd's tree) and every farmer has a secret mampoer distillery. Bosman's characters are backveld takhaars – poor, simple farmers who wear homemade veldskoens, smear cattle dung on their floors and travel in mule carts. They are conservative, superstitious folk, distrustful of novelty or change and resentful of the faraway influence of Pretoria represented by the occasional tax collector or mounted policeman.

Bosman builds on the tradition of the fireside yarn that stretches back to the early days of the South African hunting tale. As academic Craig MacKenzie notes, he was to perfect this oral-style narrative, weaving his own rich imaginings into the storehouse of local folklore. Outwardly, the stories seem artless, even simple, but Bosman's control of pace and rhythm, his deft use of irony, pathos and humour, mark him as one of our finest short-story writers. Another much admired attribute is Bosman's use of language: in a sense, it is Afrikaans written in English, what one might call 'Englikaans'. Bosman honed a style that translated the texture, rhythm and idioms of Afrikaans, even its sentence structure, into English. When reading these stories, you can almost hear the slow and steady rumble of the words rolling off Oom Schalk's tongue 'with the red dust of the road in their sound'.

———✷———

It was my intention to visit the Marico and see how much of Bosman's world could still be unearthed. I knew that some places and characters were purely fictional, but many were real, or at least adaptations of the real. On this particular journey, I decided to invite my elderly, bibliophile mother, Suzanne, to join me. Ma has always loved the Oom Schalk stories and her brother (the poet Uys Krige) was a friend of Bosman in post-war Johannesburg, making her an ideal travelling companion.

Early one midwinter's morning, we left Pretoria in a hired car, heading west on the N4 via Rustenburg and Swartruggens, bound for the Bushveld. Although the locale of Bosman's stories is further north, the village of Groot Marico has become synonymous with the writer. This quaint dorp, 220 kilometres west of Pretoria, still has a pioneer feel and is home to the Herman Charles Bosman Literary Society.

At the information centre – which doubles as Bosman Mecca – we met Santa and Egbert van Bart, the driving forces behind the literary society. With a Biblical beard, flowing grey hair, threadbare cardigan and veldskoens peeling from their soles, Egbert was a pretty good facsimile of Oom Schalk. Egbert and Santa had supervised the building of an exact replica of the school where the author taught (the original, on a farm near Nietverdiend, has fallen into ruin) and this serves as a living museum and home for cultural activities in the Marico. Each year on the third weekend of October, the society and its many fans gather for the Bosman Festival to celebrate the author's life, swap anecdotes, attend shows and drink mampoer.

Egbert told me about the genesis of the project. 'At sunset on the twentieth of March 1993, a group of us came together on Groot Lotteringskop in the

Dwarsberge to found the literary society,' he said in his thick Afrikaans accent. 'Our aim was to commemorate both Bosman and the Marico, source of his inspiration. Later that year, we gathered by firelight at the old schoolhouse where he had taught, to discuss how the crumbling structure could be restored. The poet and Bosman protégé Lionel Abrahams was there in his wheelchair to reminisce, and actor Patrick Mynhardt did one of his marvellous Oom Schalk impersonations. A full Marico moon came up through the thorn trees. It was just marvellous! But come, Justin and Suzanne, let me give you a little tour.'

He led us through the complex, pointing out the open-air theatre, ox wagons, bakoond and barn-like schoolhouse. 'Originally, we planned to restore the Bosman school at Heimweeberg,' he said, rummaging in his pockets for the keys. 'It was such a nice example of old Transvaal vernacular architecture. The walls were cracked and the thatch rotten, but we thought we could resurrect it. However, there was trouble getting permission from the farmer, Oom Gielie Haasbroek, who'd survived from Bosman's day and didn't think much of the troublesome schoolteacher. Then the farm changed hands, negotiations dragged on and on, and finally the structure collapsed after a storm in 2001. So we decided on Plan B: to build an exact replica here in Groot Marico.'

Unlocking the door, he led us into the one-room structure with its earth-coloured walls, dung floor, tamboti windows and, in the corner, a bronze bust of Bosman wearing his trademark fedora. 'The whole project was a labour of love for the society's members,' said Egbert. 'Our volunteers spent weekends felling poplars for the roof beams, cutting thatch and combing the sheaves, collecting clay and cattle dung for plastering. The walls are made of half-baked bricks salvaged from derelict buildings in the district. We inaugurated the schoolhouse on the centenary of Bosman's birth, the fifth of February 2005, and christened it by smashing a bottle of peach brandy against the wall.'

Egbert explained that back in the 1920s, the school principal and his family lived behind a curtain, forming a makeshift second room, while Bosman boarded on an adjacent farm. I tried to picture the precocious, twenty-year-old stadsjapie standing before a class of Bushveld children, the alphabet chalked on the blackboard behind him, the 'Groen Boek' syllabus open on the table, a low Marico sun shafting through the windows. Bosman's short story 'Circumstantial Evidence' has a description of the end of a school day, after the children have left on foot or been collected by donkey cart. 'The only sounds in that peaceful classroom, with the day drawing to a close, were the even scratchings of the schoolmaster's red ink pen in double-ruled exercise books supplied by the Transvaal Education Department.'

I remembered that the schoolhouse had also been used for church services and concerts, and in the evenings for lamp-lit meetings of the Dwarsberg Farmers' Union and the Drogevlei Debating Society. It was at such events that Bosman discovered the simple eloquence of the locals and learnt some of the rhetorical techniques that were to characterise his stories.

Later that day, sipping strong Marico coffee (chased with a shot of honey mampoer) on the Van Barts' stoep, conversation drifted the way it should, of a bosveld afternoon, to topics such as the threat of drought, modern-day cattle rustling, the merits of peach versus marula mampoer and the ills of the city. I fetched a map from the car and Egbert helped me plan our Bosman route, up the R49 and over the Dwarsberge, pencilling in sites of interest along the way.

'Lots of the important places have fallen into ruin, such as the Heimweeberg School and Jurie Steyn's famous voorkamer cum post office,' said Egbert. 'The bush takes over quickly here and buildings simply melt back into the earth. I went one time to try to find Jurie Steyn's house with Craig MacKenzie when he was preparing the new edition of Bosman's works. Jurie Steyn's fictional post office was modelled on the real-life one run by Jurie Prinsloo, and it lay just off the Nietverdiend–Abjaterskop road. The ruin was still standing in 1964 when David Goldblatt photographed it and his photo appears on the cover of *The Complete Voorkamer Stories*. But Craig and I had no luck – the building had long since disappeared.'

I was pleased to notice that my mother and Santa were hitting it off. 'You know, my brother and Herman used to spar verbally,' I overheard Ma saying. 'There's a story about the time Uys was coming out of Broadcast House in Joburg and saw Bosman scolding a black man for flogging his donkey. "That's right, Herman," Uys called out, "your good deed for the day. Tell him that after his mother, a man's best friend is his horse."

'Bosman retorted: "Ag Uys, you were always the master of the cliché."

'To which my brother replied, "Ah, but do you know what a cliché is? It's that which is worn threadbare next to the hearts of men."'

I heard Santa chuckling as Egbert poured more coffee. 'We're all slaves to a good story, aren't we?' he said. 'And if the story makes you kuier longer than you intended, so much the better. Stories flow through this town like a second artery – after the Groot Marico River, that is. I mean, you head off to the shop in the morning to buy some bread and you get chatting and find yourself only getting home at blimmin' four in the afternoon. It can be a real problem in this dorp. It's not for nothing that the clock on our church steeple has no hands.'

Ma and I spent the night in a cottage on River Still Guest Farm, situated in a wooded kloof on the banks of the Groot Marico River. Apparently, the owner bought the citrus farm with the proceeds of a fifty-cent pull on a casino fruit machine (perhaps three lemons?), or so the Marico rumour goes. We had the leafy stone cottage to ourselves, with swings suspended above the river and a raft for summer fun, but it was far too cold to venture in. On the opposite bank lay pure bushveld dotted with leadwoods, aloes and euphorbias.

While Ma unpacked, I went exploring and found farmer Jacques du Plessis pressing lemons and oranges using a contraption that looked like part of a Victorian steam engine (I didn't ask him about the fruit machine). Jacques and a farmhand were working their way through a large, sunny pile of citrus.

'Hallo Justin, ou maat, do you like mampoer?'

'Yes, in small doses.'

'Ag, we don't know what a small dose is around here.' He winked. 'As Oom Piet "Rympies" Swanepoel says of our local brew: "Dit het krag, dit het skop / Dit het vonk, dit het vuur / Dit is meer as net dop / Dis Marico kultuur" (It has power, it has kick / It has spark, it has fire / It's more than just drink / It's Marico culture).'

'How much mampoer will you get from a pile like this?' I asked.

'Only about ten per cent of the fermented sap ends up as mampoer, so maybe eighty litres from this lot,' he said, tossing another spent rind into a bucket.

'I thought Marico mampoer was normally made from peaches.'

'Man, you can make it with just about anything. If you remember in the story "Mampoer", Oom Schalk talks about using kareeboom berries, marulas, Kei apples and even red milkwood. You can use apricots, pears, plums. Figs are my favourite. Ag, we'd make it from old veldskoens if we could.'

Later, I lit a braai fire as dusty yellow light sifted through the trees. River Still was succumbing to that species of peace you find nowhere else but in the bushveld on a drowsy afternoon. Ma sat in a comfy chair on the stoep reading *Mafeking Road* for the umpteenth time. The cobbled gurgle of water over boulders was punctuated by the occasional 'kwê!' of a go-away bird.

After sunset it turned icy cold. We ate our wors, sosaties and salad indoors and Ma went to bed early, but I lingered with my maps and notes spread out on the dining-room table. Through the window, the moon was all but full, snared in a thorn tree, and I found myself thinking about Oom Schalk's lunar musings in 'Drieka and the Moon':

> There is a queer witchery about the moon when it is full ... It does strange things to your mind, the Marico moon, and in your heart are wild and fragrant fancies, and your thoughts go very far away ... I have seen the moon in other places besides the Marico. But it is not the same there ... Always when the moon shines full like that, it does something to our hearts that we wonder very much about and that we never understand.

About 40 kilometres west of Groot Marico, the literary traveller arrives at the first major co-ordinate in Oom Schalk's geography. No doubt Zeerust was once a pretty Western Transvaal town, but it has suffered the depredations of tawdry modern architecture and garish signage, and is now more Shoprite and Wimpy than ye olde backveld. Oom Schalk's bioscope is no more and bottle stores have replaced the traditional pub. However, Zeerust is worth a stop, if only to soak up a bit of vestigial Bosman atmosphere. The commonage of the NG Kerk (the former church has made way for an ugly red-brick affair) is where ox wagons once outspanned and tents were erected for Nagmaal. Many a tale was spun of the goings-on at this religious gathering of Marico families. Oom Schalk recalls courting his first crush, Lettie de Bruyn, during Nagmaal: pale cheeks and a long white dress, a tantalising kiss under the Marico moon and how he experienced the elation but also 'the age-old sorrow of first love'.

Zeerust came to symbolise the disruption of timeless Marico life. It was from here that young lovers absconded on the train, or men ran away to the bright lights of Joburg and the mines, despite the predikant's warnings about the carnality, wild living and sinful riches of the diggings (or perhaps because of them). Zeerust presented other vices too. Oom Schalk occasionally played truant from church to see performances by the conjurer in the town hall, visit the bioscope or go drinking at the bar. He notes with disapproval how he spotted other sheepish farmers sitting in the pub when they were supposed to be attending Nagmaal services. On one occasion, he even bumped into the predikant in the bar and was himself made to feel guilty. What the predikant was doing there is not recorded.

Escaping iniquitous Zeerust, Ma and I travelled north on the R49 – the famous 'Mafeking Road' – into the heart of Oom Schalk country. In Bosman's day, this was a simple dirt track with a grass middelmannetjie winding through untamed bushveld. I thought of the wagons returning to the Marico along this road after Nagmaal, an archetypal scene of Afrikaners on trek. Inside the canvas wagon tents sat the women and children; beside the oxen walked the drivers, cracking their whips. Oom Schalk tells of outspanning along this road, singing songs and telling ghost stories around the campfire, and waking to a bright morning after rain, when 'a low wind stirs the wet grass, and you feel, for a little while, that you know the same thing that the veld knows, and in your heart are whisperings.'

We traversed Sephton's Nek, setting of the tale 'Dopper and Papist' about Catholic farmer Piet Reilly and his Dopper wife Gertruida, who lived just north of the pass. It was at the Reilly homestead that Oom Schalk, Gert

Bekker and two churchmen stopped for coffee and, after tending to a sick child, came away with their prejudice against Catholics dented and the humanism of simple Marico folk asserted once more.

We drove on through cattle and game-ranch country, chatting about Oom Schalk and his world. 'You know, it's Bosman's knowledge of the earthiness of Afrikaans that makes his English so unique,' said Ma. 'There's that story about when he and a junior colleague were compiling an anthology of South African poetry. My brother submitted something that wasn't going to make the cut and the young colleague was agonising over how to write the rejection letter.'

I'd read the story in the Bosman biography by Valerie Rosenberg. The young man started with something highfalutin like, 'Geagte Meneer Krige, Hiermee stuur ons u gedig terug (Dear Mr Krige, We are herewith returning your poem).' Bosman read it and exclaimed, 'Hell, you don't write a letter like that to Uys. He will never understand such Afrikaans.' He grabbed a sheet of paper and wrote: 'Liewe Uys, [That's how you start off a letter to him. Now let me see. He'll want to know how I am.] Ek het baie siek gewees met die griep (I have been very sick with flu). [This is about the most common form of Afrikaans you can write: real low-class stuff, but it's beautiful. Then we have to ask how he is.] Hoe gaan dit met jou? [Now to the point.] Hierdie gedig is sommer 'n klomp kak. Jou vriend, Herman (This poem is simply a pile of shit. Your friend, Herman).'

'Bosman died of a heart attack soon after, while he was still working on that anthology,' said Ma as the long, straight Marico road stretched out before us.

After half an hour, we reached Nietverdiend, a small, strung-out dorp that is home to the fictional grave of Hans Welman from the story 'Unto Dust', although there was some controversy about the identity of the grave's occupant. Suspicion arose that Welman's bones had got themselves mixed up with those of the black warrior who'd killed him (before himself being shot) during a commando skirmish. In fact, six months later, when the burial party finally returned to the site of the clash, they had great difficulty telling the black man's bones from the white. And it was indeed strange how for months thereafter the dog belonging to the black warrior frequented Hans Welman's grave.

Nietverdiend is still home to the district police station, famous in many a Marico tale. Bosman's characters are in a continuous cat-and-mouse game with the constables, mostly concerning cattle rustling or the illegal distillation of mampoer. We paused to doff our caps at the police compound, much bigger than the outpost of Oom Schalk's day, but there wasn't much else to detain us in Nietverdiend, so on we pressed.

Somewhere along the stretch of road we now traversed lie the remains of Jurie Steyn's house, which Egbert had failed to find. I imagined farmers sitting around the famous voorkamer offering their opinion on current affairs and rehashing the perennial topics of white ants, droughts, bank managers and ghosts, their coffee-fuelled conversations filling many a long and lazy Marico afternoon. As MacKenzie has pointed out, these stories take place a generation after Oom Schalk's time, when the unbounded liberties of frontier life had been curtailed by external forces – the authorities in Pretoria, the Land Bank and stricter border policing. The mule cart and ox wagon had been supplanted by the government lorry that brought post, visitors and gossip from the outside world. The freedom of the pioneering days was gone and the old-world charm was slipping away. Jurie Steyn's voorkamer was a life-raft to which the bosvelders clung and where, for a few hours, they could ignore the encroachments on their way of life. Strong coffee and tall tales well told were their tragicomic defence against the ravages of time, soaked with Bosman's own empathy and nostalgia.

About fifteen kilometres north of Nietverdiend, we pulled off at a wayside shop with the words 'Zwingli Cash Store' emblazoned in red and white on the facade. My heart skipped a faster tattoo. Here was brick-and-mortar tangibility meeting fictional chimera at last. Zwingli had been Bosman's local store and post office, and was used as partial inspiration for Jurie Steyn's voorkamer.

We parked beside a rusted petrol pump and got out to stretch our creaky road legs. The store with its large signs advertising Joko tea was boarded up – another Bosman link falling into ruin. Peering through a window at the darkened interior, I recalled a David Goldblatt photograph taken in Krisjan Geel's Zwingli Store depicting a young farmer with piles of blankets stacked on shelves behind him. He stands confidently, one hand on his hip, the other on the counter, a sweat-stained bush hat pushed back from his open sunburnt face.

Goldblatt was a great admirer of Bosman and in *Some Afrikaners Revisited* he writes: 'Unaffected in language, economic of means, deceptively simple in plot, [Bosman's stories] conveyed in near poetry, with humour, irony and profound understanding, what must surely have been the truth and particularity of Boer life in the Marico Bushveld in the late 19th and early 20th centuries. Presumptuously, I aspired somehow to bring similar qualities to my photographs.' During the summer of 1964/65, Goldblatt visited the Marico to see if he could find the characters and settings of the tales and to photograph Oom Schalk's dying world. 'It was exciting and strangely affirming to discover, as I went from farm to farm and met the local people, the extraordinary correlations between the facts, the spirit of the place and Bosman's stories.'

Goldblatt was grabbing the tail-end of an era: many farms had already been abandoned as poor soil, drought, overgrazing and poverty drove bosvelders off the land. His photographs record a changing Marico, images imbued with a complicated nostalgia for the bygone age of pioneer farmers and the world of Bosman's tales.

I knew that the Zwingli store lay within walking distance of Bosman's Heimweeberg School and the Middelrand homestead where he lodged. We backtracked down the road a few hundred metres and took a dirt track that led west. In my research, I'd found an old map that showed the Heimweeberg schoolhouse about a kilometre from Zwingli. What remained of its ruins had to be somewhere here, so we searched the veld, but game fencing and thick bush soon forced us to give up.

'As long as you know it's here, Justie, you don't actually have to see the ruin,' said my mother.

'But, Ma—'

'There's probably nothing left of it at all.'

'Ja, okay, Ma, you're probably right.'

In the absence of a ruin, I held in my mind the snapshot of a farmer's son with his black nursemaid, taken by Goldblatt on Heimweeberg farm in 1964. The young white boy rests his hands on the girl's back in an apparent gesture of ownership. But rather than being subservient, she returns the gesture by holding his bare foot, an enigmatic smile playing on her lips. The pose is carelessly intimate, an image from the height of apartheid in an archly conservative corner of South Africa, showing both familiarity and humanity. In this respect, there is an echo of Bosman's empathic treatment of all his Marico characters.

A farmer's son with his nursemaid, Heimweeberg, Nietverdiend, Western Transvaal, 1964

© The David Goldblatt Legacy Trust
Courtesy The David Goldblatt Legacy Trust and Goodman Gallery

We continued up the R49, swinging northeast to skirt a mountain that slowly resolved itself into the camel-like double hump of Abjaterskop. I pulled off and we got out to survey this mountain that was so important in Bosman's world. The portly koppie with its diagonal striations and bushy slopes appeared underwhelming in the white light of midday. To lend it more gravitas, you needed to narrow your eyes and let your imagination conjure a mountain in the shape of Oom Schalk's boot, plucked from one of his best-loved stories, 'In the Withaak's Shade'. It begins:

Leopards? – Oom Schalk Lourens said – Oh, yes, there are two varieties on this side of the Limpopo. The chief difference between them is that the one kind of leopard has got a few more spots on it than the other kind. But when you meet a leopard in the veld, unexpectedly, you seldom trouble to count his spots to find out which kind he belongs to. That is unnecessary. Because, whatever kind of leopard it is that you come across in this way, you only do one kind of running. And that is the fastest kind.

In this famous tale, Oom Schalk gives up on a search for his stray cattle and decides instead to snooze away the heat of the day in the shade of a withaak. As he dozes off, he thinks the tip of his boot looks just like Abjaterskop in the distance. Later, he wakes to find a hungry-looking leopard sniffing at those very same boots. 'I was uncomfortable,' he recounts. 'I knew that nothing I could do would ever convince that leopard that my toe was Abjaterskop. He was not that sort of leopard.' I pictured Oom Schalk lying in the shade next to the R49, his boots pointing at the kop's double hump, wondering what exactly to do about the overly familiar leopard.

Ma hauled out the apple juice and biltong and we found our own patch of shade. Narrowing and 'mistifying' my eyes once more, the R49 shrank back to its sandy, meandering forebear. This stretch of road often features in Bosman's stories because it was said to be haunted and the adjacent Abjaterskop a home of witches. Oom Schalk warns that it's never a good idea to come this way at night, and never ever on foot. In one tale, he attends a dance at Willem Prinsloo's homestead on the slopes of Abjaterskop, a story inspired by Bosman's own twenty-first birthday on the real-life farm of John Callaghan. Although Oom Schalk doesn't believe in ghosts, on his way to the dance he spurs his horse to a gallop through the dark poort, because 'a horse is sensitive about things like ghosts and witches, and it was my duty to see my horse was not frightened unnecessarily.'

Many of the farms described by Bosman no longer exist and others have been incorporated into one of South Africa's largest game reserves. Madikwe is a conservation success story. By the late Twentieth Century, the wildlife that had been so plentiful in Oom Schalk's day had mostly been shot out and it was nigh impossible to imagine a leopard disturbing your siesta in the region of Abjaterskop. But that's all changed and today there are plenty of leopards in the neighbourhood – and bigger cats too – for the famous mountain now marks the western boundary of Madikwe.

By 1991, when this Big Five reserve was founded, the area had been reduced to a series of degraded cattle farms and an extensive wildlife restocking programme had to be undertaken. Operation Phoenix was reputedly the largest reintroduction of game in the world. Lying in a transition zone where bushveld meets Kalahari, Madikwe is a magical place of big skies, pristine wilderness and wide-open plains cut by perennial rivers and dotted with volcanic inselbergs.

I'd planned to spend a few days in Madikwe to see how much of Bosman we could find inside the reserve and because it's a jolly nice place to spend a few days. I also wanted to treat my ma to a bit of safari luxury. We entered via Abjaterskop Gate and headed for the park's headquarters at Vleisfontein, once the site of a Jesuit Mission Station often mentioned by Bosman. Oom Schalk recalls how the local predikant used to rile against the mission's papists and their proselytising activities among the Bapedi.

Vleischfontein (Vleisfontein today) was founded in 1884 as a replenishment station on the road to the Jesuit outpost in Bulawayo. Gardens and orchards were laid out and streams dammed to provide catfish and barbel for Friday meals. The mission became a well-known landmark for those trekking along the Mafeking Road and many a weary traveller stopped to enjoy the priests' hospitality. In 1894, the mission was handed over to the Order of the Oblates of Mary Immaculate (Marists), as the Jesuits no longer needed a halfway house due to the opening of the Bechuanaland railroad. The Marists, together with the Holy Family Sisters and Dominican Sisters, developed the school and built a church, convent, grotto and priests' house.

We parked in the shade of a thorn tree and took a walk around the old mission. Centrepiece was the elegant, double-storey convent that today serves as the Parks Board head office. Gabled and cream coloured with brown trimmings, its entrance was flanked by two mature frangipani trees and a free-standing belfry topped with pinnacles. Nearby lay a stone ruin with alcoves housing an altar and statue of the Virgin Mary; beside it, a tiny, barrel-vaulted chapel with a sky-blue roof and another lifelike Virgin – incongruous Catholic vestiges in the heart of a Bushveld game reserve.

There are more than twenty safari lodges in Madikwe, but I had chosen Thakadu River Camp for its location in the reserve's south-east corner. According to my research, Oom Schalk's fictional home lay somewhere in this quadrant. Bosman tells us that the Lourens farm was located in the Derdepoort district, north of the Dwarsberge and south-east of Abjaterskop (which could be seen in the distance over a spur of the Dwarsberge).

Community-owned Thakadu Camp is a lovely creation of thatch, stone and canvas, tucked into a leafy thicket overlooking the Marico River. That afternoon, I relaxed in a deckchair beside the pool armed with a tall drink and binoculars, occasionally dipping into *Bosman at his Best*, but mostly scanning the trees. The bird life was splendid and it wasn't long before I'd ticked off crimson-breasted shrike, pied barbet, Meyer's parrot, white-throated robin, Jameson's firefinch and paradise whydah.

I marvelled, too, at the variety of flora visible from my perch and opened Bosman to reread his celebration of bushveld trees in 'Marico Revisited':

> Withaaks and kameeldorings. The kremetart-boom. Swarthaak and blinkblaar and wag-'n-bietjie. Moepels and maroelas. The sun-baked vlakte and the thorn-tree and South Africa. Trees are more than vegetation and more than symbols and more than pallid sentimentality ... What the oak and the ash and the cypress are to Europe, the thorn-tree is to South Africa. And if laurel and myrtle and bay are for chaplet and wreath, thorns are for a crown.

We set off on a late-afternoon game drive with guide André Nel – rosy cheeked and clad from head to toe in khaki. Red termite mounds, green magic-guarri bushes, blond grass and grey thorn trees. As Oom Schalk would have it in 'The Wind in the Trees': 'From one horizon to the other the heavens were a deep and intense blue. Bush and koppie, withaak and kremetart and kameel-doorn were dreaming languidly under a cloudless sky.' The wildlife sightings came at regular intervals – waterbuck, zebra, giraffe, buffalo – and André pointed out Bosman locations as we went. Stopping beside the ruin of a farmhouse he said, 'This is all that's left of Tommiesrus, the farm that Bosman mentions in *A Cask of Jerepigo*. And over that bult is the Lemmer farm—'

'You don't mean Krisjan Lemmer, the biggest liar in the Bushveld?' I exclaimed.

'The same!' said André. 'Bosman used real people in his stories; he just mixed them up a bit. The Lemmer family became the liars, but in real life they were actually big cattle rustlers. Then again, who isn't, I mean wasn't.' He winked. Another bloody liar, I thought.

We had to negotiate our way around a white rhino standing stubbornly in the road – a majestic specimen with beautiful scimitar horns – in order to reach the waterhole for sundowner drinks. The dam's fringes were already occupied by a herd of elephants playfully spraying themselves with red mud. Teenagers jousted with one another, then turned their attention to our vehicle and we had to back off smartly.

Parked a little way off to give the elephants some elbow room, André told us more about Operation Phoenix. Over a period of seven years, more than 8 000 animals of 28 species were introduced into Madikwe. Whole families of elephants were brought from drought-stricken Gonarezhou National Park in Zimbabwe, along with youngsters left over from culling in the Kruger. Then came lions. Park officials wanted to find the biggest, handsomest lions in southern Africa, which they sourced from Etosha in Namibia. Wild dogs have also been a great success story in Madikwe, an introduction and breeding programme that would not have pleased Oom Schalk or any other stock farmer in the district. I recalled the story of how one pack of wild dogs, forced out of the Kalahari after rinderpest wiped out the game, killed 300 of Flip Malherbe's sheep (or so he claimed, despite the fact that he owned only 50 sheep).

Once the elephants were done with their cavorting, we moved to the water's edge. The light had softened and the veld was undergoing its daily metamorphosis from dull fawn to gold. André poured G&Ts and passed around nutty nibbles as the sun set over Abjaterskop in a pyrotechnic display. How right Bosman had been when he said 'sunsets in the Marico Bushveld are incredible things, heavily striped like prison bars and flamboyant like their kaffir blankets.'

The mirrored dam gave back tree reflections in the shape of delicate thorn-tree calligraphy and leafless leadwood spires knotted with nests. Umbrella trees stretched to the southern horizon where the lumpy grey Dwarsberge tailed away to the west – the evocative, ever-present backdrop to so many Oom Schalk tales. Perhaps this very dam lay within the boundaries of his fictional farm? In fact, upon further consideration and another G&T, I was certain it did. A lone hippo honked his baritone honk at us and the sky turned salmon, then lilac, as the first stars made their discreet entrance.

The next morning's game drive provided an icy dawn start. Ma and I donned beanies, gloves and scarves against the sniping breeze. 'Jislaaik, dis vrek koud,' said André, pulling on his fleece and breathing clouds of steam. Bosman loved this time of day in the veld, before the garish colours of sunrise, when 'the blurred horizons are wrapped in theology' and the morning is still a wonder of 'griseous tones, leaden and ashen-silver tints and neutral greens, and patches that are the colour of doves' wings'.

It was turning out to be an uneventful game drive until André spotted a lioness, crouched in the long grass, a bundle of excitedly quivering muscles. She was trying to sneak up on a wildebeest herd, but her male companion was trailing behind and didn't appear in the mood for a breakfast hunt. He flopped down under a tree while the lioness worked herself into a position where she could have a feasible crack at the approaching beasts. She pawed the ground, ears flattened – wound up like a spring. But there was no backup from the male and he rolled over, exposing a white belly to the sky, paws aloft.

'He's mulling over the attack plan,' whispered André. 'Forget about the boykie. You go, girl, give it your best shot.' Tension mounted as the distance between the antagonists narrowed. Just then, the wildebeests noticed something amiss, perhaps the periscopic paws of the 'boykie', and they took off as though a starting pistol had been fired. The female trudged back to the male who was, by now, snoring loudly in the shade of a withaak.

North of the Dwarsberge, the land descends gradually towards the border and it was along this stretch of frontier that many Bosman characters conducted their cattle rustling. Oom Schalk learnt a number of cunning methods to outwit the authorities, such as bending the fence posts and covering the barbed wire with canvas, thereby allowing the animals to cross, or grazing fowls over an area to disguise the tracks of illicit stock.

Retracing this old smuggler route, we crossed into Botswana at Kopfontein and drove via Gaborone to Ramoutsa (Ramotswa today), a town central to Bosman's world. I found the Lutheran mission station and school mentioned by Oom Schalk, but not the Indian store where farmers used to gather and socialise. It has no doubt been replaced by the many spaza shops and minimarts that now line Ramotswa's streets. We stopped at Choppies Superstore (the closest incarnation to the Indian shop I could find) and stocked up on padkos. A century later, social gathering and gossiping still appeared to be the order of the day at the store.

In Bosman's time, Marico boers regularly visited Ramoutsa to buy fencing wire, cattle dip and other provisions, wait for the train or simply while away the day 'discussing politics, mealie-crops and the miltsiekte. They stood there, talking, to give their mules a chance to rest. Sometimes a mule got sunstroke, from resting for such a long time in the sun, while his owner was talking.'

The farmers would marvel, and scoff, at the newfangled items for sale in the store, such as gramophones and paraffin candles in packets, and the strange white grease that came in a tube for polishing plates and spoons (although some suggested it could also be used for brushing teeth). They grumbled about how the Indian added roasted baobab roots to the coffee and Kalahari sand to the yellow sugar, but the thing that most upset Oom Schalk was how the storekeeper had set himself up as a rival storyteller, trading in even taller tales than his own. How could the poor old oom compete with a liar who used unfair methods, like putting princesses and palaces into his stories,

> and elephants that were all dressed up with yellow and red hangings and that were trained to trample on the king's enemies at the word of command. Whereas the only kind of elephants I could talk about were those that didn't wear red hangings or gold

bangles, and that didn't worry about whether or not you were the king's enemy: they just trampled on you first, anyhow, and without any sort of training, either.

In 'Marico Revisited', Bosman tells of his return to the region two decades after leaving his teaching post and how he was once again enraptured by the Bushveld. He stepped off the train at Ramoutsa siding, back into a world he had in the intervening years completely recast in fiction. We found the century-old railway station – green roof, sky-blue veranda, red fire buckets, echoing offices. It could hardly have changed a jot since Bosman's visit. But we didn't linger: the day was getting long in the shadows and, our journey almost done, we needed to make tracks for the Big Smoke.

We crossed the border at Swartkopfontein, re-entering the Marico at the western end of the Dwarsberge. As we drove, I was thinking about Bosman's nostalgic return described in 'Marico Revisited', probably along this very road: 'We travelled on through the bush over stony paths that were little more than tracks going in between the trees and underneath their branches, the thorns tearing at the windscreen and the hood of the car in the same way as they had done years before, when I had first visited the Marico. I was glad to find that nothing had changed.'

We passed the spot where, if you're wearing your fictional hat, you'll find the grave of Paulus Oberholzer, a young man disowned by his father when he ran off with a black woman from Ramoutsa. Oberholzer senior forbade the burial of his son on the family farm after he'd hanged himself. Oom Schalk helped dig the grave beside the Ramoutsa road in the shade of a stand of withaak trees.

On we drove, past Koedoesrand farm, where Lenie Venter fell in love with a travelling insurance salesman but was eventually persuaded not to marry him. By now, the sun was low, the light turning syrupy. The thorn trees on either side pressed closer and the Dwarsberge formed an undulating green mamba on our left. The road traversed a vast sunflower field, the yellow-flamed, honeycomb faces bending towards us, and Ma began to recite one of her favourite Krige poems, 'Sonneblom' (Sunflower): 'Na die bron / van alles, die son, / één beurende drang / één goue verlang!' (To the source of everything, the sun, / one striving urge / one golden yearning!)

'Aren't those the words on Uys's gravestone?' I asked.

My mother nodded. 'And Jan Rabie planted sunflowers on the grave. They were my brother's favourite flower.'

Next came fields filled with cattle, possibly descendants of those smuggled across the border in Oom Schalk's day. Up ahead a magnificent white cow with a bell around her neck stood foursquare in the road. We drew to a halt. She didn't want to let us pass. I thought of the memoir 'Reminiscences' and the apparition said to haunt the Ramoutsa road at night, a ghost in the form of a white donkey with its forelegs set firmly in the road beside a stand of marula trees. Bosman writes: 'Nobody was quite certain where the hind legs of the donkey were planted because the lonely traveller would decide to turn back just about then ... I visited that part of the Marico again about two years ago. The clump of maroelas by the side of the Government road has been cut down, since those days. But the donkey is still there.' Perhaps the cow, I was beginning to think, now that I looked at her more closely as my car inched forward to coax her off the road, did in fact look not altogether unlike a donkey.

Chasing the light, we pushed on towards the R49, again passing close to the site of the Heimweeberg school. Bosman's words echoed in my head once more: 'And so I arrived back in that part of the country to which the Transvaal Education Department in its wisdom had sent me years before. There is no other place I know that is so heavy with atmosphere, so strangely and darkly impregnated with that stuff of life that bears the authentic stamp of South Africa.'

Bosman's journey back to the Marico, not long before his own death, must have been a remarkable encounter with his past. 'I found, what I should have known all along, of course, that it was the present that was haunted, and that the past was not full of ghosts,' he wrote. 'The phantoms are what you carry around with you, in your head, like you carry your dreams under your arm.' And I realised that my ma and I had also been crisscrossing the Marico in search of phantoms – the characters and places of old, beloved stories – and had been experiencing that strange nostalgia brought on by literature, where the line between fact and fiction is deliciously blurred and your phantoms stand foursquare in the road, as real and present as a white donkey-cow.

———✵———

ALONE IN ALL THAT VASTNESS

JM Coetzee's Moordenaars Karoo

As an undergraduate at UCT in the 1980s, I opted for a course tutored by Stephen Watson on apocalyptic South African fiction. Our studies focused on *July's People* by Nadine Gordimer, Karel Schoeman's *Promised Land* and JM Coetzee's *Life & Times of Michael K*. The latter left a particular impression on me and, at the time, I thought it the finest South African novel I'd ever read. I think I probably still do.

Michael K continued to haunt me in my post-university life and was top of the list when I started to plan this lit-fossicking road-trip project. I have always had a curious relationship with UCT's Great Writer. In certain territories, I felt I could relate to Coetzee: he and I had similar backgrounds, being 'brought up English' in big, old, landed, Cape Afrikaner families. Both of us had a host of gentle, soft-spoken aunts and uncles and hordes of cousins who gathered annually for the familie samesyn. We both grew up in the southern suburbs, attended UCT, studied abroad and later taught in the UCT English Department. That's where the similarities skid to a halt (he, of course, went on to conquer the literary world; I did not), but his presence on the upper corridor of the Arts Block continued to exert an influence on me, and many others, even long after he'd emigrated to Australia.

Winner of the Booker Prize in 1983, *Life & Times of Michael K* is the allegorical story of an idiot-sage. Although his race is not revealed, Michael K is doubtless coloured, living in a fictionalised version of late-apartheid South Africa. The novel is set in a time of low-key civil war with curfews, travel restrictions and internment camps. The oppressive political system, its institutions and bureaucracy, become Michael K's principal antagonists.

Michael is an uneducated, working-class man with a harelip who has been fatherless since childhood. Raised by his domestic-worker mother, he spent some of his childhood in an orphanage. One day, his sickly mother announces that she wants to return to the farm of her youth in the Karoo.

Travel permits are not forthcoming, so Michael constructs a wagon from the chassis of a wheelbarrow to carry his mother and the pair set off from their home in Sea Point, bound for the interior.

Reaching Stellenbosch, her health deteriorates and after a short period of hospitalisation she dies. Michael abandons the wagon and continues the journey on foot. After considerable adversity he reaches the Karoo and finds the farm he assumes to be his mother's birthplace. He is captivated by the landscape, thinking he has found a patch of earth where he can escape the authorities and the outside world, and decides to remain on the farm.

His attempts to make a home for himself and cultivate a garden are cut short by the arrival of the farmer's grandson, a deserter from the army. Not wanting to be a servant or subject, or to join the guerrillas, Michael takes refuge in the Swartberg mountains. Hunger eventually drives him to the village of Prince Albert where he is hospitalised and then interned in a work camp. Michael escapes and goes back to the farm where he tries to eke out an existence once more, but he is discovered by soldiers, falsely accused of aiding the guerrillas, transferred to Cape Town and placed in a rehabilitation camp, from which he again escapes. The novel ends with him returning to Sea Point and joining a group of vagrants living on Signal Hill.

Born in 1940, JM Coetzee spent the holidays of his youth on the family farm in the central Karoo. His connection to that environment is important to our understanding of a number of his novels, as well as his non-fiction work, *White Writing*, in which he explores the history and potency of the plaasroman. In *Life & Times of Michael K*, Coetzee presents a critique of both the plaasroman and traditional renderings of landscape, particularly the Karoo, in South African literature. In this light, we can see Michael's engagement with the land and its cultivation as standing in opposition, and perhaps even as an antidote, to former colonial narratives.

There are a number of South African founding myths that become themes and questions in *Michael K*: the Eden-like garden established by the first Dutch settlers at the Cape, the Great Trek to the Promised Land, and the iconic place of the farm in Afrikaner culture that established a close bond between volk and land. Furthermore, are the settlers and their farms at war with the wilderness and with the black inhabitants of the land, or living in harmony with them? And can the English language ever truly represent the South African landscape, or is this only possible in indigenous languages … or in the muteness of a character like Michael K?

Another dimension to the novel is the Romantic notion of an escape from the city to the country and finding a refuge from civilisation. It is in nature that Michael (and Coetzee) find relief from the tyrannies of the modern world. As Eckard Smuts has noted, the affinity that Coetzee feels for the family farm and the Karoo, and the possibility of a more fully realised identity that it evokes, draws on the English Romantic literary ideal of achieving a unified sense of self through creative acts of identification with the natural environment. This identification is often linked to powerful childhood experiences of nature, forever compromised for Coetzee by the knowledge that he will never be able to live permanently on the farm, and by the problematic idea of 'ownership', tainted by the act of dispossession wrought by colonialism and apartheid.

———✳———

My principal goal of this literary quest was to visit the Coetzee family farm, Voëlfontein, where *Life & Times of Michael K* is partly and loosely set. The farm and surrounding lands are fictionalised, and Michael K is as slippery a signifier as ever walked the pages of a South African novel, but I wanted to try to find the places where the veil between reality and narrative were thinnest. In the novel, the farm is situated on the Moordenaars River, north of Prince Albert and east of the R353 towards Kruidfontein, but Coetzee's geography remains deliberately vague and his family farm (further north) is clearly the inspiration for the novel.

Voëlfontein belonged to Coetzee's grandfather and is an important palimpsest in many of his novels, non-fiction and autobiographical works. His connection to the farms of both his parents' families, but particularly Voëlfontein, distinguished the young Coetzee from his classmates at school. 'Through the farms,' he writes in his fictionalised memoir *Boyhood*, 'he is rooted in the past; through the farms he has substance … Farms are places of freedom, of life.'

As a child, Coetzee spent considerable time on Voëlfontein, usually during school holidays – sojourns that left him with powerful memories. He recalls that on his first visit, at about the age of four, he was playing with the labourers' children one day when he discovered he could speak Afrikaans. John and the other Coetzee children would roam the veld as free as wild animals, and the farm's horses, donkeys, cows, pigs, ducks and goats provided constant entertainment. His uncles and aunts were good-natured and the atmosphere idyllic. He remembers lazy afternoons when his family would sit on the stoep after their nap and talk about the old days, about their father the boordjie-boer (collar-and-tie farmer) and their schoolmasters with their buttock-warming canes.

Coetzee's love of the farm and the Karoo grew to a point where he wanted to live nowhere else. However, just like Michael K, he did not wish to share it with anyone. In *Boyhood* he writes:

> Is there no way of living in the Karoo – the only place in the world where he wants to be – as he wants to live: without belonging to a family? … In his imagination Voëlfontein is a kingdom in its own right. There is not enough time in a single life to know all of Voëlfontein, know its every stone and bush. No time can be enough when one loves a place with such devouring love.

If I wanted to get closer to Michael K – and by extension his brilliant, reclusive, émigré creator – I needed to visit the farm. Voëlfontein is Coetzee's ground zero.

My first attempt was via the novelist himself. As we had done some work together in the past, I still had John's contact details and sent him an email asking about the farm. He wrote back promptly: 'As for Voëlfontein, the cousin of mine who owns the farm has been somewhat plagued by people who have read *Boyhood* and want to see the place. He doesn't take kindly to strangers, and I would hesitate to arm you with an introduction since he and I have had no contact in half a century.'

Undeterred, but not wanting to give offence, I tried other avenues. Coetzee scholars offered me what leads they could. Professor Carrol Clarkson of the University of the Western Cape suggested I contact Hermann Wittenberg, also at UWC. Retired Professor David Attwell of York University had visited the farm and sent me photos and vague directions, saying the turn-off was somewhere between the N1 and Merweville. He'd visited it in 2012 while researching his own book: 'My contact with Gerald Coetzee, John's cousin at Voëlfontein, was very brief and came via the filmmaker Anton Naudé (based in Stellenbosch), who was close to Coetzee's biographer, John Kannemeyer.'

Kannemeyer had since died, I had trouble tracking down Naudé and Wittenberg was unable to help. Attwell did, however, furnish me with Gerald Coetzee's email address. I wrote to 'Oom Gerald', explained my project and asked whether it would be possible to visit the farm: there was no reply. Perhaps John was right about pestering literary fans.

Next, I contacted the Fransie Pienaar Museum in Prince Albert and various guesthouses in the area to try to establish the location of Voëlfontein. These ends proved similarly dead. But then came a breakthrough: Kallie le Roux, owner of Springbok Lodge in Merweville, replied to my email with Oom Gerald's cell phone number. I sent a text message in my most formal and polite Afrikaans. There was no response.

In the meantime, I'd taken to trawling the Moordenaars Karoo (the driest, harshest section of the Koup region) on Google Maps. Back and forth, my mouse played across the brown and khaki wastes north of the N1, looking for farmhouses. From Attwell's photographs, I knew the homestead had two front gables, a grey roof, a pentagonal lawn and a stoep with a green-and-white-striped afdak. But the Karoo haystack was vast and the farmhouse needles well camouflaged.

At last, one evening, my mouse hit the jackpot. Clicking its way along a dry riverbed it happened upon a promising structure. Zooming in, I could make out the blurry shadows of two gables ... and a green-and-white roof over the stoep. Although the house was more than twenty kilometres from the main road down a farm track, I reckoned I might be able to find my way there, even without Oom Gerald's invitation, and even if I had to climb over a few fences and indulge in a spot of light trespassing.

My luck had turned the corner. A few days later, I received a reply to my text message from Oom Gerald: yes, I was welcome to visit the farm, as long as it wasn't a Tuesday. He supplied me with directions, stressing that I would need a 4x4 or at least a 'proper bakkie' if I came from the west, and we arranged a meeting for 10.30 a.m. the following Friday. I was inordinately, perhaps even disproportionately, excited. In some strange way, it felt as though I was going to meet Michael K himself.

It was a misty winter morning on Sea Point promenade and a grey-fingered cold front crawled across the Atlantic towards me. A salt-laden westerly blew fresh off the whitecaps as I strolled towards Rocklands, passing the homeless man from Dar es Salaam seated on his regular bench – threadbare clothes, holey socks, broken sandals – with his backpack and sleeping bag beside him.

'Morning, Eric.'

'Salaam, Justin.'

'No work yet?'

'Not a ting,' he said with a broad smile. How on earth did he keep his spirits buoyant in this kwerekwere-hating corner of the south?

I ambled on past the sculptures of the wonky white horses, outsize steel spectacles and disembodied rhino, my eyes scanning the seafront for Michael K's haunts. He'd lived with his domestic-worker mother in the basement of one of these apartment blocks. It was from here that the pair set off with a homemade cart in the dead of winter, and it is to one of these beaches, perhaps Rocklands or Queen's, that Michael returned at the end of the novel and was adopted by a group of vagrants.

Back in my own seafront flat, I finished the last of my packing, loaded the car and set off along Beach Road, past Somerset Hospital, seat of colonial medicine and all got up in Victorian finery with crenellations and broekie-lace fretwork. Michael collected his mother from this hospital after her discharge … and here on my right was the bus stop where they waited endlessly for a ride back to Sea Point. To the left lay the docks – now upmarket marina apartments, but in the novel a wasteland of burnt-out warehouses where the homeless took refuge.

I joined the elevated freeway, driving out of the city against the tail end of rush-hour traffic. The pylons below were ringed with the makeshift shelters – plastic sheeting, wooden frames, cardboard walls – of the modern homeless. Michael's people. Passing Paarden Island, I pictured the highway blocked by a checkpoint where mother and son were turned back because they couldn't produce the necessary papers to proceed into the interior. Instead, they took a detour south through the suburbs, over Mowbray railway bridge, past the Children's Hospital and along Klipfontein Road. I, too, deviated through the suburbs and onto the N2, heading for Stellenbosch. I stopped outside the Boland town's austere white hospital and thought of Michael, sleeping in an alley on flattened cartons, waiting for news of his mother.

After her death, he set off once more, heading north carrying a box with her ashes. I followed him along the R44, rejoining the N1, past orchards, pine plantations and farms set against the saw-tooth crags of Du Toitskloof, looking architectural in the cold morning shadow. Michael avoided the Huguenot Tunnel with its guard post and ascended the pass instead. I spotted him trudging through wet brush, shunning the road and its convoys. Reaching the saddle at nightfall, he must have turned to look back at a distant Table Mountain and the green flats between. No regrets, I should think, apart from the loss of his mother.

Descending the eastern side of the pass, he would perhaps have stopped to drink from the gnashing Molenaars River. Grey buttresses and sandstone ramparts on either side, waves of cloud breaking overhead, waterfalls pouring from the cliffs in twisting spindles of thread. The landscape here is more European than African – Germanic, Alpine. A Romantic painting of this gorge would need only a Friedrich-like Rückenfigur in the foreground, staring in awe at the sublime cliffs. But Michael could never be a Rückenfigur. Head down, he remains a moving target, representative of the dispossessed on a ghostly traverse of the berg.

The slopes of the descent were thick with fynbos, richly green and smelling of damp fecundity. Maybe Michael felt the first inkling of freedom here, perhaps as a by-product of the land's powerful indifference. But ahead of him lay many hours of trudging … mere minutes in my car. The mountain walls opened to reveal the wide valley of the Breede River. Back into settler farmland, Michael passed unending vineyards, stripped to bark in their winter livery. Against the light, into the sun, the tar glistened. These are inhospitable flatlands, especially on a winter's day with a cold, white glare and icy wind. Slowly Worcester began to take shape up ahead on my right: it was somewhere in the outskirts of this Boland town that Michael was stopped at a roadblock and detained.

I turned onto the R60 and entered the dull suburb of Reunion Park, situated between the railway line and the N1. Coetzee's parents moved to Worcester in the late 1940s and John attended school here. Reunion Park was an unattractive new suburb with sparse vegetation – a boring, conservative platteland environment. In *Boyhood*, Coetzee writes of his upbringing: 'Perhaps Worcester is a purgatory one must pass through.' Near his home lay the railway yards and John crossed the line most days on his bicycle. It is to this railway junction that Michael is brought and loaded into a carriage along with other detainees for transfer into the Karoo. I crossed the tracks and drove through a bleak industrial area filled with queues of rolling stock, then returned to the N1 and headed northeast, following the railway line into the Hex River Valley. Just before Sandhills, I pulled into a layby and got out. In the novel, the tracks hereabouts were blocked by a rockfall, perhaps as a result of sabotage, and the detainees were unloaded to help clear the line. In a corner of the valley below lay Kanetvlei, the farm of my own childhood holidays whose homestead I could just make out among distant trees.

When my father opened an architectural practice in Worcester in the 1950s and designed his first, Modernist houses, one of his early projects was the restoration of Kanetvlei, home to the Conradie family. The owners became friends and the Foxes used to visit the farm each autumn after harvest when the vines were dressed in scarlet. My recollections are filled with whitewashed cottages, the smell of fermenting grapes, a hang bridge over a stony stream. I remember delicate San rock art in caves above the vineyards and sheep being herded into the kraal each evening, their hooves turning the dust to gold. I explored the farm on the back of a motorbike with the farmer's son and hiked into steep-sided kloofs. I had not returned to Kanetvlei for three decades, but I could still picture every corner of the farm. This distant view from the N1 seemed a pale and unreliable facsimile beside my Kodachrome recollections.

Pressing on up the highway, road signs warned drivers not to stop: 'Highjacking hotspot for 30 kilometres'. There'd been recent attacks on vehicles, particularly trucks, on the stretch through De Doorns, and bridges over the road were covered with wire mesh to prevent rocks being dropped on passing cars. Shacks lined the N1, plastic bags decorated the fences, the ground sparkled with broken glass. Powder-keg youths milled about on the verges: unemployed, idle, hungry, angry – the modern incarnation of *Michael K*'s rebels. The vineyards were surrounded by razor wire, but above and beyond the valley's agri-political mess stood the Matroosberg's upper slopes, glinting in sheets of virgin snow.

Next came the long, grinding ascent of Moordhoogte Pass, overtaking shongololo trucks, finally to reach the plains of the Karoo. The veld in every direction was bleached grey and bone dry with only the daisy-strewn verges and culverts holding any colour. Insects exploded on my windscreen; ostriches pecked at barren ground; pied crows and police cars patrolled the highway. At Touws River – low hills, behemoth fuel stations – I paused to pay my respects at the vast railway yard where Michael was disembarked and set free.

The Shosholoza Meyl train, resplendent in purple and turquoise livery, thundered past, billowing clouds of dust. I recalled that as a boy, John used to take the train up the line from Worcester to visit the farm and how their humble passenger train had to pull in to sidings to let the more illustrious and important express trains race past.

From Touws River, Michael made for the eastern hills on foot, preferring to head across open country and avoid the N1 – symbol of authority, artery for army trucks, place of roadblocks, searches and the threat of reincarceration. To this day, the N1 remains an unloved alimentary canal. Apart from hijackings, stone throwing and (more recently) petrol bombing, the Karoo's long, straight, sleep-inducing stretches are notorious for horror crashes. Like Michael, I wanted to be free of it.

Many Coetzee holidays involved this journey up the N1 to Voëlfontein or Prince Albert, home to his grandparents. Plenty of its coordinates find a home in his writing, such as Laingsburg, where Michael was offered shelter for the night, and the Anglo-Boer War blockhouses protecting the bridges that flashed by. Indeed, *Michael K* is filled with echoes of that earlier South African war, so powerfully evoked by Deneys Reitz in *Commando*.

I turned onto the R407 and crossed the dry Vlakkraal River, bound for Prince Albert. Free of the highway at last, and slowing to a more sedate pace, I registered an immediate change. The N1 had felt like a contaminating force that poisoned the land along its flanks, but as I drew away from it, the veld began to work its magic. Somewhere in the middle of nowhere, far from any sign of habitation, I passed a lone man wearing a shapeless coat and hat pulled low over his eyes. I pictured Michael wrapped in his mother's coat doing the same, and was reminded of Boesman and Lena, two of Athol Fugard's most memorable characters, walking the back roads of the Eastern Cape, trapped in a loop of Beckettian futility, bent forward against the wind, against adversity, against history.

And I found myself thinking of Krisjan Swart, a Karoo itinerant captured in the paintings of my uncle, François Krige. Like Michael, Krisjan was a wanderer and a 'vagrant' who would occasionally turn up in Montagu asking for food or gardening work. Krige often set him to work, but rather than tending flowers, Krisjan sat for my uncle and had his portrait painted. In the many sketches and oils, he is rendered as a loner, a rover, an icon – a timeless figure imbued with almost saintly dignity. Krisjan is usually depicted with his billycan, staff and sack of belongings, tramping the Karoo roads in veldskoens and greatcoat. Breyten Breytenbach writes of these portraits in *Dog Heart*:

> Krisjan is painted as the emblem of a broken humanity. The folds in his face are pages blackened by history, marked in a foreign tongue. Krisjan is King Lear. His majesty and his massive presence fill the cloth. Krisjan is a deposed ruler seen through the eyes of Rembrandt. He comes from a long way away down the ages. Then François Krige paints Krisjan as Montagu knows him: a hang-about, bum, drifter, beggar, sleeping wherever the alcohol closes in upon him in rain or in sun, the sad nomad with filthy rags twisted around the head, an oversized and shapeless and torn overcoat, all his belongings in the one bag slung across his shoulder. In the past the old people trek through the mountains with across their shoulders all their belongings in bags made of soft skin.

Ahead of me, the Swartberg rose out of the plains – battleship-grey, sinuous, muscular – with the name 'Prince Albert' painted in white letters on the side of a koppie. Somewhere in these scrubby flats, about five kilometres north of the town, is the site of Jakkalsdrif camp, where Michael was interned after being apprehended for vagrancy. My mind's eye populated the veld with wood-and-iron buildings, barbed-wire fences and tents, imaginings borrowed from photos of similar camps in the Anglo-Boer War.

I drove through the former coloured township of North End and into Prince Albert, drawing up at Haven on Church where I'd booked to stay. The B&B had the advantage of being next door to the home of a friend, Kevin Jacobs, with only a garden gate separating the two. The Haven's owner, Elsabe Koen, met me in the driveway accompanied by a geriatric shar pei that was deaf, blind in one eye and overly protective of Elsabe. The dog took an instant dislike to me and started barking even before I'd alighted.

'Don't mind Polo,' she said. 'He's a softie at heart, although he's not very keen on men. He just needs to get used to you.' Over the ensuing days, Polo barked, growled, huffed, made mock charges and never really did get used to me.

'I'm from PE, but moved here in April to start the B&B,' said Elsabe as she led me to the guest cottage in her back yard. 'It was always part of my five-year plan to settle here – I've loved PA since coming with my dad when I was a kid – but the plan had to be brought forward 'cause of BEE. The usual story: they retrenched me for a black person, but hey, I'm not sorry, the PA folk have been so welcoming. Our market on Saturdays is where it all happens: farm produce, Pete Reinders' legendary vegetables, lekker local eggs, cheese and yoghurt from our famous PA dairy. You must go see it.'

The cottage was flanked by an open field and a dam – the ideal spot to write, ponder Michael's wanderings and reread the five kilograms of Coetzee works in my duffel bag. Unpacking, I laid out the books, photocopied maps and notes on my bed. Tomorrow was to be a big day. Looking at the Google Maps printout again, I reckoned it would take an hour and a half to reach Voëlfontein and, as John had warned me about the nuisance of literary stalkers, I didn't want to be late for my appointment with Oom Gerald.

Kevin came over to say hello. He and his wife Toni Younghusband had moved to Prince Albert six years earlier and adored their adopted dorp. They'd wanted to find somewhere 'charming and friendly' that was 'far, but not too far' from Cape Town. 'Friends who'd moved here raved about it,' said Kevin. 'We bought a place and started fixing it up slowly while still living in Cape Town. When we eventually took the plunge and relocated, we were embraced by the community as soon as we moved in. I started editing the village newspaper and took up painting; Toni got involved in animal welfare. It's a move we haven't regretted for a single minute.'

Later that afternoon, I strolled up Church Street to the Fransie Pienaar

Museum where I met curator Lydia Barrella at the reception. A formidable woman in her seventies, she wore thick spectacles, a blue cardigan, Crocs on her stockinged feet and large blue clips in her hair. Lydia led me through to her office at the back of the museum where she seated me among piles of dusty files and imparted what she knew of the connections between the Coetzee family and Prince Albert.

'Back in the 1930s and '40s, John's grandparents, the De Beers, were important people in this town,' she said. 'His grandfather, Gerrit Maxwell Coetzee, was mayor, and their home, called Ruimte and built in 1852, was just behind the museum on the corner of Pastorie and De Beer streets. The beautiful old gable has unfortunately been removed.'

'I suppose John would have visited that house often as a child,' I said.

'Definitely. You know, I had a very odd experience last month. An elderly gentleman pitched up here and, like you, asked about the De Beer connection, so I showed him some of our old photos and chatted to him for a bit, just like I'm doing with you. It was only after he left that I realised it was wragtig-waar JM Coetzee himself, visiting from Australia! Can you believe it. I felt like such a clot. What a shy man ... too modest to even say who he was, but I did give him my email address and we've corresponded since.'

She switched on her computer and called up images of the De Beer house and a shop owned by the family on Church Street, currently the Showroom Theatre. 'John emailed me with a list of questions about his family,' said Lydia. 'I sent him everything I had and asked if he remembered which house he'd lived in. You might recall from the Kannemeyer biography that John stayed in PA with his mother and brother in 1944. He would have been about four years old. At the time, his father was serving up north with the South African Army and his mother rented a room from Miss Florence Forsythe. John wrote back and said he couldn't recall which house, but that it must have been summer because of all the mosquitoes, the long hot nights and days of boredom sheltering indoors from the sun.'

Thanking Lydia, I took a stroll down Pastorie Street, lined with stately Cape Dutch townhouses, until I came to the old De Beer home. A high wall, carport and line of cypress trees shielded the building from the road, but I tried a gate and found my way into the field behind, where gardeners were tending vines, lemon and olive trees. The house had the same green-and-white-striped veranda roof as the photos I'd seen of Voëlfontein – a family preference. I was getting closer to the source.

Standing in the De Beers' field, I was thinking about the genteel, settled, platteland-dorp existence I knew from childhood holidays in Montagu, staying with Uncle François. I remember the soporific afternoons, the dry heat and trilling doves, the leiwater gurgling in the sluits on either side of Long Street. Just like Prince Albert, Montagu comprised a patchwork of orchards, gardens, vineyards and dams, and rugged mountains rising at the edge of town – all of it perfect for boys' adventuring.

François's home was typical of the mid-Nineteenth Century with a simple gable, thatched roof, green shutters and vine pergola; its creaky interiors were dark and cool, smelling of wood polish and oil paint. There was a larder filled with produce from the garden, jars of chutney, jam, pickles and cherry liqueur. The furniture was Cape Dutch, much of it from our ancestral family farm, Bontebokskloof, near Swellendam.

My stroll through Prince Albert took me past the police station, screened by a high fence, to which a delirious Michael was briefly brought after his spell in the mountains, before being sent to hospital for treatment. Turning left into Odendaal Street, I came to the very hospital – a low, nondescript edifice fronted by a cactus garden. This building was perhaps too modern for the novel, but did it really matter? As far as my imagination was concerned, Michael was admitted here and convalesced in a wood-and-iron extension at the back.

I climbed a koppie to the west of town and found a boulder with a commanding aspect. Prince Albert was laid out below – neat, tree-lined streets and white buildings with grey or red tin roofs. This was the first view Michael had had of the town after his long walk from Touws River. How secure and settled the village looked, so at home in the landscape, surrounded by nurturing farmlands with open plains to the north and the Swartberg to the south, a peaceful oasis fed by perennial water from the mountains. At its heart lay the Dutch Reformed Church with its silver spire, speaking to and for the landed establishment. Michael could never have found a place here.

I returned to the B&B and was intercepted by Polo, who replied to my warm greeting with growls, his low-cropped ears and swollen eye adding to the menace. As I opened the gate, he broke into a frenzy of barking and only once I was safely in my room did he return to more placatory snorting. It was rather disconcerting, almost as though I, a paying guest, was not entirely welcome.

That evening, Kevin invited me to the opening of a new restaurant run by local chef Jeremy Freemantle. It was a festive affair in a newly converted cottage with a buffet of charcuterie starters, chicken in a Japanese sauce and a dessert of pears in wine. I was seated between old-timers Pete Reinders, a retired doctor, and Nick Dover, a former British Airways pilot.

'In all my long-haul travels with BA, I'd never been to a place quite like PA,' said Nick. 'I just fell in love with the town and bought a house here. My wife doesn't quite see the charm and stays in London or Wiltshire, where we have homes, but I'm absolutely smitten. The mountains, the climate, the restaurants and the unbelievably welcoming people. When I'm back in the UK, I have to remind myself not to greet everyone I pass in the street.'

'So, you remain optimistic, despite South Africa's woes?' I asked.

'Yes. How could you lot have expected anything different from a post-liberation African country, but that doesn't mean I want to leave.'

Pete Reinders, on my left, had been the town doctor for decades and Kevin had told me how much the man was loved in Prince Albert. Many of his patients weren't able to pay, others settled their accounts with farm produce or even live chickens. When he retired, Pete's debtors' book was overflowing, but he didn't have the heart to pursue anyone.

'Me and the wife love camping wild in the veld,' said Pete. 'We've got a fully kitted-out 4x4 and just sommer stop and make camp beside the road in far-flung corners of the Karoo. Although my wife has been getting a bit nervous lately, what with the crime and all. She's overreacting, of course, but when the nagging gets too much I sleep with a pistol under my pillow.'

Glancing around the room, I noticed that the clientele was exclusively white. A quarter of a century into democracy and Michael K's people have barely gained a foothold in the middle-class world of platteland towns. The old racial divisions remain largely intact. Looking out the window at the dark mountains, I thought of Michael taking refuge in the Swartberg heights: perhaps his spirit was still up there, staring back at the lights of the town. How did our sumptuous restaurant fare compare to his frugal diet?

I remembered my own encounter with Coetzee's fastidiousness around food. There was an occasion in the 1980s when I was asked to invite the novelist to lunch at our home in Newlands. Family friend Breyten Breytenbach had recently been released from prison and was staying with us. He wanted to meet Coetzee and asked me to help. I was a UCT student at the time and, like most undergraduates in the English Department, knew and feared 'God', the ascetic Booker Prize winner on the upper corridor. Until then, I'd never dared speak to Him. Perhaps concerned about Coetzee's notorious diffidence, Breyten suggested I also invite poet Stephen Watson to make things more gesellig.

My mother served fish, but Coetzee announced that he was vegetarian and nibbled on hastily produced Provita biscuits and cheese, to my ma's mortification. It was an awkward lunch for me, seated amid three of my literary heroes with nothing to contribute other than 'may I pass you the salt?'. Breyten was his gregarious self, Watson chimed in where he could, Coetzee spoke little, his words carefully chosen. In *Boyhood* he states, 'Part of being prudent is always to tell less rather than more.' Ours was a prudent lunch. Coetzee was, however, surprised and pleased to discover that Uys Krige was my mother's brother. I recall almost nothing else about the conversation, apart from my own tongue-tied awe at being seated beside the man who had given birth to Michael K.

---*---

Driving north next morning, bound for Voëlfontein, I followed the route Michael would have walked when he escaped from Jakkalsdrif camp and returned to the farm. I pictured him trudging across stony ground beside the road, a dado line of blue mountains behind, the empty vlaktes of the

Koup ahead. It was an icy morning, the veld holding to its pale fastness. For Michael, 'the landscape was so empty that it was not hard to believe at times that his was the first foot ever to tread a particular inch of earth or disturb a particular pebble. But every mile or two there was a fence to remind him that he was a trespasser as well as a runaway.'

Crossing the N1, I took the road to Merweville, not encountering a single car along the way. The land grew drier, the vegetation sparser, the earth turning to bare rock. After about 30 kilometres, I found the sign 'Voëlfontein 21 km', and pulled off to open the farm gate, feeling as though I was stepping into the pages of a book, both Coetzee's and my own.

The act of opening the gate to a farm has resonance for me, as it does for Coetzee. I'd grown up with Uys Krige's poem 'Plaashek', which articulates a prodigal return (although written in the Lowveld) to the hallowed ground of a farm:

> Na al die jare maak ek weer
> 'n plaashek oop.
> Waar het my paaie
> tog nie geloop
> om my hier by 'n hek te bring
> van al my waan gestroop,
> maar met my denke helder
> en in my hart die hoop?
>
> Die hek staan in die skad'wee van
> 'n kremetart.
> Die stilte in my's volkome met
> niks troebels, niks verward.
> Ek lig die knop ... Ek maak
> 'n hek oop in my hart.
>
>
> Now after all the years I'll open
> a gate again.
> Where have my paths
> till now not led

to bring me to this farm gate
with all illusions shed
but hope, hope in my heart
and clear dreams in my head?

The gate stands in
a baobab's shade.
A wholeness in me, harmony
and no bitterness, no hate.
I lift the catch ... and in my heart
open a gate.

Opening a farm gate – Bontebokskloof for Krige, Voëlfontein for Coetzee – suggests entry into a timeless realm that represents their childhood and is thus sanctified and reachable only through memory. In *White Writing*, Coetzee refers to this Krige poem, describing how a wanderer returning to the farm of his birth experiences 'in the act of opening the farm gate the same intimation of a return to the true self and primitive moral sources that Wordsworth feels in returning to the dales and fells'.

My brother Revel remembers visiting Uncle Uys at his home in Onrus some time in the early 1970s, back when he too was an English undergraduate at UCT. Uys was holding court on the stoep, as was his wont, regaling a guest with one of his amusing, digressive, entertaining stories. The guest, sitting captivated on a low stool at the feet of the poet, looked vaguely familiar. It took my brother a moment to register that it was one of his lecturers – a certain JM Coetzee. Revel was shocked: already back then, Coetzee had acquired his ascetic, guru-like reputation.

Closing the gate behind me, I drove down a straight dirt track, thinking how twenty-one kilometres constituted rather a long driveway. The land was flat and dotted with sparse, stunted shrubs; the fence posts were of stone and the wire between them taut as bowstring. There were many gates and the road deteriorated, compelling me to drive slowly over sections of splintered shale. I was behind schedule and making my 10.30 appointment on time was looking unlikely. Worse, there was no cell phone reception to notify Oom Gerald and I really, really didn't want to start off on the wrong foot and be lumped with those pesky literary fans Coetzee had warned me about. No one likes to be on the wrong side of both a Nobel Laureate and a Karoo farmer. Yet there I was, slipping further and further behind schedule. The road split. Which way? I examined the tyre tracks and opted for the more trafficked, right-hand fork. Coming to a homestead, I slid to a halt in a cloud of dust as an elderly woman poked her head from a cottage window.

'Ek's op soek na Voëlfontein, Mevrou!' I shouted.

'Reguit, meneer, en hou links, keep left!'

My Suzuki's tyres spat dirt. The track bisected again. This time I went left, against my better judgement and influenced by the woman's advice. There was another gate; the track worsened. I raced past a herd of startled sheep. Another gate. The road turned to boulders, forcing me to engage four-wheel drive. No, this couldn't be right. Oom Gerald had said the road was bad, but surely not this bad. By now, I was properly late and my slow immersion into Michael's world over the course of a meditative drive was long forgotten.

Eventually, thankfully, I found the right road and came to a gate marked 'Voëlfontein': it was time to take a deep breath and slow things down. I drove the last few kilometres at a more leisurely pace, traversed a ridge and swung past a graveyard down into a riverbed. My tyres crunched on loose sand as I skirted a sheep pen and climbed a low rise to the house. My first impression was of beauty – an old homestead graced with classic lines set in a lovely garden. The geography of valley, house and ridge fitted the novel, but it was not a precise fit. My second impression was through Michael's eyes: how Voëlfontein was a place of settlers; how he could never be at home in a house like this; how a hut or a hollow in the veld was where he felt more comfortable. I was with Michael as he 'approached the house and circled it. The shutters were closed and a rock-pigeon flew in at a hole where one of the gables had crumbled, leaving timbers exposed and galvanized roof-plates buckled. A loose plate flapped monotonously in the wind.'

The scene was just as I'd imagined it: a cloudless sky, bright green lawn and a pair of white gables, elegant in their simplicity. The right-hand gable, I noticed, sported an unfortunate satellite dish. A farm hand busy loading a bakkie directed me to an open door at the north end of the long façade.

'Kom in, kom in, Justin. Koppie koffie?' said Oom Gerald, shaking my hand with a rough paw. Short, bespectacled, thinning hair, beer boep and an engaging smile, he was dressed in a shabby blue jersey and jeans. Gerald ushered me to an office chair beside his desk. My opening salvos were in cobwebbed Afrikaans, the old Cape Afrikaans of my family, uncontaminated by modern slang or neologisms. Coetzee writes about the awkwardness of his own Afrikaans while staying on the farm and I, too, soldiered on, mealy-mouthed, for a while, then Gerald switched to English.

'I'm John's younger cousin by seven years,' he said. 'Our oupa bought the farm in 1916 and when he died in 1946, his son – my pa, Sonny – took over. I inherited Voëlfontein in 1979 when Pa died. I've been farming for four decades and this current drought we're experiencing is the worst I've ever known. Must be global warming or something. It's tough, man, there isn't much left of the veld and I'm forced to buy in feed for my sheep, otherwise they wouldn't survive.'

He pulled a map from a drawer and unravelled it over the keyboard. The farmhouse sat at the southern end of a web of large enclosures.

'Goodness, Oom Gerald, how big is Voëlfontein?' I asked.

'About 6 000 hectares. The northern part of the farm has just had a bit of rain, so that's where I've got most of my sheep at the moment.'

'When last did John visit?'

'Ag, he came here a couple of times in the Eighties, but he hasn't been back since.'

I remarked on the Kannemeyer biography on a shelf above Gerald's head and he took it down, flipping through the pages until he came to a photograph of four people standing beside a Chevy. 'That's me, my sister, my ma and pa. John took the photo outside their Plumstead home in 1954. That old Chevy is still in my garage, all dusty and unused, but I think of it as a piece of history.'

'Do you get many visitors coming to walk in John's footsteps?'

'No, not really. Kannemeyer was here, of course, and Attwell. Hermann Giliomee came with some film people and there have been a few admirers of his books, even a Chinese couple, kan jy dit glo? But not John, he hasn't returned.'

After my experiences in the Lowveld, Waterberg and North West, I asked about farm security. 'Ja, nee, we're all right here, so far from everything, but we do have to be on the lookout, just in case. The other day someone saw a skollie walking through the farm and I immediately got a call from my neighbour and from the police. We have to be careful. When you leave here, someone will spot you and there'll be a phone call to check up with me, jy weet.'

Gerald suggested a tour of the house. Little did he know that I was looking at it through Michael's eyes, seeing a ruined kitchen with birds flitting in and out of a hole in the roof, a pile of masonry where the gable had collapsed, a strung-up goat carcass covered in flies. Michael soon realised he could never live comfortably in the shell of this settler home: 'It is not for the house that I have come.'

Gerald showed me how a former entrance had been bricked up and where plaster had been removed to reveal old stonework. Although the house still had its original yellowwood ceilings, darkened with age, many of the Oregon pine floors had been ripped out and replaced with loud tiling. The modern furniture was out of character and the back stoep had been bricked in, creating an awkward space. This wasn't a branch of the Coetzees that went in for aesthetic refinement. These were the productive, working Coetzees, not the ones with literary pretentions who frittered away their time 'writing poetry'.

A long corridor offered bedrooms and bathrooms on either side and I thought of the big family gatherings described in *Boyhood*, and reprised in the novel when the Visagie grandson tells Michael, 'Day after day my grandmother would pile the table with food, good country food, and we would eat every last scrap. Karoo lamb like you never taste any more.'

I said to Gerald: 'John writes about the big samesyns at Christmas and Easter when all the Coetzees descended and the house was filled to overflowing with mattresses and stretchers in every room. Does that still happen?'

'Nee, man, not any more, all the uncles and aunts are dead now. There are too few of us Coetzees left. You know, when we had those gatherings, John would always be off walking the farm. He'd get up at five, before the rest of us were even awake, and be out there in the veld until eleven. Walking, walking.'

Gerald had not read *Michael K*, so I gave him a brief plot summary, foregrounding the farm, and asked whether I could have a look around. 'Certainly, but let me drive you,' he said. We climbed into his bakkie and one of the farm's working dogs, a border collie named Nero, jumped in the back, quivering with excitement at the prospect of an outing.

'We've just finished shearing,' said Gerald as we pulled away. 'My coloured foreman basically runs Voëlfontein these days and I trust him with everything. He recently won a prize for being the best foreman in the region.'

I recalled the description of shearing in *Boyhood*, how thrilled the young John had been by the annual event, and how he helped stuff the bales, 'jumping up and down on the mass of thick, hot, oily wool'. One year, he was given the task of doling out dried-bean tokens to the workers for each sheep shorn.

We drove through a dry riverbed and along the cracked-earth rim of an empty dam. 'Due to the drought, our dam hasn't had proper water in four years,' said Gerald. I was reminded of how John deliberately drank very little water when visiting the farm, so as to stand him in good stead if he ever got lost in the veld: 'He wants to be a creature of the desert, this desert, like a lizard' ... just like his creation, Michael K.

Gerald parked on a rise and we got out, joined by Nero, who chased a pair of Karoo korhaans into the air. The collie returned to lead us up onto the dam wall from where we had a good view of the farm – homestead to our right, thick bush below and a couple of windmills downstream in the dry riverbed.

'Outa Jaap had his little house over to the left among the trees, but it fell into ruin long ago,' said Gerald. 'He was here even before my grandfather.' In

Boyhood, the old coloured man is referred to as belonging to the farm: 'Outa Jaap came with it, knew more about it, about sheep, veld, weather, than the newcomer would ever know.' He was a part of the land in a way the Coetzees could never be, and a spiritual forebear, perhaps, of Michael K.

Coming from conservative Worcester, where coloured people were forced into subservience – 'Asseblief my nooi! Asseblief my basie!' – John admired how correct and dignified the relations were between his uncle and the farm workers. They, too, were Michael's forebears.

'In the novel, the hero cultivates a patch of pumpkins beside a dam,' I said. 'Do you think John would have had this place in mind?'

'No, more likely the stone dam beside the windmill over there.' He pointed beyond the homestead.

Back at the house, I asked Gerald if I could have a wander, visit the second dam and take some photos. 'Of course,' he said and disappeared into his office.

I walked round the side of the house with Nero trotting at my heels and peered into the shed, where I found the grey Chevy with split windscreen and flamboyant wings photographed by John back in 1954. It was covered in dust, but the tyres were hard and it looked ready for the road.

When staying on the farm, the young John would watch sheep being slaughtered behind the shed (perhaps this shed) every Friday. Freek held down the legs while Ros slit its throat with a pocket knife. John vividly recalls the flaying of the still warm carcass, blue stomach and intestines spilling into a basin – an act Michael replicates when he slaughters a goat on the farm.

The hillside behind the house was patterned with drystone enclosures that looked like ancient calligraphy. 'The kraal walls are two feet thick and higher than his head; they are made of flat blue-grey stones, every one of them trundled here by donkey cart,' Coetzee writes in *Boyhood*. Even as a child, his vision was tinged with nostalgia: 'He tries to picture the herds of sheep, all of them dead and gone now, that must have sheltered from the sun in the lee of these walls … And the kraals, without a use, are sliding into ruin.'

It was probably in one of the seep lines on this koppie, some distance from the house and the threat of passing soldiers, that Michael K constructed his rudimentary shelter from fence posts and corrugated iron. Traversing the hillside – my eye half-heartedly, foolishly, searching for the shelter's remains

– I felt the overlapping presence of both Michael and Coetzee. I was thinking, too, about Michael's return to the farm after his escape, 'across the veld to the dam and the field where once he had scattered his mother's ashes. Every stone, every bush along the way he recognised. He felt at home at the dam as he had never felt in the house … I want to live here, he thought: I want to live here forever.'

Approaching the windmill and adjacent labourers' cottages, I remembered that Michael had wondered whether his mother had been born in one of those buildings. A flock of sheep watched me with vague interest, Nero with more concern as he found a hole in the fence and led me to a small square dam. This, according to Gerald, was the most likely location of the garden where Michael 'planted a small patch of pumpkins and a small patch of mealies … His deepest pleasure came at sunset when he turned open the cock at the dam wall and watched the stream of water run down its channels to soak the earth, turning it from fawn to deep brown.'

There is a description of the farm in the short story 'Nietverloren', in which Coetzee talks of these irrigated plots: 'An acre of land had been given over to the growing of wheat, just as there had been an acre given over to pumpkin and squash and watermelon and beans … From the bounty of those two acres the table was stocked not only of his grandfather but of all the families who worked for him.'

I found myself listening for Michael, but the farm gave back only silence. I looked for pumpkin shoots, a hint of green, or the sacred orb of a melon, but saw nothing but desiccated earth. No matter, Michael's world had inhabited my head for more than three decades and to finally tread the soil of his 'garden' was strange, intoxicating and enough.

I walked back to the house through stands of aloes and palms, cypress and orange trees. Three sheep dogs lay dozing on the lawn, the gables were cut-outs against a navy-blue sky. I saw the Coetzee uncles sitting on the stoep swapping tales, heard the laughter of children playing cricket on the lawn, smelt the aroma of roast lamb emanating from the doorway. But I also remembered the adult John's difficult visit to the farm after his time studying and teaching in America. Pale, scrawny, awkward, impecunious, he sits uncomfortably at the dining table. Having become a vegetarian, he can no longer stomach the lamb. In a prefiguring of Michael K, he feels himself an outsider who no longer belongs.

Gerald emerged from the house to say goodbye and I asked him if he knew Maraisdal, the farm where Coetzee penned his first novel. 'Ja, I do,' he said. 'When John came back from America he had boggerall money, so I arranged for him to stay for free in a vacant house on Maraisdal.' Gerald asked for my notebook and drew a map. 'As you come into Leeu Gamka on the N1, turn left at the butcher, go through three gates and left through a riverbed. You'll see the little house on the top of the hill, here.' He drew a wonky square.

I climbed into my car and wound down the window. 'You know, I don't think John will ever see the farm again,' said Gerald. 'Antjie Krog was here the other day with some people to make a video, record the bird sounds, wat ook al. They're going to send it to John for his eightieth birthday, which is coming up in a few months. To Adelaide. I think John loved this place more than anything. I think he also loved my pa more than his own father.'

Gerald gave a cursory wave and strode back to the house with Nero at his heels. I drove through the riverbed and stopped at the graveyard in a fenced enclosure on the slope opposite the homestead. There were about twenty graves covered with sheets of slate and gravel. Rock upon rock. I found the big, marble headstone of Gert Coetzee, the patriarch who died in 1946. John's memory of his grandfather was of a formidable gentleman farmer who ruled over the family, but also of 'a stooped, grouchy old man with a bristly chin'.

Another headstone read: 'In loving memory of Gerald (Sonny) Coetzee passed away 5 Aug 1979 age 68 years, a name and character which the tide will never wash away' – the uncle who John loved 'more than his own father'. The grave was adorned with an upended jar of plastic roses. I wondered what it meant to be reminded of your family line every time you used the driveway, your forebears occupying the earth you lived on and tended. Coetzee writes in *Boyhood* that he wished to be buried on the farm or, if cremated, have his ashes scattered there, just as Michael's mother had wanted.

I drove back to the main road, thinking of John and Michael roaming this veld, their kontrei, the dry crunch of their veldskoens echoing in my head. In *Boyhood*, Coetzee tells of how as a child he used to rub his palms in the dust as though a ritual form of washing: 'He loves every stone of it, every bush, every blade of grass, loves the birds that give it its name ... It is not conceivable that another person could love the farm as he does.'

But neither John nor Michael could ever truly belong to Voëlfontein. This is made clear in *Boyhood* and remains an abiding ache:

> Since as far back as he can remember this love has had an edge of pain. He may visit the farm but he will never live there. The farm is not his home; he will never be more than a guest, an uneasy guest. Even now, day by day, the farm and he are travelling different roads, separating, growing not closer but further apart. One day the farm will be wholly gone, wholly lost; already he is grieving at that loss.

If he (like Michael) does not belong *on* the farm, then perhaps, ultimately, he can belong *to* the farm, a kind of belonging that excludes ownership and inheritance. 'In his secret heart he knows what the farm in its way knows too: that Voëlfontein belongs to no one. The farm is greater than all of them.'

Reaching the main road, I closed the gate behind me and turned north, bound for Merweville. It was somewhere along this road, during one of his later visits to the farm, that John and his cousin Agnes (referred to as Margot in *Summertime*) were forced to spend the night when their bakkie broke down. The pair were 'rescued' the next morning by one of the farm workers in a donkey cart.

It was to Agnes that John confided his secrets as a child and he did so again during this visit in the early 1970s. He told her that the thing he was mulling over, that was closest to his heart, was the same realisation that appears at dusk to the male baboon in Eugène Marais's book. When the sun starts to set, the old troop leader thinks to himself: '*Just one life and then never again. Never, never, never.* That is what the Karoo does to me too. It fills me with melancholy. It spoils me for life.' Agnes doesn't understand what her cousin is going on about. 'This place wrenches my heart,' he continues. 'It wrenched my heart when I was a child, and I have never been right since.'

Merweville rose out of the veld and I crawled up a main drag lined with Cape Dutch and Victorian houses on large plots – an attractive village set around an elegant church of grey stone and white icing. Coetzee's grandfather – a go-getter of his era – was once mayor of the town. In the 1970s, John had considered buying a house here, a place his retired father might live and where John could visit from Cape Town on weekends, but the idea came to nought.

It was Friday afternoon and not a soul about. I stopped in the middle of town to take a few photographs, then headed back out the way I'd come. Reaching Leeu Gamka, I followed Gerald's crude map and, turning left just after the butcher, followed tyre tracks across open veld, past a scrapyard of vintage cars, through three farm gates and a riverbed to find the Maraisdal house perched on a rise – a white cottage with a pitched iron roof and a stoep at front and back. The place appeared deserted.

Coetzee and his young family stayed in this house in 1971, and it was here that he wrote part of his first novel, *Dusklands*. It's significant that after living in urban America, he should choose a cottage in the semi-desert so far from Cape Town (but close to Voëlfontein). He had not yet given up the idea of making a home in the Karoo. But the accommodation was basic with the barest furniture and his two children had to sleep on newspapers on the floor. Water needed to be collected in buckets, wood had to be chopped for fuel and reading was done by the light of paraffin lamps.

I opened a rickety gate and circled the house. Out back I found a thicket of thorn trees and a derelict caravan. It was among these acacias that Coetzee built a shelter for privacy, away from the children and noise of the house, so that he could write in peace. Nearby stood a clanking windmill and a concrete dam. Watching the water gush in rhythmic squirts, timed with the breeze and rotation of the blades, I thought again of Michael harbouring just such a pump and rationing the water for his pumpkins.

It was almost time to return to Cape Town, but there was one last *Michael K* site to visit. Up early next morning, I headed south, bound for the Swartberg. Prince Albert glistened in pale winter light, the air was crisp and a great cleft in the mountain's façade offered entry to the famous pass. Cliffs closed in as I entered the first kloof, lime-coloured rock rising on either flank. A single shaft of sunlight illuminated a patch of stream as I snaked through the shadowy poort, my tyres splashing through successive drifts.

I pulled off the road, got out and knelt to drink the fynbos-infused water, doffing my cap to poet Guy Butler, who celebrates such acts in his poem 'Sweetwater'. Looking up, I saw a pair of grey rheboks staring at me and I froze, letting their doe eyes explore the alien creature in their midst.

ALONE IN ALL THAT VASTNESS

Quivering flanks, quizzical expressions, pricked ears, nostrils tasting the air. Then, spooked, they took flight up the slope in graceful bounds, hooves clinking on shale, white tails bobbing bunny-like between the boulders.

The pass grew more spectacular with each turn, its vistas opening and closing like stage sets. Some offered serrations sunk in shadow, others were sunlit Impressionist renditions in ochres, tangerines and yellows. It was among these crags that the rebels of Coetzee's novel took refuge – spectral figures who raided the towns and conducted acts of sabotage before returning to the Swartberg's heights. Here again, the novel harks back to the Anglo-Boer War when commandos (Deneys Reitz among them) moved through these mountains, harassing or evading the British.

Topping out in undulant uplands, my dashboard thermometer registered 3°C and warned of ice on the road. One of Coetzee's earliest memories, recounted in *Boyhood*, is of travelling with his mother on a bus over this pass. The child throws a sweet wrapper out the window and watches it flutter away. 'He thinks all the time of the scrap of paper, alone in all that vastness, that he abandoned when he should not have abandoned it. One day he must go back to the Swartberg Pass and find it and rescue it. This is his duty: he may not die until he has done it.'

I took the Gamkaskloof turnoff, once again making for the valley of Die Hel through highlands that looked more Scottish than Karoo. 'Dangerous road, 48 kilometres,' read the sign. The sky roiled with angry clouds; snow decorated the slopes on either side of a route lined with anthills and aloes, restio grasses and proteas. Finding an overgrown side track, I engaged four-wheel drive and headed off-road. Sandstone boulders required careful negotiating, the loose sections needed a bit of speed. I came to a ridge and got out to stretch my legs, but even the simple act of walking was made difficult by sharp shale and brittle bush. It was somewhere among these peaks that Michael retreated after leaving the farm, living rough and eking an existence in this rocky fastness. And, at the end of the novel, he imagines returning once more to the Karoo, perhaps to these very heights.

So, Michael, I said to myself as I took a seat on a comfortable boulder, did you ever make it back here again? If so, what do you live on? Roots and bulbs like your Khoisan ancestors? Lizards and ants? There aren't any colonial pumpkins up here among the crags. I picture you alone at night, finding shelter in a cave or beneath an overhang, the freezing temperatures and the impossibly remote stars ... remote just like you, like Coetzee, like all of us who, when push comes to shove, exist so many light-years apart. 'Now surely I have come as far as a man can come; surely no one will be mad enough to cross these plains, climb these mountains, search these rocks to find me; surely now that in all the world only I know where I am, I can think of myself as lost.'

Michael's hardy self-reliance allowed him to turn in upon himself in an act that was beyond loneliness. It was, rather, a state of the purest emptiness: waiting for nothing, wanting nothing. In the words of his doctor, Michael is 'a soul blessedly untouched by doctrine, untouched by history'. He is a nugget, a kernel: a stone passing through institutions, camps, hospitals and the intestines of civil war. Or perhaps he is a seed, ready to germinate when the weather turns, when the political winds begin to blow from another direction. The Karoo has always been described as silent, indifferent, mute; the stories of its Khoisan keepers erased. Perhaps Michael is its silent voice?

And if that wind did eventually change direction, Michael would instinctively know that he must not replicate the path of the settler. When he made his crude shelter near the farmhouse, he had been careful not to plunder its material trappings – cooking-pot, folding chair, grid – preferring wood and leather, materials the insects could devour. He'd been careful not to establish 'a new house, a rival line'. His future path would be anti-capitalist, ecologically grounded ... millennial. In his dreams, he conjured a Karoo emptied of roads, emptied of farmhouses.

Below me, water tinkled through the kloof; high above, a Verreaux's eagle twirled on its gyre, a black crucifix against the blue. Wind rustled the mountain fynbos; a faint buchu perfume wafted on the breeze. The longer I sat, the more I noticed: the white lichen encrusting my boulder, a beetle negotiating a crack in the rock, a tiny pink flower nodding to the wind. The pulse of blood in my ears.

The sandstone cliffs around me had been contorted and rumpled by unimaginable forces. The whole landscape tilted exaggeratedly, green slopes leaning southward, the north faces exposing raw meat, as though the berg had been hacked by a cleaver. François Krige spent decades painting Karoo rocks, trying to capture them with brush and oils. I thought of his Cogmanskloof, Koo Valley and Matroosberg works, how the rocks are rendered in bold, almost Fauvist strokes of cream, ochre and burnt sienna, the proteas in Impressionistic dabs of yellow and scarlet. And of how he spent half a lifetime studying this landscape, learning the way of its folds, twists and eruptions, the way it manifests its colours with the help of water and iron, lime and lichen, painting itself into beauty.

It was perhaps inevitable that an artist of Coetzee's sensitivity would develop an intense love for the Karoo, particularly as he was exposed to it at such a young age. Anyone who has lived there understands this kind of passion, one that often reveals itself in an almost unquenchable yearning. Perhaps it's a combination of the stark beauty, barrenness and silence that helps forge this strong attachment. Even in a work such as *Life & Times of Michael K*, where the novelist has tried to pare down the language to its barest architecture and leach the autobiographical particularities, his love for the land still seeps to the surface like water from an underground spring, irrigating the text from below.

Sitting on my rock, I was thinking how Michael's places – Worcester, the Swartberg, Prince Albert, the farm – are also the significant places of Coetzee's childhood. It is the landscape of his heart. I recalled John's conversation with his cousin Agnes in *Summertime*:

> *Best to cut yourself free of what you love*, he had said during their walk – *cut yourself free and hope the wound heals* … That is what they share above all: not just a love of this farm, this *kontrei*, this Karoo, but an understanding that goes with that love, an understanding that love can be too much. To him and to her it was granted to spend their childhood summers in a sacred space. That glory can never be regained; best not to haunt old sites and come away from them mourning what is for ever gone.

And so it comes to pass that you find you can move to Australia, you can even somehow stay away from the farm for the rest of your life. You can 'put it behind you'. But you will always carry the scar of that place. Indeed, you returned here only last month, to this district, but not the farm. The farm would be too much.

Two decades after writing *Michael K*, Coetzee describes an alternative dispensation for the Karoo and for farms like Voëlfontein. Once, these islands in the wilderness had been self-sufficient, growing all their own produce; now they are simply sheep ranches or game farms producing a commercial 'crop'. In the short story 'Nietverloren', he wistfully imagines a future in which the original farm workers return to the land:

> What did it mean for the land as a whole, and the conception the land had of itself, that huge tracts of it should be sliding back into prehistory? In the larger picture, was it really better that families who in the old days lived on the land by the sweat of their brow should now be mouldering in the windswept townships of Cape Town? Could one not imagine a different history and a different social order in which the Karoo was reclaimed, its scattered sons and daughters reassembled, the earth tilled again?

In *Boyhood*, *Summertime* and 'Nietverloren', he repeatedly writes his swansong to the Karoo, a place now fallen from the grace of his childhood memories: depopulated, drought-ravaged, turned to purely commercial or wildlife farming. And yet the love – palpably, achingly – remains.

My eyes made a final, panoramic sweep of the mountains, then I walked back to the car. I left Michael up there, still refusing to be part of any camp, any ideology, waiting for time to pass, for a new, gentler era to be born.

Michael K, creature of being, not yet of becoming. Still waiting.

———✳———

LIKE WINGS WITHOUT BODIES

Dalene Matthee's Knysna Forest

> *The axe falls silent and the towering yellowwood emits a strange, keening sound as it begins to lean like the mast of a ship. The last wooden strands between the gashes at its base tear loose with a loud snap and the leviathan topples, scything through the surrounding trees, bringing down everything in its path. Turacos take flight, crying in consternation; a terrified bushbuck scuttles through the underbrush. Dust rises from the fallen monster as leaves rain down like funereal confetti. There's a wide blue gap in the forest canopy now, letting in too much light. The giant yellowwood, king of the forest, is dead, ready to be flayed by the little men swarming about its carcass.*

---※---

Knysna's ancient Afrotemperate forest has achieved a mythical place in South African literature thanks to the works of Dalene Matthee (1938–2005). For my next literary quest, I wanted to immerse myself in this leafy corner of the Garden Route and trace the circuitous paths of her most famous novel, *Circles in a Forest*, seeking out the places that had inspired her.

Heading east out of Knysna on the N2, I turned north onto the R339 and, after half an hour of climbing along a gravel road, reached Diepwalle (Deep Walls) Forest Station, home to a SANParks camp set deep in the forest's heart. The accommodation, such as it was, comprised a handful of raised timber decks, each with a lean-to dining area. I pitched a tent on one of these platforms and unpacked my sleeping bag and braai equipment. In less than ten minutes, I had a comfortable home with not another soul in the campsite to disturb the peace. Surrounding me on three sides were living walls of yellowwood, wild pomegranate and Cape beech, the forest floor softened by ferns and thick with fallen leaves. It was idyllic in a mildly unnerving way.

Knysna's rainforest of subtropical broadleaf trees is a feral, sequestered world set beside the Garden Route's affluent tourist playgrounds. Few travellers venture far off the beaten N2 into its gloomy vastness, an evergreen realm home to enormous Outeniqua yellowwoods (kalanders), some of them a thousand years old, and inhabited by a host of shy creatures, including five mammals listed in South Africa's Red Data Book – Samango monkey, honey badger, blue duiker, tree hyrax and giant golden mole – while the long-tailed forest shrew is practically endemic. The few remaining forest elephants – the southernmost in the world and the only free-ranging pachyderms in South Africa – are the last survivors of the great herds of old. It's estimated that in 1870 there were as many as 500 living in the forest; by 1970, only 10 remained.

My camp established, I strolled over to the administration building where I met head ranger Klaas Havenga, a man of the forest who's lived at Diepwalle for more than twenty years. Klaas had a Voortrekker beard with grey flecks and eyes that sparkled with golden flecks of their own.

'You must really love forests,' I said. 'I'd probably suffer from the claustrophobia of leaves if I stayed here too long.'

'Either you hate it or you love it,' said Klaas. 'Most days I feel uplifted but sometimes, especially when it's dry and windy, there's a kind of violence here. It feels threatening. Over time, you get to know its many moods and parts: the birds, the insects, the flowers. When I'm worried or upset, I go and sit among the trees and it calms me.

'A forest is a miraculous thing, a precious thing. It stores carbon, enriches the soil, cleans the air and it needs no maintenance. I'm not a hippie or anything, but I must admit that I do think of it as one huge living organism with its own consciousness. There are no individuals in a forest; everything is connected; trees communicate through the air and via their root systems and funguses that meet underground. They save water, nourish their offspring and warn each other when danger is near. A third of the food a tree produces goes into feeding other organisms. It all fits together like one giant jigsaw puzzle.'

'Have you ever seen the mythical elephants?' I asked.

'Elephant. There's only one, a female of about fifty years old, and yes, I've seen her a few times. We follow her spoor when she comes into our section of the forest or damages park property.'

'What kind of damage?'

'Ag, sometimes she takes exception to a picnic table, a gate or a sign. She's a bit of an anarchist. We follow her for a while after she's had one of her quarrels with our equipment, but she travels vast distances each day, so it's blimmin' hard to keep up with her. Come, let me show you a video.'

Klaas led me through to his office, flipped open a laptop and clicked on a file. The screen showed night-time camera-trap footage that at first made little sense, but slowly a lighter shade of dots emerged from the grainy charcoal – a ghostly gathering of pixels that suggested a mammalian blob. Now an eye, a tusk, and suddenly the agglomeration resolved itself into brief elephant magnificence before she stepped out of frame. It was electrifying: my first sighting of a legendary Knysna elephant in the virtual flesh!

---*---

Dalene Matthee's novelistic presence is everywhere apparent in the Garden Route National Park. There's Jubilee Creek where, in *Circles in a Forest*, the novel's hero Saul Barnard pans for gold; so too the remains of Millwood town, where Saul's beloved Kate teaches the miners' children; as well as hamlets like Diepwalle, home to his brother Jozef, and Gouna, where the woodcutters buy their provisions. Matthee found such a wealth of inspiration in the region's history that she often used its stories and locations almost unaltered. Her four forest books are tremendously evocative of place and, with millions of copies sold, have entered the public imagination, colouring the experience of many who visit the area.

Matthee was born in Riversdale in 1938 and began her career writing short stories and children's books, but she is best known for her forest novels: *Circles in a Forest*, *Fiela's Child*, *The Mulberry Forest* and *Dreamforest*. Her fascination for the Knysna landscape was sparked during a hike through the forest in 1978. She subsequently visited Karatara, a village to which many of the Afrikaner woodcutters had retired after tree felling was banned. She conducted many interviews, treating the old-timers with great respect, and they in turn shared their knowledge with the woman they affectionately called the 'bostannie' (forest aunty). She learnt about a way of life and a world that had long since passed. The woodcutters had spent most of their working lives in forest clearings and were simple, religious folk with rich storytelling traditions and an intimate, at times uncanny, knowledge of their environment.

One of the notable features of Matthee's forest novels is her ability to capture the spirit of the Knysna wilderness and its backwoods inhabitants. Her use of language, particularly in the original Afrikaans but somewhat lost in the English translation, conveys the colloquialism and unique cultural references of the region. Woodcutters developed a way of life, belief system and language suited to their environment, with 'endemic' ways of describing the topography, weather, fauna and flora. As critics Willie Cloete and Marita Wenzel note, the forest determined their income, diet, clothing, dwelling type, level of education, social standing, occupation and their experience of religion.

Over time, Matthee also developed a powerful connection with the forest, sometimes sleeping alone in the wild, and became a vocal advocate for its preservation. She described the Knysna wilderness as a mighty 'power station' and cautioned visitors not to enter it with a negative attitude. In her essay 'Enchanted Forest Land', she writes:

> The longer you explore a rainforest the more captivating it becomes, and all the time its mysteries deepen … You tread with caution and speak with a subdued voice, for you have entered a world that transcends human understanding – primeval forest … Gradually your sense of wonderment becomes one of veneration. Even one of uneasiness … The mind is overwhelmed by the complexity of this wonder-world.

Such was her empathy that Matthee would ask the forest's permission before doing research or bringing guests. She would greet the forest and wipe her feet before entering, as though crossing the lintel into a space, a home, that deserved the utmost respect. 'When I walk into it, I get a feeling right here,' she said in an interview, pointing to her stomach.

In Thomas Hardy's *The Woodlanders*, the forest is portrayed as a force in its own right, a character that dominates the story and strongly influences those who live in it. Similarly, the forest of Matthee's novels is rendered as a unifying element, a life force, a protagonist and even, at times, as an antagonist. For her readers, as much as for her characters, the experience of the fictional forest is a visceral one, making a strong impression on the senses. In her novel, the elderly sage and Khoi tracker, Maska, describes this relationship in personified terms:

> The Forest is angry … Because strangers are taking him over … The spirit of the stones does not want to lie still for ever, they get too big for the stones and then they move into the things that are growing. The small stones take the small plants, the larger stones the larger plants. The mountain cliffs take for themselves the biggest kalanders and the highest uprights because they have room for the larger spirits.

But the spirits of place grow restless when humans desecrate the land.

Circles in a Forest is a work of popular fiction, at times sentimental, but it nevertheless remains a compelling evocation of Knysna's wilderness. It has become a South African classic, much loved, much translated (into a dozen languages) and much prescribed for school syllabi.

The novel's protagonist, Saul Barnard, is a woodcutter with a restless spirit who, like Matthee, feels protective over the forest and wants to prevent its destruction by the forces of greed and 'progress'. Saul comes to the conclusion that life is a circle of exploitation: 'The woodcutter killed the Forest, the wood-buyer killed the woodcutter. Round and round and round you walked the crooked circle.'

The forest is a Garden of Eden and Saul has eaten the fruit of knowledge which compels him to try to save it. He shares a bond with Old Foot, a solitary elephant bull that roams the forest. Man and beast are brothers, walking similar circular paths, both literal and figurative, through the wilderness. Saul has been rejected by his people and humiliated by unscrupulous timber merchants, while Old Foot has left the herd and is being tracked by hunters who want his ivory. Man and beast are presented as custodians of an ancient realm that is about to be destroyed by timber merchants, hunters and gold diggers.

The novel opens with Saul standing on the deck of a sailing ship in Knysna Lagoon, poised to leave his past behind him: the forest, his lover, Old Foot, his responsibilities. Maska arrives with news that Saul's nephew has been gored by Old Foot, and that a hunting party has set out to shoot the elephant.

Saul feels that he owes it to Old Foot to save him from the humiliation of falling to a hunter's gun and if anyone is going pull the trigger, it must be him.

And so, with four days to go before the ship is due to sail, Saul borrows a rifle and sets off to find his kindred soul. Returning once more to the forest, he feels as though he's walking backwards into himself and begins reliving his past: the felling of the great kalander; his encounters with Old Foot; falling in love with Kate; his conflict with MacDonald, the malevolent wood merchant; the discovery of gold at Millwood and his wasted years as a gold-digger. These flashbacks provide the substance of the plot until the climax when he crosses paths once more with Old Foot.

———✳———

There's a small building close to the Diepwalle administration block that houses the Forest Legends Museum with exhibits ranging from the lives of woodcutters to the region's ecology. Part of the museum is dedicated to local fauna and one room is filled with the skeleton of an elephant bull, discovered in 1983. I stepped into the eerie space, illuminated with green lighting to simulate woodland, an enlarged photograph of vegetation as backdrop. The bones glowed in this pseudo forest and I reached up to stroke the tip of a tusk, its ivory smooth and cool to the touch. It was for this toothy commodity that you had to die, Old Foot. The experience was unsettling: an elephant too big for the room. I thought, just then, of Saul reaching out to touch the body of Old Foot after the giant had been shot: 'He feels the thick, rough skin stretching over the bulging skull – his hand gropes over the cold and lifeless eye, the spiny eyelashes prick the soft flesh of his palm.'

The display in an adjacent room presented the world of the woodcutter: tin plates, a dimpled kettle, simple wood furnishings and a set of double-handed trek saws. Once a tree was felled, the men dug trenches and used pit-saws with one man on top, two below, wielding the long blade in a perpendicular motion to cut the trunk into planks. Where the terrain was difficult, men had to stand in for oxen, lashing themselves to the logs with leather thongs and dragging them out.

In this manner, the forest was gradually denuded to feed the insatiable demand for timber, fuel, railway sleepers and material for the building of houses, wagons and boats. The precious hardwoods were shipped from Knysna to the Cape and beyond, but the woodcutters themselves earned a meagre living, exploited by merchants who made vast profits at their expense. By the early Twentieth Century, the forest was greatly reduced and legislation was finally passed in 1939 to halt the deforestation and withdraw the woodcutters' permits. Today, much of the remaining forest lies within the Garden Route National Park and most tree felling is done according to sustainable harvesting regulations.

———✳———

Eager to explore some of the trails that radiate from Diepwalle, I went walkabout with SANParks ranger Wilfred Oraai, who'd been living in the forest for nearly three decades. A gentle soul with the features of a San hunter-gatherer, Wilfred has an unquenchable love affair with the forest. As we picked our way along a leafy track, he confided that his wife and children didn't really understand his passion. They lived in Plettenberg Bay and only saw him when he emerged from the trees for the occasional weekend or at holiday time. He told me that he suffers from headaches when he leaves the forest and I pictured him stepping from the treeline into the bright light of the Plettenberg metropole, wide-eyed, with twigs and leaves clinging to his clothes, a forest dweller out of place amid all that sea and space, noise and glare.

Wilfred spoke in a guttural, idiomatic Afrikaans, all the while stroking his salt-and-pepper moustache: 'Die bome praat met 'n mens. Jy moet net goed en mooi kan luister ... The trees talk to you. You must just listen carefully.'

I followed him through dense foliage, his footfall making no sound; his short, ground-hugging body and gait completely attuned to the surroundings. The leaves did not stir as he slipped between low-hanging branches, pointing out plants and insects as we went, me galumphing along noisily behind. Peering into the cleft of a yellowwood trunk, he showed me the cancerous fungus eating away at the old tree's heart.

'She won't have much longer in this world,' he said softly. 'But when she falls, her work won't be done: her dead body will provide food and shelter for fungi, woodlice, beetles, termites and millipedes, until she finally decomposes to enrich the soil. It's a beautiful thing. You know, Justin, there's a tree for every purpose in God's heaven. They are like giant factories producing wax, gum, resin, tannin, fats and sugars. Us humans don't yet even know half the things trees can make.'

As we walked on, he explained how he wanted to pass on his forest knowledge to those who were willing to listen. 'I have a son, but he's not interested, so I give to others what I know, like how to track a forest elephant. These things must not die with me.'

He told me about the many animals he'd encountered on the trails, such as caracal, wildcat, bush pig and blue duiker. 'I once saw a monkey stalking and managing to catch a loerie; another time I spotted a leopard on the road near Diepwalle. She let her two cubs cross ahead of her, then she charged my car, spitting and hissing.'

Exposed roots lay across our path like the tentacles of vegetable octopi and fern fronds in the shape of hairy parasols bent overhead. From somewhere in the viridian depths came the soft conversation of a stream; birds chirruped and insects pinged their forest sonar. Not one sound overwhelmed another, as though this vast, disparate orchestra were playing a faultless tune.

Wilfred held up his hand. 'Boslourie,' he whispered. Above us on a bough sat a Narina trogon, its scarlet-and-green body haloed by a leafy dapple. 'Hoot-hoot, hoot-hoot,' it said and Wilfred smiled. Then, with one majestic beat of its wings, the bird vanished. On we walked.

Through Wilfred's eyes, I began to notice the details of my environment: the textures of bark, the myriad leaf colours and forms, the tiny creatures of the forest floor. We stopped to allow a millipede to pass, its banks of oars rowing it across our path. A bit further on, Wilfred helped a dwarf chameleon onto a branch. 'At night, these little guys turn white and sleep curled up in the heart of a fern,' he said. 'Is it not just wonderful?'

He showed me how the slow-growing stinkwood takes advantage of its fallen kin by 'grafting' itself onto the older root system of its forebears, thus gaining a few hundred years' head start through coppicing.

'So many of these plants have medicinal qualities,' he said, and I had a momentary flashback to Saul being taught the lore of the forest and the uses of plants by his father. 'If you have breathing problems, there's wild garlic or suikerbos. For headaches, you grind stinkwood bark; for indigestion there's renosterbos or fennel; for ear infections you use tree fuchsia leaves; for general aches and pains there's the camphor bush.

'The forest has also always been our people's kitchen. There are vegetables such as agapanthus roots and wild cauliflower, and so many different kinds of fruit: turkey berry, num-num, sour fig, wild olive. You can make candles by boiling waxberry and brew a lekker tea from the honey bush. My ancestors even made lovely soft bedding from everlastings.

'Look there, elephant spoor!' he said, crouching down and pointing to a soggy indentation. Beside it was a patch of crushed vegetation where the giant had lain down. Wilfred told me the path we were on used to be a route frequented by elephants each spring and autumn, migrating from their winter feeding grounds in Harkerville to Gouna Forest for the summer season. 'I've had a few encounters with the female that visits Diepwalle,' he said under his breath. 'Haai, that lady, she can move fast! If she gets a whiff of my scent, it can take me a whole day of tracking to catch up with her again.'

He told me of the dark night when he bumped into her while walking to

Knysna. 'Suddenly, I noticed these four big black poles in the road ahead of me. "That's funny," I thought. Then I walked a bit closer and saw the rest of the elephant, so I stopped and put my rucksack down. She gave a little blow through her trunk but didn't move out of the way. I just stood there and she just stood there and neither of us said a word. Then she mos stepped back into the forest and let me pass. As I continued down the road, I heard her following along in the trees beside me, all the way to the tar. I think she was, you know, watching over me.'

'Have you ever felt threatened?' I asked.

'No, no, never ever. Once I was up in a pine tree trying to photograph her and she came closer and closer. There was no escape. Just then, I lost my footing and fell at her feet, but she didn't charge or anything, she just looked at me for a while with those old, wise eyes, before moving off.'

'How many elephants are left, do you think?'

'Officially, just the one, but maybe a couple more … I think it might be a male doing all the damage when he's in musth.'

I'd chatted to naturalist Gareth Patterson while preparing for my trip and his research seems to point to more elephants. Some years ago, Gareth relocated to Knysna and switched from studying lions to pachyderms. He analysed dung, took DNA samples, measured scars on trees made by elephants and came to the conclusion that there were at least six females and three bulls. If he's right, they're the most secretive elephants on the planet.

'What vegetation do they eat?' I asked.

'Ag, a bit of everything, sommer the whole salad,' he said. 'Some people say elephant dung is medicine because it's so rich and diverse.' He stopped and looked me in the eye. 'Justin, you must understand that these creatures are bladdy clever: they remember everything. They know exactly what happened to their ancestors and that's why they're so shy. They choose who is allowed to see them. So, I feel very, how can I say … privileged.'

We completed our circular trail and found ourselves back at Diepwalle. 'This has been very special for me,' I said. 'It's like the forest is part of you.'

'Ja, well, good things has gotta come to an end. Retirement is not far off.'

'What will you do?'

'Plett,' he said. It sounded flat and hollow, like a bad word, a dead-end word. He looked away.

'You can always visit the forest. Plett isn't far.'

'Ja, I suppose you're right.' We shook hands and I watched him vanish behind a curtain of leaves.

———✳———

Late afternoon, I sat on my deck dipping into *Circles in a Forest* once again. A breeze off the ocean cooled the air and a low sun added dusty columns to the forest architecture. I put the book aside, lit a fire and placed a sweet potato and an onion wrapped in tinfoil beside the flames. A vervet monkey eyed my packet of chips, but upon careful reflection, and taking note of my brandished braai tongs (and bared teeth), decided against a raid. Hadeda ibises clattered about in the trees overhead like furniture movers; greater double-collared sunbirds tweeted shrilly from all sides; unidentified choristers accompanied them from deep in the wood. I'd already worked my way through the better part of a bottle of red juice o' the vine, and was singing along to their calls: 'And the coloured birds go, "Doo, da doo, da doo, da do do doo …"' as one does when all on one's lonesome in a very big, slightly spooky forest.

I remembered how Matthee eulogises the solitary camper and turned to the relevant passage in *Circles*:

> Peacefulness comes to a man when he sits by his own fire and rakes out his own sweet potatoes from under his own ash. As if something inside opens up slowly … Your eyes see things you did not see yesterday: the gossamer-fine moss twining round the blue buck rope … the specks of mauve in the feathers of the grey cuckoo-shrike, the same mauve as the moss on the saffron's bark. Then one day, sitting in front of your shelter, you suddenly realise that the old leaves do not fall from the forest roof – they fluttered to the ground in a slow twirling flight like wings without bodies.

A dusky softness settled over Diepwalle. I placed a snake of boerewors and a lamb chop on the grid and the aroma of sizzling meat began to waft across my deck. When darkness crept out from the underbrush, the mood began to change. My head-torch was playing up and my candle offered only the barest light, inviting the forest to edge in more closely from all sides.

I could see no stars. Although it was springtime, the temperature dropped to single figures. I pulled on a second jersey and sat staring at the wall of vegetation, fending off a hint of primal fear: elephant, leopard, adder, thingamajig?

Later, I hunkered down in my summer sleeping bag, a rolled-up jacket for a pillow, as rain pecked the tent and drew peaty smells from the earth. With my head-torch restored to working order, I continued reading *Circles* and found the passage recounting the young Saul's first meeting with Old Foot. He and his brother are on their way to Diepwalle. It's just after midday and they're having a rest at Skuins Bush. They notice movement in the bushes, but it takes a moment before they make out two big, flapping ears. The boys are petrified and Saul's brother scrambles into the branches of a stinkwood, yelling, 'It's Old Foot!'

The elephant approaches Saul, who has remained rooted to the spot. Despite his fear, the lad takes note of the enormous tusks: smooth like butter, and yellow. 'Under the eye that was turned towards him, a wet patch stained the rough, wrinkled skin dark and it looked as if he was weeping. Over his massive rump was a deep trench scored by a bullet years ago and in one ear there was a round bullet hole that had healed too.' Saul has come face to face with his double.

The first blush of dawn lit my tent and a red-chested cuckoo shattered the stillness with a loud 'Piet my vrou!' Wriggling out of the sleeping bag, I unzipped the flaps and stepped out into a misty scene, curtains of vapour ghosting among the trees. I boiled a kettle on the previous night's coals and had my coffee and rusk on the deck, staring at a foggy vista of muffled peacefulness.

When the mist burnt off, I drove up Prince Alfred Pass to Spitzkop lookout point. This rough road, completed by Thomas Bain in 1867, was one of the famous engineer's greatest challenges. His labourers had to hack through seemingly impenetrable forest to construct a route that climbed 700 metres in just 14 kilometres.

Reaching the top of the pass, I stepped from the vehicle into a sea of aloes, restios and proteas in flowering abundance. It was a bright morning, the sun just up and the air still icy. The mountaintop was windless and free of trees, the views in every direction godly. Below me, the earth fell away in serrated lines: to the northwest, the Outeniqua Mountains stood tall and blue; to the northeast, the shark-fin pinnacles of the Tsitsikamma; far to south, Knysna's knobbly Heads, and beyond them, the Indian Ocean stretched away in a vast denim carpet.

From somewhere in the valley below came the harsh sound of a chainsaw, nibbling away at the forest fringes. Looking more closely at the landscape, I noticed patches of ugly, monochromatic green – the encroachment of pine and eucalyptus plantation – but for the most part, my view was filled with a rich tapestry of myriad greens: the ancient forest of Old Foot.

Back in camp, I set off on my own to hike one of the other trails Wilfred had recommended. Within minutes, I was embraced once more by foliage and recalled Saul's response when he returned to the woods after spending time in Knysna: 'The more the Forest closed around him, the lighter his body felt. He wanted to stretch out his hands and touch the nearest trees. He wanted to sit down and feel the cool, clammy moss under his fingers. He drew the forest air deep into his lungs as if to fill himself with it. It was like coming home.'

I imagined the vegetation all around me exhaling damp fecundity; the earth was spongy underfoot; spiderwebs stretched across my path. At times, the leaf cover was so thick that it grew dark; then, moments later, I'd emerge into a patch of spotlit benediction dancing with butterflies. The dapples created a chequerboard that sparkled like a forest disco accompanied by the creak and moan of ancient trees, the intimate rubbing of bark on bark. When gusts of wind passed through the canopy, the uppermost branches swayed with the rhythm of an oceanic swell, but at ground level it remained breathless.

The forest floor was a teeming underworld: flowering plants and creepers, ants, spiders and all manner of critters busily breaking down the fallen giants. Craving light in the gloom were paintbrush lilies, wild irises and carrot ferns; higher up were climbers and lianas using the trees as ladders to reach the sun's rays. Up there, far above, most of the photosynthesis was taking place, the driving force of the forest engine and the underpinning of all creation. I tried to visualise all this promiscuous growing, this upward yearning for the canopy.

As I walked, I listened to the multifarious sounds: the officious scuffling of Cape spurfowl, the warbling song of unseen white-eyes, a chorus of cicadas, oboe frogs, insect percussion. From glade to glade, it changed. The deeper I went, the more subtlety and variety I recognised.

I also began to notice forest patterns amid the apparent anarchy of disparate shapes. The sensual, curled perfection of a fern bud, the black spiral of a coiled millipede, bracket fungi as large as plates, the delicate orbs of minuscule mushrooms, the complicated quilts formed by dead leaves and the variegated pot-pourri of composted soil.

And textures. The striated smoothness and corky spots of ironwood, the soft forgiveness of moss, a spiderweb's dewdrop gossamer, the plastic carapace of crab. Rough bark, brittle fungus. I stopped to run my hand over the hoary trunk of a stinkwood and recalled how Saul believed this to be the finest wood of all: 'The colour of the brown forest streams and with the most beautiful grain, it was formed over thousands of days of sunshine and rain.'

Colours too. So many shades of green, beyond any palette's wild imagining: apple, teal, chartreuse, lime, pistachio, malachite, emerald. The orange flash of an olive thrush in the underbrush; the foam-white underside of a mushroom; a scarlet leaf on a wet black bough; luminous lichen peeling like paint; the bleached trunk of a white pear tree.

I sensed that I was beginning to gain some understanding of the forest, that I was getting under its bark, but realised in the same instant that this was foolish hubris. Saul knew the sensation:

> There are times when he gets the feeling, however, that between man and the Forest lies but a thin veil. Like a cobweb. Like an invisible mist through which you would be able to see if only you could open your eyes wide enough. But the next moment he knows it is only a dream. The Forest is like someone you can hear talking, but whose language you do not understand. You hear him, you see him, you touch him, you see the signs he makes, but you do not know what he says.

At least I could claim that I was gaining a better understanding of how its component parts fitted together. Klaas Havenga had said the forest is one big organism, an ecosystem in which each element – both living and non-living – interacts with the others and is dependent on them to create forest harmony. Soil, earth, air, flora, fauna – all fulfil essential roles in the functioning of the One. Take, for instance, the Outeniqua yellowwood.

The female tree bears fleshy fruit that are feasted on by bats and turacos, but some of the fruit falls to the ground where bush pigs gorge on the delicacy. The seeds aren't digested properly and end up in the pigs' droppings, which germinate elsewhere to create a new generation of yellowwoods.

The forest is a perfect, fully evolved system with no extraneous element, except, perhaps, clay-footed *Homo sapiens*. Maybe our species started to lose its way, its oneness, when it forsook the trees for solid ground and chose to be bipedal. We gained so much from that giant leap … and lost so much, forgetting that we had been shaped by the forest long before we were even human, not realising what it meant to still share almost half our DNA with trees.

———*———

After a few days of full forest immersion, it was time to put a toe back in civilisation's pond. Knysna provided a nasty shock. I was struck by the town's daunting openness, the abundance of unnecessary sky, the brutality of traffic. I missed the comfort of leaves, the freshness of upland air, the sibilance of forest sounds. Matthee describes just such a descent from forest to town: 'One moment the Forest was still around and above them, the next moment it started thinning out, getting lighter … more sun and then suddenly the world was lying open. Naked. Like someone without a hat. Without a roof.'

On his first visit to Knysna, Saul was both scared and entranced by the sights: a church with coloured windows, double-storeyed buildings, gardens with foreign plants, people wearing fancier clothes than he'd ever seen and sailing ships that looked like trees without leaves.

I wanted to retrace Saul's footsteps in and around Knysna and knew that Millwood House would be a good place to start. This charming little museum – red-roofed with a wooden, broekie-lace veranda – commemorates the abandoned forest town that features prominently in *Circles*. Gold was discovered near Millwood in 1876, but yields were not as rich as expected and after a few boom years, the town was abandoned. Today's museum started life as a quaint yellowwood house, built in Millwood during the 1880s, then dismantled and re-erected in Knysna.

Almost nothing remains of the hilltop mining town, but the house preserves artefacts and photographs from that heady era of gold rush. The museum complex comprises a number of buildings that present aspects of the region's history, including the gold mines, timber industry and Knysna's enigmatic founder, George Rex, rumoured to be the illegitimate son of George III, Prince of Wales, but who Matthee denounced as 'the first destroyer of the forest'.

The creaky interiors of Millwood House are decorated with period artefacts, including wicker prams, Victorian clothing, sewing machines and a kitchen cluttered with paraphernalia. The exhibits evoke the austerity and hardships of mining life, and the god-fearing nature of the town's inhabitants. There's an English homeliness about this set of wood-and-corrugated-iron houses surrounded by white picket fences that once held the forest wildness at bay.

After visiting Millwood, I took a walk around town in search of locations from the novel. Just up the street lay Woodmill Lane shopping centre, site of the town's original sawmill. I recalled Saul's shock when he first saw the mountains of wood, stacked and ready for shipping, evidence that the forest he so loved was being siphoned through this timber factory. In 1984, after more than a century in operation, the sawmill was closed down. The warehouses, smokestack and steam engines once fed by wood chips are still there, but now the place is gentrified and thronging with shoppers. The mall was filled with machinery – a giant crosscut saw, a geriatric generator – all brightly painted and recycled as sculptural elements, dinosaurs all.

I wandered up the hill to Memorial Square and came to the library, a gabled sandstone building with large doors of black stinkwood, its ceilings and sash windows of wit els. A timid and curious Saul once tried to gain entry here. Clad in woodcutter clothes and stumbling over his broken English, he was chased away by a stiff-collared, bespectacled librarian who shouted, 'You will not lay your dirty hands on any of these books!'

At the corner of Main and Queen streets, I came upon the rundown, double-storeyed Royal Hotel, formerly known as St George's Tavern. Captain Thomas Horn operated this thatched hostelry, frequented by Saul, and it was here in 1867 that Queen Victoria's son, Prince Alfred, Duke of Edinburgh, spent his first night in Knysna on his way to shoot forest elephants. In *Circles*, it is Saul's father who leads the prince to the elephants, with half of Knysna in tow, all dressed to the nines in their Sunday best and armed with anything that could put a hole in an animal. After the well-satisfied prince set sail for Simon's Town, with one elephant skin and two trophy heads, Horn's tavern was renamed The Royal Hotel.

Also on Main Street is St George's Church (1849), looking more Kentish than African with its neo-Gothic lines and mossy graves. Saul felt alienated from the 'English God' whose house this was and never dared go inside. I, however, passed through the teak-and-ironstone lynch gate and entered its verdant grounds. Erected on land donated by George Rex, the sandstone building has wide yellowwood floorboards and a timber ceiling with exposed hammer trusses, its charming whitewashed interior lit by stained-glass windows.

Next, I strolled down Long Street and over a bridge to Thesen Island whose shores are thick with modern waterfront development. On the quay, I noticed the remains of narrow-gauge railway tracks embedded in the concrete, and recalled that a little steam engine, affectionately known as the Coffee Pot, used to transport timber all the way from Diepwalle to the harbour. In its heyday, almost a hundred vessels docked here annually (the port was closed to shipping in 1954) and each year up to 28 000 tons of wood was loaded onto the ships.

I imagined barques and schooners, brigs and steamers tying up to embark goods and timber: the furling of thunderous canvas, bustle of wagons and shouting of stevedores. I recalled how Saul would watch the sailing ships ghosting up the lagoon like seabirds with great white wings angled to catch the breeze, and how he fantasised about escaping to the wide blue beyond the Heads. With a few nuggets of Millwood gold in your pocket, you could board a ship and venture out to explore the world of Pax Britannica.

Late afternoon found me on the western shores of Knysna Lagoon at Belvidere Manor, an old Rex/Duthie home built in 1849 and fictionally frequented by Saul's wood-merchant nemesis, MacDonald. Today it's a posh hotel with rolling lawns down to the water where I found The Bell, a tavern with low yellowwood ceilings and ironwood-block floors. There were lanterns and charts, stable doors and mugs hooked to a beam, and the wine cellar was visible through a window in the floor where, in times of yore, freshly caught game used to hang.

Ordering a beer, burger and chips (well-deserved to offset the shock of urbanity), I felt like a gold prospector of old, down from the mountains for some hearty grub, a few pints and good cheer. Staring out across the lagoon, I imagined a Nineteenth-Century world of sailing ships and woodcutters, the comings and goings of ivory hunters and frontiersmen ... now all of it transformed into a holiday playground on the international tourist circuit.

---*---

The following day, I headed northwest into hills that had once elicited a gold rush. When the precious metal was first discovered, fortune hunters poured in to Millwood and within weeks, a tent town had sprung up in the forest. Even Saul was seduced, and tried his hand at panning for alluvial gold in the Homtini River, but was appalled by the destruction of the forest caused by the miners.

Millwood town mushroomed before Saul's eyes. Soon there were six hotels, two churches, three banks, a post office, three newspapers (!), a brothel, music hall, four bakeries and thirty-two shops to provide for the horde of hopefuls. In 1886, reef gold was discovered, sparking a second rush, and within two years there were 1 400 claims being worked, but yields soon dwindled and the town began to contract. Many miners lost everything. Of the abandoned town, only one building remains, Mother Holly, also known as Materolli (a mispronunciation by local Italians of the Gouna settlement), which serves as a small museum and tearoom.

I left the N2 and drove inland to Rheenendal, paid for a permit to enter the national park, and followed a gravel track that wound uphill through dense forest. During the mining era, wagons would often get bogged down in the mud along this section of road. Topping out into open country, I drew up at Mother Holly where I'd arranged to meet James Haupt.

'You'd better hop in my 4x4 – your car will struggle,' said tall, fresh-faced James, a tuna fisherman turned guide who offers tours of the old mining settlement. We bounced up the hill to Bendigo Mine, one of the larger operations during the gold rush, where James stopped beside a shed to show me the restored mining equipment, including a heavy crusher, stamp battery, steam engine, boiler and cocopans. Most of the gear had been hauled here by oxen more than a century ago and abandoned where it stood when mining ceased.

'Here, put this on,' said James, getting out the car and handing me a yellow hard hat and torch.

'The Bendigo Adit has recently been restored and fitted with lights and ventilation. You don't get claustrophobia or anything, hey?'

'Ah, no, not really,' I said.

'Good, I'll lead the way.'

He started a generator, unlocked a gate and flicked on the lights of a tunnel that disappeared into the mountain.

'How far does it go?' I asked.

'About 250 metres.'

We picked our way down the tunnel, water trickling along the floor, the dark oesophagus squeezing tighter. Perhaps I was, after all, a little bit claustrophobic. We came to a wall of dark rock.

'When the miners struck dolerite, which is super hard, they gave up. It was yet another disappointment for them.' Thankfully, we didn't linger and returned to the entrance.

'The news that gold had been found in these forests spread like wildfire through the colony,' said James as we drove back down the hill. 'But within five years, disillusioned diggers began leaving for the Transvaal where prospects were better. Millwood was pretty much reduced to a ghost town and all that's left today are a couple of empty streets. I'll drop you there if you want to have a look around.'

We came to a fork, where I got out and James directed me up a side track towards two old oaks standing like the gateposts to an aborted Victorian dream. I'd read that it was during a hike in 1978 that this pair of alien trees – so incongruous amid the fynbos – had provided Matthee with the spark for an idea that led to research which ultimately resulted in her forest novels.

Signposts in the bush marked former streets and missing buildings, some of them vaguely distinguishable by their overgrown foundations. I noticed foxgloves and fuchsias, proper English damsels from the gardens of Millwood, now feral and mixing with the fynbos riff-raff. But really, there was nothing much to see other than the graveyard which was, appropriately, the town's most prominent landmark and boasted two large headstones and a few burial mounds melting back into the earth.

I stood in the middle of Main Street, in the heart of a non-existent town, trying to imagine life during the gold rush: rows of tents and makeshift houses, the valley ringing with the sound of pickaxes and rumble of dynamite.

I was picturing it through Saul's eyes: 'Damp chickens stood between the dwellings; here and there was a shivering dog tied to a tent-pole; all over the large, hacked-out clearing, raw tree-stumps stuck out like dead bodies not yet buried.' All gone.

I drove back down the hill to my next appointment with *Circles*. Parking beside the Dalene Matthee Big Tree Memorial at Krisjan-se-Nek, I joined a group of hikers gathered around Meagan Vermaas, a local guide who uses the forest novels as inspiration for her walking trails. Meagan is a Pre-Raphaelite-lookalike – red hair (complemented by a bright orange scarf), high cheekbones, pale blue eyes – and has made Knysna Forest her focus of study and passionate cause.

After introducing ourselves, we took a closer look at the pedimented memorial, erected soon after Matthee's death in 2005. 'Dalene often came to Krisjan-se-Nek to replenish her soul and gain inspiration for her wonderful stories,' said Meagan. 'And her ashes were scattered right here. The Outeniqua yellowwood behind me is 40 metres high and nearly 900 years old. It was one of Dalene's favourite kalanders and is named after her. You might remember that in her famous novel, Saul Barnard considers the Knysna yellowwood to be the biblical tree of good and evil. Apparently, when Dalene finished writing a book, she would return to this spot and read passages from it back to the forest.'

Before we set off on Meagan's 'Circles in a Forest' Trail, she stressed that we should practise conservation etiquette and stick to the path as the forest floor was fragile. 'The topsoil here is very thin, the root systems often less than thirty centimetres deep,' she said. 'Even the giant trees spread their roots laterally, so tread lightly: we are guests in the forest.'

Meagan talked about the novels as we walked, pointing out interesting plants and describing how Matthee often compared her characters to trees. 'For instance, Saul's father Joram was like an ironwood, strong and true with a beautiful heart,' she said. 'Oh, by the way, do you see those wit els trees in the glade? Because they grow a bit crooked, they're the easiest ones to climb. You might want to remember that if you're being chased by an elephant.'

We crossed a tea-coloured stream embowered with branches, the water gurgling over polished boulders, the banks greasy and tall ferns filtering the light. Meagan showed us furrows that lead from the river to a series of old sluice boxes for extracting gold. I thought of Saul panning in the icy water until he was blue with cold and of his growing dejection as days passed without even a grain of gold to show for his efforts.

'Miners used to burrow away with pick and shovel, digging these precarious shafts,' she said, pointing to a tunnel in the rock. 'It was terribly hard labour, and dangerous too.'

At the end of a narrow kloof, we came to a waterfall that stepped down in two cascades. 'Elephants sometimes bathe here,' whispered Meagan, as though the Big Feet were listening. I imagined great, grey, forest ghosts splashing about in the pond and rolling in the mud – a bathing ritual in the forest's heart. I thought, too, about how elephants were the spiritual guardians of this place. Even if their numbers were tragically reduced, perhaps even to a solitary female, they remained the apex mammal of this wilderness … its totem.

Before turning back, Meagan read us a short piece from Matthee's essay 'Enchanted Forest Land': 'Those who have experienced the forest in all its moods return home enriched. They do so in the knowledge that should man destroy the last of the forests, some of his inner peace, freedom and joy will be lost forever. The enchantment of the rainforest transcends its physical presence, leaving the human soul touched in mysterious ways that even science cannot fathom.'

---—✳︎———

At the end of the novel, Saul comes upon the carcass of Old Foot, shot by the hunters before he could intervene. Devastated, he runs his hand over the skin of the fallen beast: 'Elephant of his childhood dreams. Old Foot, the most feared. Animal-brother in Maska's tongue. King of the Forest … Was there ever a more beautiful creature destroyed by the will of man? … Like the Forest you must cry out in silence.'

Today, Knysna Forest is one third the size it was in the Nineteenth Century when buffaloes and lions frequented its shadows and hippos wallowed in its streams; before the intervention of the diggers, hunters and timber merchants. 'For some reason or other man is always the spoiler and destroyer,' Saul laments.

But all has not been lost. It is fortuitous that Millwood did not yield enough gold and the town was returned to the bush. Indeed, the reader of *Circles* can take pleasure in Matthee's description of the forest reclaiming the town as abandoned houses fall into disrepair and pigeons colonise the ruins. The woodcutters have also been retired and much of the region declared a national park. Sometimes, all too rarely, the outcome is in nature's favour. It is in no small measure due to Matthee's work that this forest is held in such high regard by the public, and it is ultimately the public who will decide its fate in the greedy years to come.

On my last night at Diepwalle, I walked into the forest and sat at the foot of a giant kalander. 'Like a mighty king it stood towering above the white alder and mountain saffron, stinkwood, assegai and hard pear,' writes Matthee. 'As if God had planted it there long before the others.' I was cradled by its flying-buttress roots; its bark scaled off in flakes across my spine. Gone were my fears of the first evening. The enormous trunk stretched to the sky packed with elevator veins and arteries bearing water aloft and sending sun-made sustenance below. Up there, clouds of leaves inked the shaggy darkness and old man's beard moss hung from the branches like strands of pale-green hair. Below and beside me, tentacle roots tethered the great tower of living wood to the earth. I pressed my cheek to its rough trunk, my body to its ancient, craggy frame. I sensed the centuries of upward yearning and downward anchoring, felt the old yellowwood's power coursing through me.

A fragrant muskiness leaked from the soil. I registered the forest's breathing – gently in, gently out – the barely perceptible susurration of the single, great creature that it surely was. Matthee had known that the forest was one, perfectly whole, fully evolved system. It needed nothing more, nothing less. Only man could destroy its harmony.

A dark softness settled over the forest. If I wasn't careful, I might well lose myself completely to its leafy embrace.

———※———

RED IN TRUTH AND LORE
Zakes Mda's Wild Coast

When I was a boy, the R61 from Mthatha to Port St Johns seemed to me a conduit into a fantastical realm. Growing up under apartheid with closed borders, this was an exotic escape into a subtropical African world. I remember village children calling 'Sweets!' from the verges and lads running beside the car selling clay models of oxen and cars complete with roof racks bearing wooden surfboards. Bantustans were part of the venal apartheid system, but for a young boy there was something magical about leaving a wet, wintery Cape Town and crossing a border into this other, African 'state' with its warm ocean, lush shoreline and traditional way of life.

I remember meals tended by suited waiters in the echoing dining hall of Cape Hermes Hotel, and playing Cowboys and Indians in its cascading gardens dotted with thatched umbrellas. Port St Johns was overgrown with flamboyant vegetation, and colonial villas ringed by wide verandas gave the place a languid, tropical air. Women wore traditional ochre garb with oblong headgear, covered their faces in cream-coloured paint and smoked long pipes. I remember rondavels perched on hilltops, roofs packed with pumpkins, boys herding cattle on the slopes and mielie cobs drying in the sun.

The Heart of Redness by Zakes Mda (born in 1948) is a novel that captures the enchantment of the rural Eastern Cape I recall from my childhood. I wanted to revisit the Wild Coast, using Mda's text as my guide, and spend time in the village of Qolora (spelt Qolorha in the novel) where much of the story is set. Mutual friend Mandla Langa put me in touch with Mda and I emailed him outlining the project. He replied within the hour:

> That's wonderful! I haven't been there for years! I suggest you book at the Trennerys which is one of the two hotels almost at Qolorha Mouth. The other one is Seagull Hotel. Near these hotels is a trading store owned by Rufus Hulley, a very resourceful man who is a walking encyclopaedia on the history of that area ... The ladies

who manage the Trennerys (if they are still there) are a rich source of information as well.

---*---

About thirty-five kilometres east of East London, I turned off the N2 at the sign for Haga Haga and Morgan Bay. As the road wended its way coastwise through rolling country, I was thinking about the Xhosa Cattle Killing and how these peaceful hills and valleys had once been filled with the starving and the dying. Hundreds of thousands of cattle were slaughtered during that terrible episode in our history and it is thought that 40 000 people died, mostly of hunger. Mda paints an apocalyptic picture in the novel: 'At first it was mostly old people and children. Then men and women in their prime. Dying everywhere. Corpses and skeletons were a common sight. In the dongas. On the veld. Even around the homesteads. No one had the strength to bury them.'

Central to *The Heart of Redness* (2000) is this great 'national suicide' of 1856-57, precipitated by a teenage prophetess, Nongqawuse, who preached salvation for the Xhosa people. If they killed all their cattle, burnt their crops and put an end to witchcraft, the spirits of their ancestors would rise up and drive the colonising British into the sea, after which the cattle would be resurrected and the crops restored. Nongqawuse's prophecy split the Xhosa nation into Unbelievers and Believers, many of the latter adopting the millenarian cult and destroying their livelihoods, an act that resulted in years of misery, starvation and death.

The road came to an end at the mouth of the Great Kei River and I parked in the shade to wait for the ferry. In the bad old days, a bridge further upstream marked the border between apartheid South Africa and the Republic of Transkei. You even had to show a passport to enter the Land of Chief Matanzima.

After a short wait, the ferry appeared, nosing its bows against the slipway as a skipper with a red cap, fake Ray-Ban sunglasses and gold chain revved the engine. I eased my rental car onto the deck and paid the skipper as a line of locals laden with shopping bags stepped aboard and found a seat on the benches that lined either side of the ferry. With a grumble of the outboard engine, we were off, crabbing across the chocolate waters of the Kei, the wind whipping up a short chop from the southeast. In a moment of nostalgia, I imagined the verdant banks of my childhood Transkei heaving into view.

The road now led inland for a dozen kilometres before bending back to the coast. The afternoon light was softening, the valleys already sunk in shadow. An old gent held out a hand and called 'Christmas!' with a broad smile as I passed; a group of boys shouted 'Sweets, sweets!' – transporting me straight back to the 1970s. I was tripping on memories as my car rumbled into Qolora by Sea, a settlement of widely scattered homesteads in pale shades of green, pink and yellow, some circular rondavels, others hexagonal. There was a row of white-owned beach houses along the shore, a hilltop school and beside it a large trading store painted cream and brown with a red roof and colonnaded stoep. This had to be the Vulindlela Store that features so prominently in the novel, or at least its inspiration (the geography was slightly off).

I pulled over and got out, picturing an early scene in *The Heart of Redness* in which old Bhonco comes trudging up the hill in overalls and gumboots, cursing the trader for building the store on the summit. 'But the breathtaking view from the top compensates for the arduous climb,' writes Mda. 'Down below, on his right, he can see the wild sea smashing gigantic waves against the rocks, creating mountains of snow-white surf. On his left his eyes feast on the green valleys and the patches of villages with beautiful houses painted pink, powder blue, yellow and white.'

The store was typical of the rural Eastern Cape with wide counters behind chicken wire, an old-fashioned scale with weights, and shelves packed with non-perishable necessities such as mielie-meal, cooking oil, long-life milk and sweets in tall glass jars. A woman with cropped grey hair and sparkling eyes served at one of the counters.

'Excuse me, but are you by any chance Mrs Hulley?' I asked.

'Yes, I am, young man, how may I help?'

'Pleased to meet you. I wrote to your husband a while back. I'm here to research Zakes Mda's *Heart of Redness*.'

'Oh yes, Rufus told me about you. Justin, is it? Such a nice man, that Zakes chap. Rufus showed him around Qolora, oh, it must be twenty years ago now. My husband is ill at the moment, but do come for tea tomorrow afternoon.'

Thanking her, I drove down the hill towards the ocean, remembering the novel's protagonist, Camagu, doing the same and remarking that 'a generous artist painted the village of Qolorha-by-Sea, using splashes of lush colour. It is a canvas where blue and green dominate. It is the blue of the skies and the distant hills, of the ocean and the rivers that flow into it. The green is of the meadows and the valleys, the tall grass and the usundu palms.'

Trennerys Hotel is reached down a lush, embowered road, and the century-old establishment – recast as the Blue Flamingo Hotel in the novel – is a delightful hotchpotch of thatched chalets, villas and lawns encircled by forest with no sea views, just its proximate roar. It's the kind of Transkei family hotel I fondly remember from childhood, with all-you-can-eat seafood evenings, fishing expeditions, afternoon teas and games after dinner.

'Welcome to our little slice of paradise!' said a beaming Deoni Barnard as I entered the reception. 'You said you wanted to write, so we've put you far from the main lodge.' She unhooked a key and led me past the pub and swimming pool to a chalet set among the trees. 'Supper is from seven, but come through earlier if you like and have a drink at the Barrel and Gecko.'

After unpacking, I pulled on shorts and flip-flops, crossed the lawn, past the tennis court and down a path through thick vegetation that closed overhead. I stepped from the forest onto a wide sweep of beach echoing with the din of surf. Mist probed gaps in the dunes; pink clouds drifted off the ocean; there was not a soul in sight. I wandered along a tide line strewn with the sea's detritus – limpets, perlemoen shells, the bodies of crabs – then cut across the beach to the lagoon where I found a jetty and a handful of boats pulled up on the sand. Two Xhosa boys pumping for prawns waved and shouted 'mholo' as I passed.

The lagoon was fringed with indigenous forest – milkwood and yellowwood, wild date palm, wild plum and strelitzias nodding their shaggy heads to the breeze. A pair of blacksmith lapwings sounded their anvil-tapping call at my approach and pied kingfishers in natty black-and-white livery dived for minnows. A fish eagle perched in the top of a tree on the opposite bank threw back its head and let out its cry. My way was blocked by a river so I retraced my steps, finding a shorter route back to the hotel through the forest, the last rays of sunlight filtering in angled shafts across the path's green tunnel.

There were only three other guests in a dining hall adorned with garish paintings of women in traditional garb, lazy fans ticking overhead. I chose a table with a view of the swimming pool with faux waterfall feature and blue lights. A posse of smiling Xhosa waitrons was on hand to serve. I ordered a bottle of Merlot and jotted notes as tinny Eighties music leaked from the bar. Carrot soup was followed by peppery kudu steak, then ice cream and hot chocolate sauce.

One of the staff had the gaunt features and ashen complexion that suggested she might be an Aids sufferer. Not only had the Xhosa nation been decimated in the aftermath of the Great Cattle Killing, but another tsunami had swept through these parts in the shape of HIV. I thought of Sweetness, the daughter of Bruman and Alice Magxwalisa, who had worked for my parents at our family home in Simon's Town. The couple had lived in a cottage on the property with their four children. Sweetness was the eldest and an embodiment of her name with a gentle nature and an infectious smile that permanently lit up her face.

At the age of nineteen, she met a sailor serving in the local naval base and it's rumoured that he gave her 'the disease'. Sweetness grew thin, weak and listless; her face turned grey but her smile remained. We implored her to go to hospital. By then, antiretrovirals were widely available, despite President Mbeki's head-in-the-sand policies, but her mother was a sangoma and thought otherwise. Alice took Sweetness back home to the Eastern Cape to consult with the ancestors and to try to heal her. Alice threw herself at the task, using all the traditional means and medicines at her disposal, to no avail. Alice did not return to Cape Town after Sweetness died and remained at the family kraal, tending to the fields and practising her arcane craft.

A few years ago, I was travelling through the Eastern Cape and decided to make a detour to pay my respects. It was a Saturday and almost every village had a marquee set up on the commonage for funerals ... Aids funerals. I'd been given loose directions to a hamlet near Dwesa and eventually found the house. It was an emotional reunion with Alice, whom I'd not seen for many years. There were gifts from my mother – practical items and food – and much to catch up on. I asked about Sweetness, but Alice did not want to speak about her daughter and instead directed me to a mielie patch behind the house. 'There is Sweetness,' she said and looked away.

The grave, just a mound of Transkei earth, lay in the middle of a field among dry corn stalks with no cross or headstone to mark the spot. I stood beside the knoll, tears pouring down my cheeks: what a waste, I thought.

What a laying waste. In a few years, maybe sooner, no trace of her grave would remain and Alice's plough would no longer have to make a detour around the mound.

The Heart of Redness is a multigenerational saga that interweaves history, myth and realist fiction. A novel of broad scope and compassion, it tells the story of contemporary rural life set against the backdrop of the Cattle Killing. In Mda's story, the conflict between Believers and Unbelievers has persisted down the generations to the present day. Believers still claim that the prophecies of Nongqawuse would have come true if *all* Xhosa people had participated in the destruction. The ancestors had failed to rise up because of the doubters. Unbelievers argue that the folly of the original Believers led not only to decades of suffering, but that the Killing enhanced the power of the colonisers, forcing the Xhosa to leave their decimated homeland and sell their labour to white settlers and rival tribes.

The age-old conflict between Believers and Unbelievers is reflected in opposing attitudes towards a proposed casino and tourist resort in Qolorha. Unbelievers support the development because it will create jobs and inject money into the region; Believers are dead set against the proposal, claiming it will destroy their traditional way of life.

The novel's protagonist is Camagu, a middle-aged man recently returned from exile in the USA armed with a PhD in economic development and wanting to help build the new South Africa. He tries to make a go of things in Johannesburg, but can't find suitable work and soon becomes disillusioned by the many ills of the new democracy. When he meets a beautiful woman who is about to return home to Qolorha-by-Sea, he decides to follow her. Camagu settles in the village and becomes embroiled in the battle between Believers and Unbelievers, as well as in love affairs with two women, Xoliswa and Qukezwa, one from each side of the conflict.

The chief Believer is Zim (father of Qukezwa) while his arch rival and chief Unbeliever is Bhonco (father of Xoliswa). Bhonco riles against the traditionalists who 'want us to remain in our wildness! To remain red all our lives! To stay in the darkness of redness!' Indeed, Bhonco even refuses to wear traditional, red-ochre-coloured garb and will only dress in Western clothes.

He also demands that his wife abandon the 'red ochre of unenlightenment' that she smears on her body and on her isikhakha dresses.

By contrast, Zim and his Believers seek to retain their traditions and preserve the pristine natural world of Qolorha. If there has to be tourism, they argue, it should take the form of the kind of eco-tourism that preserves the forests, rivers and their way of life. The white store owner, John Dalton, whose ancestor killed both Zim and Bhonco's forefather, Xikixa, sides with the Believers in the casino controversy.

Mda gives both factions a fair hearing: while the Believers look exclusively to the past for direction and risk falling into the trap of superstition and arch conservatism, the Unbelievers have little insight into the damage that unbridled development might cause. Caught between the two camps, Camagu needs to chart a course of personal integrity. Although Mda bends the reader's sympathies in favour of the Believers, he resists any definitive position and we are led back and forth through the intricacies and ironies of village politics, wondering who will win this archetypal battle for the soul of rural South Africa.

My own interest in *The Heart of Redness* relates to Mda's evocation of the spirit of the Wild Coast through his portrayal of its topography as well as his characters' relationship with the land, no doubt coloured by his own childhood memories of growing up in the Eastern Cape, recalled in his autobiography, *Sometimes there is a Void*. The extensive use of Xhosa lexicon in his description of plants, birds, sights and smells as well as his evocative depiction of landscape create a powerful sense of place.

In *Dance of Life*, Gail Fincham notes how Mda's story-worlds are both rooted in carefully observed places and suffused with the memories of their inhabitants. She quotes Mda: 'I usually see a place and immediately decide that it is so beautiful or so ugly that it deserves a novel. The next question is: what character would live in a place like this and what memories are contained in this landscape? I see the trees and the rocks and the grass and the hills and the rivers as storing places of memory.'

Fincham goes on to suggest that in his use of setting, Mda combines memory, history, landscape and culture, and that his attitude to landscape has little in common with traditional Western perspectives that often treat geographical locales as expressions of human mastery. Mda's rendering of landscape derives from African oral traditions that refuse to separate land from people, ancestors or folklore, resulting in the creation of a powerful spirit of place. Landscape functions as an integral part of the locals' sense of identity and embodies their living heritage. Mda's settings serve to dissolve the barriers between land, body and being, and to collapse linear time, allowing the past to play itself out in the present. 'Nature and culture, divided by Western thought, fuse in African storytelling,' Fincham suggests. 'In Mda's novels place is dynamic and transformative.'

---*---

The following morning, I met Trevor Wigley, a local tour guide who'd offered to help me with my *Heart of Redness* quest. I wanted Trevor to show me Qolora's sights of natural beauty, especially the places Qukezwa takes Camagu, instilling in him a passion to protect this corner of the Wild Coast.

Trevor is something of a Qolora institution. When a tour group rolls into town, chances are they'll end up on one of Trevor's Trails. In the novel, it is Dalton, the trading-store owner, who takes tourists in his 4x4 to see the mangrove swamps and shipwrecks, to experience local customs and to visit Nongqawuse's infamous pool. Trevor Wigley would be my John Dalton.

'Hop in and let's go for a coffee at my place before we hit the trail,' said Trevor, swinging open the passenger door of his bakkie. Wearing a floppy hat and fishbowl spectacles, he was rosy of cheek, bushy of eyebrow and boyish-looking for his age. Two minutes' drive down the hill brought us to Trevor's home, set in a garden resplendent with pink hydrangeas and offering fine views of the ocean. It was an eclectic, ramshackle house filled with antiques, landscape paintings and faded surfing photographs, some of them featuring a young Trevor with board under arm contemplating epic Wild Coast waves. The stoep was decorated with buoys, shell mobiles and wind chimes.

While Trevor made coffee, I watched a video snippet from the *Ultimate Braai Master* television programme on his laptop. It showed Trevor guiding contestants to Nolokasa's kraal where they learn about traditional healing, customs and dance, and featured white folk mixing medicinal herbs, dancing without rhythm and getting tipsy on rounds of umqombothi (maize beer).

'I've been coming to Qolora since I was a pikkie,' said Trevor appearing with two steaming mugs.

'Did you grow up in Transkei?' I asked, following him to the stoep.

'Ja, then I moved away after school, worked for a while in a supermarket in East London, but gave it up and came back here about thirty years ago. You could call it very early retirement – much less income, but a happier life. I'm also a surfer, which was an added attraction as the waves around here are pretty nice.'

'Is your family originally from the Transkei?'

'Yes, both my grandfather and my father were traders. Dad's store was at Teko Springs, between Centane and Butterworth, but these days all the old trading stores are dying. Locals want the convenience and variety of supermarkets, not just staples bought from behind wire mesh, so they hop in a minibus taxi and go to the nearest town instead.'

'You see it as a loss?'

'Ja, I do; the trading stores hold a unique place in Eastern Cape history. Traders were intermediaries between black and white worlds with friendships on both sides. They spoke fluent Xhosa, sometimes married African women, even supplied arms to the chiefs fighting the British back in the day. The trading store was a community meeting place, a post office, a venue to buy, sell, store and process goods, even to mill grain.'

I had a flashback to the Indian store in Ramoutsa and Bosman's Marico farmers gathering to pass the time of day and catch up on local news.

'During the holidays, all the trading families would pack their wagons and trek down to the coast, to places such as Qolora. It's sad, man: apart from a few diehards like the Hulleys, the era of the trading store is over. Most of the families were pushed out in 1976 when the Transkei got its sham independence and the others have slowly trickled away, but their story is a damn interesting one.'

'I suppose traders also brought modernity, access to European goods, and consequently big changes to rural society.'

'Certainly.'

'And ultimately this brought about their own demise.'

'Yes. It's ironic that although traders generally admired local traditions, the goods they sold – shoes, Western clothes, corrugated iron, multicoloured paint – helped to erode the traditional culture of the Amaqaba.'

'Amaqaba?'

'The Reds. It refers to the traditional use of red ochre as a cosmetic, to dye clothes and the like. The name is often employed in a derogatory sense to mean backward, you know, like a country bumpkin. When you talk about intliziyo yobubomvu, the heart of redness, you're referring to a place where the locals are still practising their old customs.'

A long-tailed wydah flitted past the stoep. 'There goes that bloody bird again!' said Trevor. 'If one of 'em takes a fancy to your garden, it chases all the other birds away. Wydahs are nasty little buggers. If you're done with your coffee, let's hit the road.'

We set off in the bakkie and picked up Carlos Nkonki, Trevor's young guiding partner and fundi on local fauna and flora. As Trevor was suffering from a wonky knee, Carlos would accompany me on the more taxing walks. We parked in a forest clearing about a kilometre from Trennerys and Carlos led us down to an inlet of the Qolora River where a motorboat was moored. He retrieved the outboard engine from a locked container on the bank and attached it to the transom. The ignition's racket startled a pair of crowned hornbills that took to the air. Then we set off, puttering between banks thick with hardwoods and loud with the chatter of unseen birds, Carlos naming the trees and their uses as we passed: wild dagga for snake bite; sneezewood for fence poles, insect repellent and snuff; pompon bark for making rope; the quinine tree for curing stomach ailments and dressing wounds.

We came to The Gates, a dolerite portal whose vertical walls were stained with lichen, the dark water between giving back a little-altered version of the cliffs. 'Look carefully into that cleft on your right and you might see a white spot,' said Carlos. 'There! It's a barn owl checking us out.'

Our boat glided between narrowing cliffs until we reached a landing stage. Carlos helped Trevor as we climbed up onto a ledge, then along a path to a rock pool fed by two waterfalls. This was surely one of the places of 'untold beauty' referred to by Mda. Carlos scaled the highest boulder and swallow dived from four metres while I took the more sedate ladder. The water was cool but invigorating. Later, I sat on a rock beside Trevor as he regaled me with stories of his childhood holidays. 'Qolora was paradise for a young boy, totally wild and unspoilt.'

'Still is,' I said.

'Ja, for the most part, I s'pose. Qolora is still embedded in nature. I don't think I could ever leave.'

Back in the bakkie, we headed off road over summer-green hills crowned with rondavels and cattle grazing everywhere. The Wild Coast is one of the last corners of South Africa where Western property values have been kept at bay. There's much to criticise about 'tribal land' and the problems that go with its loose communality, but ill-defined property rights and vague ownership can be good for nature. There are few fences or enclosures and the land is mostly devoid of large developments or infrastructure. Wildlife and indigenous vegetation can live pretty well with this arrangement, especially around the margins.

But this form of land use is everywhere under threat. For example, the pristine northern Wild Coast is imperilled by the proposed construction of an N2 toll-road extension through its heart, as well as the mining of coastal dunes for titanium. Once again, it is traditionalists and conservationists up against the might of big business, corrupt government and mining companies – an archetypal scrap whose winner is usually the one with the biggest bank balance or the most muscle. The wheels of corruption are well oiled and all too often tribal chiefs or local officials are coerced or bribed, honchos in the ruling party are made company directors and the projects steam ahead.

The Heart of Redness concerns itself with land rights and the destiny of rural South Africa. To stop just such a development, Camagu wants to have Qolorha declared a national heritage site due to its cultural and historical significance. Ironically, a century and half after the Cattle Killing, Nongqawuse might help to save the village from the Unbelievers and neo-colonialists.

We drove to Gxara Waterfall (Gxarha in the novel) through a vast eucalyptus plantation, jackal buzzards tracking our bouncy progress from the highest branches. 'The forest is part of a communal farm, but the whole thing has gone to pot,' said Trevor. 'Corrupt government projects like these are doomed before they even start, as you'd expect.'

I recalled how forests were also contested places in *The Heart of Redness*. Bhonco rails against the Believers for wanting to preserve indigenous trees, arguing that they should plant 'civilised trees' instead, 'trees that come from across the seas. Trees that have no thorns like some of the ugly ones you want to protect. Trees like the wattle and bluegum that grow in the forest of Nogqoloza. You know that Nogqoloza is a beautiful forest because the trees there were planted in straight lines.'

By contrast, Qukezwa is the symbolic champion of ecological activism, going so far as to cut down foreign trees, such as lantana and wattle, that are choking the indigenous vegetation. She believes that the laws of the land need to change in order to protect local flora, contending that plantations and invasive plants are a form of ecological neo-colonialism and that the flora imported by the former colonisers continue to subjugate indigenous vegetation.

The descent to Gxara Waterfall was steep, so Trevor stayed in the bakkie while Carlos led me down a rocky path that came to a river. The air was filled with the heady scent of Bushman's tea and the water sparkled in the sunlight as we followed the bank until we came to a pond rimmed by a weir at the head of the falls. From a ledge, we peered over the edge and the earth fell away at our feet as water tipped over the lip and splashed into the stream far below. This, too, was one of Mda's places of 'untold beauty'.

In the novel, it is pristine environments such as these that are under threat. Camagu argues that hotels and casinos, like those proposed for Qolorha, are usually frequented by the rich and the only real beneficiaries are multinational companies, their shareholders and complicit government officials. He warns that, contrary to all the promises, few new jobs are created for locals in such deals and rural communities invariably pay a heavy price, losing both their land and their freedom.

---*---

That afternoon, Trevor accompanied me to the Hulleys for tea. In *The Heart of Redness*, the white, English-speaking perspective is embodied in two characters, both named John Dalton: the Nineteenth-Century Dalton involved in the beheading of Xikixa (the 'Headless Ancestor'), and his great-great-grandson, the trading-store owner. The contemporary Dalton was raised in Qolorha, attended initiation school, speaks fluent isiXhosa and mocks the snobbishness of his fellow English South Africans. In the novel's dedication, Mda makes it clear that Hulley should not be equated with Dalton: 'There is a real-life trader in Qolorha, whose name is Rufus Hulley, who took me to places of miracles and untold beauty. He must not be mistaken for John Dalton, the trader of *The Heart of Redness*, who is purely a fictional character.' But there can be no doubting that the fictional character is inspired by the living, breathing Hulley.

'Don't believe everything Rufus tells you,' said Trevor as we drove down the hill. 'That old rascal is big on stories, but he's a dreamer with some pretty fanciful ideas about Xhosa history. Rufus is exactly what Mda needed: more bloody fiction than fact.'

We pulled up at one of the bigger houses on the beachfront. 'My family used to own this place in the old days, before the Hulleys bought it and made it all fancy.'

Rufus met us at the door on crutches – tall, in his seventies, with grey-blond hair and a warm, if slightly diffident, smile. 'Oh, the leg, a botched operation,' he said. 'Come in and make yourselves at home.' His manner was formal, his diction clipped. Both the television and radio burbled at low volume; the hallway was filled with dark wood sculptures, most of them traditional figures. 'I got a local chap to carve these for me, told him I wanted *realistic* statues of *real* people. The man was a prodigy, but unfortunately he died a few years back.'

We were ushered into a gloomy lounge. 'Most of the old trading families left the Transkei in the 1970s, but you stayed on,' I said.

'Yes, I loved the lifestyle. I took Transkei citizenship and completely immersed myself in the community. There was mutual respect and acceptance. I got involved in building schools, clinics, even a cultural village.' I noticed Trevor rolling his eyes.

'I helped identify stock diseases and organised inoculation programmes,' Rufus continued. 'Cattle are so important to the Xhosa, and to me too. I learnt a lot about the symptoms and cures of diseases from my own herd of cattle. A farmer friend helped me when I phoned him and described the symptoms: tremors, fever, coughing and loss of appetite. He said it was heartwater and advised on the cure. I wrote a piece about it that got published, which I can show you if you'd like.' Trevor rolled his eyes again.

Conversation turned to my project. 'Mda's account of the Cattle Killing draws heavily on *The Dead Will Arise* by Jeff Peires,' said Rufus. 'Mda acknowledges as much at the outset of his novel, and he thanks me too. I was the one who took Peires and Mda to Nongqawuse's pool. It's a haunting, mystical spot. You know, when the aloes on the ridge are reflected in the water, they do look a bit like lost souls … it's quite uncanny.'

As Rufus talked, Trevor offered the occasional contradiction under his breath, just loud enough for me to hear. 'Nonsense, Zakes didn't stay here, he stayed at Trennerys,' whispered Trevor when Rufus suggested otherwise. It was like watching a practised double act and I thought how these two village elders could just as well be Bhonco and Zim. They were more similar than either would care to admit, both from good trading stock, both storytellers and mediators with rival narratives. Both of them with their dicky legs, Xhosaphilia and passion for Qolora; the one a believer of a kind, the other an unbeliever of sorts.

The pair slipped seamlessly in and out of isiXhosa, Rufus lamenting the fact that not enough whites bothered to learn the language. He held forth about the community projects he was involved in and the politicians he knew. Despite the mild affectation, he was kind and engaging, eager to remain relevant, to be of service to the community, and he seemed to need to convince me that he was.

'Rufus always has big ideas,' said Trevor as we drove back up the hill. 'He writes letters to the ANC giving advice on governing. He once even invited Mandela to his birthday party – not short on self-confidence is our Rufus.'

'But a good heart, don't you think?'

He paused, then smiled. 'Ja, that too.'

Later that evening, after a lonely lamb shank and malva pudding drowned in custard, I adjourned to the Barrel and Gecko where Mark Knopfler was crooning about the Sultans of Swing as I ordered a nightcap Amarula.

'How are you enjoying Qolora?' asked Deoni, pouring my drink.

'Very much. It's nostalgic for me. I used to come to the Wild Coast as a kid. It has such a special atmosphere.'

'I know what you mean.'

'What do you like about living here?'

'The peace and quiet, the sense of being part of a traditional way of life. I love visiting Xhosa homesteads, immersing myself in the community, meeting traditional healers, drinking umqombothi, watching the little kids dancing ...'

'Have you settled here for good?'

'Ag, I don't know for sure yet, we'll just have to see. But I came here and embraced the four Ls: learning, loving, living and laughter. The penny dropped for me one afternoon when I was sitting by the waterfall and these Xhosa boys brought me honey they'd got from a hive. We sat there eating together, straight from the comb.' She smiled and wiped the counter with a rag.

'I've got two days left,' I said. 'What do you recommend I see?'

'You must walk to the wreck of the *Jacaranda*, a cargo ship that ran aground in 1971, about four kays up the coast. There's not much left of her, so try to get there at low tide when some of the hull is visible.'

'How did she sink?'

'Oh, lots of theories, lots of stories.'

'Like?'

'One of them is that the sailors were drunk, the captain was entertaining a prostitute in his cabin and a twelve-year-old kid was at the helm. Engine trouble and strong wind is another possibility. An insurance scam is also a theory. It's funny how the ship hit the shore precisely at a small, sandy beach while everywhere else is treacherous rocks. The sailors just stepped ashore, hardly getting their feet wet: makes you wonder.' She winked.

Before bed, I strolled down the leafy corridor to the beach where the surf offered deep, booming detonations that echoed off the dunes. I sat watching the moon's reflection in the ocean and thought about Nongqawuse. Who was she and what had inspired her visions? Dalton describes her simply as a little girl who craved attention, one who'd acquired vague notions of Xhosa history and the Bible, blending them into a crude theology that gathered momentum as she gained prestige. Camagu comes to a quite different conclusion, suggesting that 'her prophecies arose out of the spiritual and material anguish of the amaXhosa nation'. Her vision conjured a sublime force that could change the terrible conditions of her time and her people.

Nongqawuse certainly had agency, implicitly espousing the rights of the Xhosa people, but also of women by calling for an end to witchcraft, adultery and incest. History is full of accounts of powerful or visionary teenage 'girls interrupted' who threaten or inspire society, from Joan of Arc to the Salem witch accusers and from Delphic priestesses to virgin sacrifices. Perhaps figures such as Greta Thunberg and Malala Yousafzai are their modern equivalents; perhaps even Olive Schreiner, to choose another gifted teenager from Nongqawuse's era. An argument could be made for both being intelligent, gifted Eastern Cape girls seeking self-expression, recognition and power through their respective (narrative) art forms: literature and prophecy.

I thought, too, of how unkind the tides of history have been to the Wild Coast: from Frontier Wars and the Cattle Killing, to the subjugations of colonialism and apartheid, and then the Aids apocalypse. But the beauty remains: kloofs and riverbanks thick with forest, sequestered lagoons and a rural way of life that, even if poor, is still vibrant and in tune with nature. Although a product of fiction, the modern Believers were perhaps right to guard their world against change. Leaking into my consciousness came the words of the Oswald Mtshali poem 'Sounds of a Cowhide Drum', a hymn to the pull of rural Africa that I'd learnt by heart as a schoolboy:

Boom! Boom! Boom!
I am the drum on your dormant soul,
cut from the black hide of a sacrificial cow.

I am the spirit of your ancestors,
habitant in hallowed huts,
eager to protect,
forever vigilant.
...

Boom! Boom! Boom!
That is the sound of a cowhide drum –
the voice of Mother Africa.

---***---

Next morning, Trevor and Carlos collected me for a visit to the pool of Nongqawuse, ground zero for the Cattle Killing. We drove inland under a threatening sky, then turned off the Kei Mouth road onto a rough track that led downhill to an overgrown thicket. Trevor filled in the backstory as he negotiated the uneven terrain: 'Nongqawuse claimed that self-destruction would bring about a golden age. Her prophesies came at a time of great strife when Xhosa land and culture were under severe threat from white settlers and the people really *needed* to believe in some kind of salvation. Historians like Peires have argued that the Cattle Killing was influenced by a combination of factors, including Governor Grey and the Frontier Wars, prophesies by diviners such as Mlanjeni, Christian beliefs, indigenous notions of regeneration, as well as the devastating impact of lung sickness, a bovine disease imported from Europe that caused the great epidemic of 1854. And, of course, faith in the power of the ancestors.'

'Where is that faith today?' I asked.

'Oh, ancestral spirits are still *so* important. No matter where you find yourself in South Africa, if you have a problem, you come home, you come here, you sacrifice an animal and ask the ancestors for advice. Witchcraft, or whatever you want to call it, is still powerful and pervasive.'

We scythed through tall grass and bounced over boulders until the bakkie could go no further. Trevor stayed in the vehicle and Carlos led me down a steep line to an elongated pond of dark water, the opposite bank covered in subtropical forest dotted with elephant-eared strelitzias. 'This is the spot where the faces of two Strangers first appeared from the fronds of an usundu palm and spoke to Nongqawuse,' said Carlos.

Her voice was in my head: 'The Strangers say that the whole community of the dead will arise and the new people will come with new cattle, horses, goats, sheep and any other animal that the people may want. There will be a new world of contentment and no one will ever lead a troubled life again.'

As if to belie its history, the pool seemed a place of utter peace. I thought of how in the novel the modern Believer, Zim, comes here with his daughter Qukezwa to look for eels and otters. He tells her that his whole life has been centred on this sacred valley: his grandfather's fields were here, he tended cattle here when he was a boy and it was in this valley that he was circumcised.

When Qukezwa brings Camagu to the pool, the valley is described as an earthly paradise thronging with guinea fowl and Egyptian geese, the vegetation thick with orchids, cycads, cerise bell flowers and wild fig trees. Qukezwa tells Camagu to throw silver coins into the pond for luck, then slips into a trance and begins to see visions that spirit her back in time. 'We stood here and saw the wonders,' she intones. 'The whole ridge was covered with people who came to see the wonders. Many things have changed. The reeds are gone. What remains is that bush over there where Nongqawuse and Nombanda first met the Strangers.'

Carlos interrupted my reverie: 'The Unbelievers stood watching from the surrounding hills and the Believers were down here in the valley.' I tried to picture the scene – a feverish excitement in the crowd, hearts overflowing with love and goodwill; carousing and laughter, too, as the valley echoed with rapturous song. Mda writes,

> Ever since Nongqawuse had ordered her followers to adorn themselves in their finery in celebration of the imminent arrival of the ancestors, Qukezwa would not be seen without her make-up of red and yellow ochre. Even old women who had long given up the practice of decorating themselves were seen covered in ochre and resplendent in ornaments. They knew that as soon as the ancestors arrived from the Otherworld, their youth would be restored.

What suspense and what tragedy! No wonder Mda was drawn to the dramatic potential of this moment in South African history when the fate of a nation hung in the balance and supernatural forces were at play as thousands gathered to await their fate. Down here, the happy throng, drunk with anticipation; up there, the silent Doubting Thomases bearing witness.

The sky was growing darker and lightning split the horizon as thunder grumbled through Nongqawuse's Valley. A forest buzzard swooped low over our heads prompting the frenetic alarm call of a troop of vervet monkeys in the trees. The muddy pool, overhung with dark, tropical vegetation, emitted a strange and powerful energy. Rain began to click among the leaves and peck at the water. It was time to go.

---*---

That afternoon, I strolled from Trennerys up the hill to Qolora by Sea Junior Secondary School. One of the children in the playground noticed my camera and ran to the gate, asking to have her picture taken. Soon there was a chattering, laughing throng, tossing school bags aside and striking poses, then gathering round to see the results on my Nikon's display screen.

In *The Heart of Redness*, this school is the setting of a stirring music concert, a scene that holds a particular resonance for me. As a teenager, I was crazy about traditional South African music and frequented backstreet record shops looking for isicathamiya and maskanda, marabi and mbaqanga albums. The music of Ladysmith Black Mambazo, Uthwalofu Namankentshane, the Soul Brothers, Letta Mbulu and Abangani filled my schoolboy bedroom. Whenever the marimba band Amampondo played in Cape Town, I persuaded my parents to give me a lift to their concerts. I was electrified by the strains of the marimbas, the high-kick dancing and melodic singing of the young women, which transported me back to the Transkei ... a naïve, urban, white teenager infatuated with (fanciful ideas about) rural, black Africa.

At the time, I was a member of a filmmakers' workshop for youngsters and on weekends we used to shoot Super-8 movies, often with liberal, pseudo-political themes and stonking mbaqanga soundtracks. In the winter of 1983, the head of our workshop, John Hill, was asked to make a documentary film for the UCT Music and Ballet schools about the disappearing dance and song of the Transkei. Fellow student Richard Stanley and I were chosen to be the two cameramen.

We drove to Umtata in John's rattletrap Land Rover and checked in to a grimy, one-star hotel frequented by sex workers. Each morning we would set off for some remote village to shoot a performance of one kind or another. As honoured guests, we were served a meal when we arrived, typically chicken and rice, no matter the time of day. Then distant singing would begin, often a haunting, warbling melody initiated by one of the women. From behind the huts would appear a line of dancers wearing red-ochre isikhakha dresses, amacici beaded earrings and big iqhiya turbans, their faces whitened and necks weighted with beadwork. Richard would set up a fixed camera on a tripod and I'd be on the second, roving camera, shooting close-ups and cut-aways.

The singing and dancing built slowly, like an incoming tide, until eventually it washed over us, drenching us in its rhythms, the slow-clap punctuation like snapping branches, dust rising from stamping feet, the drums offering their deep baritone pulse. Moved by the beauty and the emotion, we often found ourselves close to tears. Sometimes, villagers played traditional instruments, such as the umrhubhe (mouth bow), uhadi (gourd bow) or usidiphu (friction drum), and there was always dancing by local girls – the amagqiyazana – shaking their hips and kicking their legs in joyful abandon. I remember one pretty teenager of about my age, with full naked breasts, clad in traditional skirt and face paint. She had an intoxicating, enigmatic smile. I could not take my eyes off her, and she stole glances at me, but the distance, context and language barrier were too great to even attempt a conversation.

Most arresting of all was the umngqokolo overtone, or split-tone singing. In this low, rhythmic style of throat-chanting, women create a resonant buzzing sound deep in their throats and then sing above it, each woman harmonising with her own voice and those of the rest of the group. In the novel, it is Qukezwa's split-tone singing that captivates Camagu when he attends the school concert. He registers it as a form of ecstatic synaesthesia: 'Qukezwa sings in such beautiful colours. Soft colours like the ochre of yellow gullies. Reassuring colours of the earth. Red. Hot colours like blazing fire. Deep blue. Deep green. Colours of the valleys and the ocean.'

A bell rang and the children of Qolora by Sea returned to class. Standing at the school entrance, I gazed out over hamlets stretching to the north and west. The simple rondavel structures were functional and elegant, timeless even: a circular building with thatched roof, small windows, single door, mud-brick and cow-dung walls painted with colours derived from clays. Heading up the coast as a boy, I used to long for the symbolic first sighting of a rondavel, like the first impala on a visit to the Kruger Park.

But the march of progress is changing the vernacular and the unique spirit of place engendered by the rondavel. Everywhere, thatch is being replaced by corrugated iron; the circular shape of vernacular orthodoxy replaced by the square and hexagon. Indeed, 'Bhonco does not believe in this new-fangled fashion of building hexagons instead of the tried and tested rondavel.' To me, such architectural 'advancements' signify a break with a former unity with the land, symbolised by the sphere. Then again, perhaps my nostalgia is misplaced and the mud hut, with its attendant lack of amenities, is a vestige of the geography of poverty and apartheid. With the rigid square comes modernity, possibility, improvement. Maybe I'm just a conservative, die-hard Believer.

Walking back down the hill, I passed the derelict Ikhamanga Cultural Village and stopped to take a look. In the novel, Camagu is outraged at Dalton's idea of creating a fake village where tourists pay to view aspects of Xhosa culture: maidens dancing, young men stick fighting, women dressed in amahomba dresses grinding millet. He finds it contrived, dishonest even, as it venerates a changeless, pre-colonial identity that is no more. Camagu would prefer to show local culture as it exists today.

I climbed over Ikhamanga's half-collapsed fence and picked my way between derelict rondavels, many with their roofs caved in: another government-funded project in ruins. Trevor had told me that millions had been poured into this development, which had been one of Rufus Hulley's dreams. 'All gone to pot,' said Trevor. 'The locals want everything handed to them on a plate by the ANC, even if they've got no qualifications, even if they've failed matric. It's the legacy of bloody Zuma. Such entitlement, but you can hardly blame them. Government officials drive around here in flashy new cars, drawing huge salaries but doing absolutely bugger-all to uplift the community.'

Walking among Ikhamanga's ruins, I was thinking about Bulungula Lodge, blueprint for what a sensitive Wild Coast development can look like. Founded by Dave Martin, Bulungula is off-grid and completely integrated into the local community. There are no fences, no locks; guests share communal showers and eat meals en famille. If it rains, you may find a goat, or even a cow, sheltering in your rondavel.

When I first visited the backpackers lodge some years ago, Dave told me how the set-up worked as we strolled through the adjacent village of Nqileni. 'Bulungula is part-owned by the community, so they're completely invested in its success,' he explained. 'This is the way forward for the Wild Coast: low impact, community-based ecotourism. If we don't get it right, the big hotels and mining houses will move in and destroy one of the most beautiful shorelines in Africa. I mean, where else can you find rural communities living like this?' His hand swept across a pristine estuary, long white beach, clusters of traditional huts and milkwood forest, all of it free of modern buildings, tar roads or power lines. 'It's about the people. It's about us fitting into a way of life that's been largely unaffected by the ravages of colonialism and apartheid. That's what makes this so special.'

Dave is fluent in isiXhosa and we stopped frequently to enquire after neighbours, play with children and pay respects to elders. We were invited into a hut and plates of umngqusho (samp and beans) were produced. Dave shot the breeze, talking about road repairs, clinics, lobbying for government support. It struck me, sitting on a tin drum in a darkened hut with mielie cobs hanging from the rafters above our heads, that Dave was a modern castaway – like so many who have washed up on the Wild Coast down the centuries – in the venerable tradition of those who stayed, put down roots, made a difference. Since my last visit, Dave has ceded 100 per cent ownership of Bulungula to the community.

I noticed that there were no homesteads near the shoreline. Anywhere else in the world this would be prime real estate, but the coast is fortunately protected from development. Historically, the Xhosa seldom settled along the shore, seeing it as a place of danger, treacherous currents, sharks and shipwrecks. It was also the realm of the white man who came from the sea to plunder and conquer.

Black, white and brown cattle lay on the sand like plus-sized bathing belles, chewing the cud and not bothering to get up as I passed. Apparently, they choose the beach because the salt keeps ticks away. I pulled out my camera and slowly approached one of the more attractive dames with a mottled khaki-and-white coat, stubby horns, a wet nose, floppy ears and doleful eyes. 'My, how gorgeous you are,' I said as I snapped a few portraits and she blinked her acknowledgement.

Cattle have always been at the heart of Xhosa culture. Apart from meat and milk, their hides and bones are used to fashion a host of objects, and their dung fertilises the fields and provides fuel and wall plaster. Cattle are an important indicator of wealth and status, and have always been a unit of trade with men procuring wives through the payment of lobola. The animals also have a spiritual dimension in Xhosa culture and are used in ritual sacrifice to the ancestors. A homestead's cattle enclosure is regarded as a divine and sacred space. Uhuru Phalafala suggests, in a *Mail & Guardian* article, that 'the cow's function is to connect, to bridge, to invoke. Cows exist in a liminal space between the human and the divine, the physical and the spiritual, the alive and the ancestors, the worldly and the universal.'

Continuing east, I passed a handful of men fishing with rods and boys ferreting in rock pools with their dogs. Fording shallow streams and climbing a succession of bluffs, I finally came to the skeleton of the wreck, its bows lodged against the beach and only a few iron ribs protruding above the waves. I waded into the warm water and ran my hand along its weed-encrusted plates, recalling how Qukezwa brought Camagu here on one of their romantic forays. She tells him how her father had thought the *Jacaranda* was a Russian ship come to rescue the people a century too late. After the Crimean War, the idea had somehow arisen that the Russian navy would conquer the British at the Cape and liberate the Xhosa – another millenarian fantasy in circulation at the time of the Cattle Killing.

I pictured Qukezwa clambering up the side of the ship – at that stage the wreck was still largely intact – and perching on a rail. She laughs in ecstasy as a gust of wind rips away her red blanket which falls in the water and is swept out to sea. Camagu overcomes his fear and scrambles aboard to join her. Qukezwa takes his hand and places it on her pregnant belly …

———*———

It was time to return to East London and catch my flight home. I checked out of Trennerys and drove back along the road I'd come, past sections that were in the process of being tarred. Although improved access would bring convenience to isolated villages such as Qolora, it was another step in the erosion of 'redness', inviting more day trippers and overnight tourists, more buses and taxis. Bad, potholed roads have helped keep remote corners of the 'old Transkei' embalmed, but with the rolling out of tar comes the seven-league boots of Eskom, satellite dishes, street lights … the square and the hexagon. Progress.

The Heart of Redness presents Qolorha in prelapsarian terms, 'a place rich in wonders. The rivers do not cease flowing, even when the rest of the country knells a drought. The cattle are round and fat.' Zim understands its paradisiacal quality, communing with nature each day as he rests beneath his beloved wild fig tree, watching the green pigeons and amahobohobo weaverbirds building their nests in its branches, and connecting with the ancestors who visit the tree.

By the end of the novel, the Believers have claimed victory and blocked the casino development. In a final scene, Camagu drives towards Qolorha on the road I was travelling:

> He feels fortunate to be living in Qolorha. Those who want to preserve indigenous plants and birds have won the day there. At least for now. But for how long? The whole country is ruled by greed. Everyone wants to have his or her snout in the trough. Sooner or later the powers that be may decide, in the name of the people, that it is good for the people to have a gambling complex at Qolorha-by-Sea. And the gambling complex shall come into being. And of course the powers that be or their proxies – in the form of wives, sons, daughters and cousins – shall be given equity. And so the people shall be empowered.

This is how it goes in South Africa. The forces of destruction are on both sides of the spectrum, whether it's Unbelievers who hold with 'reason' and embrace development along with its attendant corruption and despoliation; or whether it's Believers who place their faith in prophesies and cling to traditions that lead them down the path of conservatism, superstition and Aids denialism. The potholes and pitfalls are everywhere.

Nearing Nongqawuse's pool, I turned onto a lumpy track and followed it as far as my hired car would go, then got out and walked to the summit of a hill that offered magnificent views of the pool, mouth of the Gxara River and ocean beyond. The sea was flecked with white horses and stained reddish brown from the land's blood. In the novel, Camagu visits this spot and is similarly captivated: 'He is moved by the view below: the waves that smash against the rocks with musical violence, the Gxarha River that flows into the Indian Ocean with misty grace, the sacred ikhamanga bushes, and the pining Nongqawuse's Valley.'

Camagu had found a home and a sense of belonging in this corner of the Wild Coast. Like many a Romantic before him, he'd been disillusioned by a revolution that had failed to live up to its promise and he'd turned away from the city to embrace a pastoral idyll where his mind could find peace in a rural setting. It is fitting that he discovers a sense of belonging among people who have a long history of being rooted in a particular landscape, affirming the overlap of place and identity, living in tune with its spirit.

All around me, non-remembering cows grazed the slopes, oblivious to the fount of their demise and the slaughter that had befallen their ancestors. This valley has been a cauldron of history, as momentous and loaded as any other historical site in South Africa, as significant as Isandlwana or Spioenkop, Cape Town's Castle or Liliesleaf Farm. Perhaps greater than all of them, for this is the place where an entire nation was brought to its knees, an act whose repercussions lasted for generations – a necropolis at the heart of the Xhosa psyche. Mandela rose from these ashes like a latter-day messiah, embodying the kind of miracle once craved by his forebears.

In the novel, Mda describes how a delegation of chiefs from all over the Xhosa nation comes to consult Nongqawuse at the mouth of the Gxara. During the meeting, she tells them to look out to sea and there, on the horizon, they spy a great horde accompanied by hundreds of cattle, appearing and disappearing in the mist. 'The new people will come only when you have killed all your cattle,' she says.

Time frames and realities collapse and I find myself standing beside Camagu among the Unbelievers, staring at the faithful, doomed masses below. There's a commotion on the beach. We look to the ocean … and there they are! The ancestors are hovering in the mist, poised to come ashore, the beheaded chiefs Xikixa and Hintsa alive once more and in the vanguard. They have joined the ethereal horde to liberate the amaXhosa and the abaThembu, the amaMpondo and the amaBhaca. Luzuko! Glory be! The white-blanketed walkers have arrived to usher in a golden age!

As prophesied, there are now two suns in the sky. The blood-red orbs come together above the sacred mountain of Ntaba kaNdoda and the world is plunged into darkness. A violent storm sweeps in and only those huts that are newly thatched in preparation for the arrival of the ancestors survive as roofs are tossed to the wind and mud walls crumble. The valley is bathed in a strange, milky light as the Believers find their voice, loudly singing the praises of the new dawn. Up here on the hill, some Unbelievers are cowering; others flee inland to find shelter from the storm.

Out of the earth and at the mouths of the rivers, the deceased begin to rise, accompanied by their cattle. My heart, too, is singing. Here at the Gxara and at the Great Kei, at the Mbashe and the Xhora, the dead are wading out of the surf. A great throng of Believers pours out of Nongqawuse's Valley onto the beach. Cries of joy, ululation and the lowing of cattle reach us up here on the hill. Finally, the time of reckoning has come: the Unbelievers, the British and their collaborators will be swallowed by the ocean, taken back to the place of creation whence they came. The time for rejoicing is now!

I blinked a few times to clear my vision. The estuary emptied itself of memories as nature worked its timeless balm ... and I wandered slowly back to the car.

———✶———

ROCK, PAPER, PEN
Stephen Watson's Cederberg

In March 1973, my father 'went to the Berg' to hike with friends. From my mother's colourful description, I decided it was a faraway, alpine realm imbued with wonder and myth. Dad returned smelling of woodsmoke, sporting a salt-and-pepper beard and telling tales of high tablelands filled with contorted sandstone formations, caves of rock art, crystal-clear mountain pools for swimming and nights spent on a bed of fynbos under the stars.

In retrospect, I learnt that my father's trip to the Cederberg* was important for other reasons. Not only had it engendered in him a love of those arid mountains to the north of Cape Town, but it made an equally strong impression on his hiker friends. Among them was Breyten Breytenbach, who tells the story of their hike in *A Season in Paradise*, the travelogue of a journey to South Africa with his Vietnamese wife Yolande after thirteen years' exile in France. Their stay caused so much controversy and media attention that the Nationalist government forbade any future visits. When he did return, clandestinely and illegally in 1975, he was arrested, tried for terrorism and sentenced to nine years' imprisonment. *A Season in Paradise* is an aching love letter to South Africa: 'Why then do I write this down … because I love this soil, this land with its people, as the eye loves the light.'

The Cederberg hike came at the end of their frenetic, three-month journey and offered an opportunity to escape the press, the tailing police and the ruckus, 'to walk the soot and the nightmares out of our bodies, to find, without it being spoken, a point of silence again'. Breytenbach had visited the Berg several times in his youth. 'Always, even from the very beginning, as far back as I can remember, the Cederberg Mountains have been a place of refuge; but more than that, a place of magic, a prehistoric place, where there are no complications and little pain, where it is possible to touch the edge of the earth, virgin, undefiled, unknown, yet devoid of all peril; mountains without questions where the moon is born from a gorge and extinguished in the sea.'

---

* Watson and Breytenbach used the less common, variant spelling 'Cedarberg'.

Paging through one of my parents' albums, I came upon Dad's photographs of that journey, faded images of a band of smiling, carefree hikers set against the backdrop of ochre mountains. What had been their exact route, I wanted to know, and who were the other members of the hiking party? I sent Breyten an email with attached pictures and received a reply from Paris the next day. He identified the other hikers as the writer Jan Rabie, publisher Daantjie Saayman and wife Nici, architect Barrie Biermann, activist James Polley, poet Barend Toerien, Quentin Otto (Breyten's brother-in-law) and Oom Frederik, a mountain guide and one of the legendary, cave-dwelling Joubert family whose donkeys transported their baggage and alcohol – 'the holy of holies in their clinking bottles'. Breyten wrote that they'd set off from Welbedacht and hiked via Langkloof and Eselbank to Wupperthal. Referring to my proposed trip to the mountains, he said, 'The Cedarberg is a good place to dance the "Jerusalema" all by your good self!' and signed himself 'Blackface', although in the email he variously called himself 'Jôrs Troelie', 'the whitish monopolist', 'the prick', 'Che Guevara' and 'the Fool'.

Dad's photos show Oom Frederik saddling up the donkeys, naked men wallowing in rock pools, Breyten riding a broomstick, Jan Rabie (who himself wrote an evocative mountain book, *Droomberge – Sederberge*) identifying fynbos and the tired, happy band arriving at Wupperthal Mission Station. As a child, I was already enthralled (partly due to these photographs) by the idea of the Berg long before visiting it.

A few months after the Breytenbach hike, my parents took me on a long holiday abroad that turned my diminutive world upside down. We travelled to Europe for a three-month tour that culminated in Greece. My own 'season in paradise' is clearly defined as that European summer of 1973 and no journey, time or setting has ever quite matched it.

A couple of years after our Grecian odyssey, I visited the Cederberg for the first time. Dad had gone hiking once more, this time with Daantjie Saayman, Barrie Biermann and Oom Frederik (by then Breyten was in prison). The plan was for my mother and me to meet them in Wupperthal at the end of the hike, where we hired a cottage for the weekend. Both the village and the mountains captivated me, spiriting me straight back to similar landscapes in Greece. On the Sunday, we were due to return to Cape Town and Oom Frederik was to lead his donkeys back over the mountains to Algeria. My father suggested that we accompany him on the first leg as far as the hamlet of Kleinvlei. This was to be my first Berg 'hike' and I took it very seriously. I was drawn to Frederik, a gentle soul with a kind, crinkly face who talked continuously to his mules as we walked. I saw the old oom as a heroic man of the mountains and walked by his side the whole way to Kleinvlei.

There's a photograph of me standing beside Frederik, him in khaki clothes, veld hat and veldskoens without socks, me in a stripy matelot top, trying to look the part of the experienced mountaineer. We reached Kleinvlei, to my boyhood eye an impossibly romantic hamlet comprising a handful of thatched cottages cut off from the outside world by wild mountains. We said goodbye to Frederik and watched him and his donkeys disappearing over a ridge before we turned back to Wupperthal. The Cederberg had me properly hooked.

Stephen Watson's childhood introduction to the Berg was not dissimilar, his father taking him on a hike from Algeria to Middelberg hut in the early Sixties. In his essay 'In these Mountains', Watson recalls that walk and his feeling of joy at finding, after a long zigzagging climb, a pair of huts 'dumpy as farm-labourers' cottages', smoke blowing from the chimney of one. Beside the door lay a pair of Wupperthal veldskoens, a walking stick cut from a sapling, a knapsack made of flayed goatskins and, out back, a tiny kraal for the donkeys.

'In this wilderness of mountains, I never imagined the sawpit of cedar chips, smelling in the rain, the wet pine-trees, black as conifers, massed behind the huts, the sound of an axe in the middle-distance of the rainy afternoon,' he writes. These signs of habitation in the wild enchanted him, as did the smells, 'of crushed slangbos, charred billy-cans, cold sweet potatoes, goatskin', that would stay with him for the rest of his life.

In the essay 'Bitter Pastoral', he again expresses his love for the Cederberg, rejoicing in 'the singularly South African poetry in its place names – Krakadouw, Wupperthal, Welbedacht, Breekkrans, Kromrivier, Tankwa – words which have for me, each one of them, the power of a mantra.' For Watson, there was a close connection between the Cederberg and his image of freedom. During his younger days, such freedom took the form of a release from the strictures of school; later the Berg provided release from other, more complicated afflictions. In these mountains, 'one could forget, at least for a while, that one was black or white, male or female, English- or Afrikaans-speaking'.

In *A Writer's Diary*, much of it written during an extended stay at Kromrivier, he describes how the Cederberg exerts a powerful hold on his imagination. He thinks of the mountains as a kind of oasis: 'As such, it has the same effect on us, spiritually and psychologically, as does any island. It is a place where we make landfall, where we can find refreshment, and where we know our journey across the barrens of sea and desert are over.' He contends that arid places like the Cederberg, Karoo and Namaqualand are central to our national identity, and that the idea of oasis is at the very heart of 'the spirit of this place, which is also the definition of so much of the South African landscape.'

———*———

Stephen Watson (1954–2011) was a poet, essayist, academic and director of the Creative Writing Programme at UCT, a man of great generosity who touched the lives of many students for whom he became a mentor, confidant and friend. But first and foremost, he was a poet – one who had, in the words of poet David Tyfield, 'a faith in the written word's ability to bring the human out of the human'. JM Coetzee concurs: 'Whether writing about the loves of men and women or about walking under the African stars, Stephen Watson is a better poet than his time (the expiring end of the Twentieth Century) and his place (squalid, beautiful Cape Town) deserve.'

Shunning ideology, or the clamour of history and politics, Watson's poetry mostly concerns landscape and is elegiac, at times confessional, in tone, often imbued with a yearning for transcendence through a deep experience of place. He blends narrative and lyric elements, often with insistent, almost incantatory rhythms. Landscapes are presences in his work, possessed of great power and serenity, and deserving of his (and our) deepest attention and love. Watson's vocabulary is arid, his palette of words curtailed; his sentences are hard bitten and hard won, painstakingly chipped from the rock of language. He strove for a mode of telling that was plain; words proofed against history and politics, truths the hand could touch … and yet there remained a yearning for ways to represent the possibility of transcendence.

Since boyhood, Watson had tried to capture his feelings about the Cederberg using short, simple, declarative sentences without narrative. In a sense, not much changed throughout his writing career. That same quest for clarity and for a representation of his love for place remained through a lifetime of trying to interpret the mountain's 'verb-less message' in a writing that was lean and powerful. In a sense, it was Orwellian 'plain speak' applied to place. In the essay 'In these Mountains' he sums up his aim:

> To reply to that which first aroused one's helpless, spontaneous love.
> To make it present, in the continuing present.
> To say that that which was there was really there.

———*———

My first encounter with Watson was in 1988 as an undergraduate at UCT. I had recently returned from a six-month voyage from Lisbon to Mossel Bay in the replica of a Fifteenth-Century Portuguese caravel. During my time at sea, I'd written a number of poems and didn't know whether they were any good (they weren't), so I showed them to the 'sympathetic poetry lecturer' on the lower corridor of the Arts Block. What he made of my doggerel – much of it of the 'lithe, golden dolphins leaping for joy' school of nautical ditty – I do not know, but he was kind and generous and offered encouragement.

Subsequently, I attended all the lectures, tutorials and courses Watson offered, from 'Novels of the Spanish Civil War' to 'Contemporary South African Literature'. We became friends and when I was a postgraduate at Oxford, I'd ask for his help with my long essays. His answers came in warm, carefully crafted letters penned in tight upright handwriting that offered just the advice I needed. Thereafter, I taught the occasional class in his Creative Writing Programme, and we would meet fairly regularly to talk about writing, life choices and women – encounters filled with his dry wit and charm.

In the last weeks of his all-too-short life, I emailed Stephen to tell him about the idea behind this book and my intention to include a chapter on his Cederberg works, focusing on two books (*A Writer's Diary* and *Presence of the Earth*) and two essays ('In these Mountains' and 'Bitter Pastoral'). I asked him where in the mountains I should go to retrace his footsteps and he wrote back:

> You could go just about anywhere: Middelberg Hut, the entire area north of Kromrivier, including the trail from Sneeuberg Hut to the bend in the Cedarberg Pass where it emerges; everywhere between Sanddrif and Sneeukop. But my Cedarberg is, as you will have gathered, as much a state of mind as one specific place. Let me know if I can be of further help. There are days now, too many, when I am v. weak and otherwise without energy. But I can still talk! Just let me know as and when it suits; and if I'm too ill on the proposed day, we can always designate another.

Tragically, there would be no other designated day: Stephen's health deteriorated rapidly and he died of cancer on 10 April 2011.

It took nearly a decade before I felt ready to visit his mountain spaces. My intention was to spend eight days in the cottage at Kromrivier he used to frequent; unfortunately, it was being renovated, so I booked an adjacent cottage often used by Stephen's friends when they visited him during his long writing sojourns.

As I drove up the N7 one bright September morning, the Swartland was decked in spring greens and canola yellows, the mountains as clear as I'd ever seen them. After Citrusdal, I took the turnoff to Algeria, crossing the swollen Olifants River on a low causeway, its tea-coloured waters and white sandbanks marking the symbolic entrance to the Cederberg. I traversed Nieuwoudt and Uitkyk passes and descended into the Driehoeks River valley flanked by the fabled peaks of Tafelberg, Sneeuberg and Wolfberg. The road skirted fields of orange daisies and high mountain vineyards still without their spring leaves, past Sanddrif, over the last spur of the Dwarsrivierberg and down into Kromrivier Valley.

Pulling up at reception, I was dismayed to see signs of extensive redevelopment: new concrete villas, a restaurant, microbrewery, shop, events centre and, inside, perched on the reception counter, a stuffed mountain leopard. The main lodge owed more to Normandy bunker design than anything vernacular. Both Tanya Wilson (Stephen's widow) and Hugh Corder (his best friend) had warned me about Kromrivier's 'modernisation', but it still came as something of a shock. I recalled how Watson had written, 'I loved only those things which did not change' ('In these Mountains') and thought how appalled he would have been by the alterations to this place that was so precious to him.

The farmer's wife, Rinda Nieuwoudt, checked me in and directed me to Bokmakierie cottage, situated a little way upstream from Stephen's beloved Riverside. 'Our construction workers are currently using Riverside for accommodation and storage, but we'll restore it once all the villas are completed,' she said. I asked Rinda about Watson's visits to the farm. 'He used to come for months at a time, often in autumn or winter. Stephen and my late mother-in-law, Olive Nieuwoudt, got on very well and chatted incessantly about poetry. Whenever Stephen stayed, she would put a pink desk in Riverside so he could write properly.'

Bokmakierie was one of the farm's original cottages and fortunately had its back to the concrete villas mushrooming south of the river. It had a cosy fireplace, covered stoep, outside bathroom and braai. The front lawn stretched to the water's edge where a narrow bridge over a weir led back to reception. I unpacked and dragged the (not pink) table to the window where I placed my laptop, a pile of books by Watson and a detailed Slingsby map of the Cederberg.

Then I took a wander downstream to have a look at 'Stephen's cottage'. Riverside was a tiny, rustic shack made of wooden packing cases and painted cream and green, with a flat corrugated-iron roof, covered stoep, squat chimney and outside toilet. Stephen described how the cottage held the heat of the day for about half an hour after sunset, then turned into an ice box. As part of a larger construction site, Riverside was a jumble of building materials, paint tins, coils of rope, wheelbarrows and bags of cement. Its front door stood ajar and the builders were not at home, so I poked my head inside: brick fireplace, minute kitchen with a high counter, an alcove with a small bed and bookcase. It was a hideaway, a snug, perfect for a poet holed up for the out-of-season months – a place to be alone, to think, to create.

Before coming to the Cederberg, I'd written to Sandra Dodson, a former girlfriend of Stephen, who accompanied him on some of his sojourns. 'I have precious memories of times together at Kromrivier,' she wrote. 'Stephen would sit outside under the oak tree every morning to write in his journal (he maintained a very disciplined writing routine). Every now and again an acorn would fall on his head, something he took to be a good omen.' Only the stump of the oak tree remains.

I could see how Riverside's position had an influence on Watson's poetry. The cottage offered a view up the valley to the twin peaks of Sugarloaf and The Pup, which he recast, reframed and refrained in so much of his writing. The stream, boulders and causeway in front of the shack also provided recurring subject matter. Significant, too, is the fact that at sunset, Watson's witching hour, you face the light when viewing the peaks. This throws the crags and contours into stark relief; everything below is in moody shadow and it is no surprise, then, that his poetry is often, to borrow from art and photography, contre-jour.

In *A Writer's Diary*, Watson describes spending nearly three months (April to July 1996) in this cottage, charting each day's course, its moods and his reflections. It was a time of intense solitude and contemplation, days of walking the mountain paths alone, chewing on the cud of words and verses, finding ways to articulate his emotional response to the landscape. There were many lonely nights, his lentils eaten, his writing done, when he would set out to wander the farm roads. 'The act of creation and the work of mourning,' he notes in *A Writer's Diary*, 'have this in common: both involve a search, circular more than linear, for an object that often cannot be articulated in advance. This wandering, apparently aimless, is only the external form this search sometimes takes.'

Leaving Riverside, I headed east down the farm road, through a stand of bluegums and into the veld beyond. Clouds of insects filled the air, seeking the moisture of my eyes and lips. The luminous-green chamomile fields and neon-orange daises of the slopes transported me into a Van Gogh painting. With the sun low in the west, my body cast a Giacometti shadow that stretched far down the jeep track. 'At this hour one's shadow is, despite its length, almost solid on the bronzed, parched bed of the road.' Yes, Stephen, I hear you.

That evening, I lit a fire, opened a packet of salt-and-vinegar chips and a bottle of everyday Cab Sauv. I planted a potato and an onion wrapped in tinfoil among the logs and briquettes, then carried a chair onto the lawn. The fire was coming along nicely, requiring only an occasional poke as I sat reading Stephen's poems. The dusk shuffled closer; frog castanets filled the air. Once the flames had mellowed, I placed a coil of Grabouw boerewors and a pair of chicken sosaties on the grid. By now, enough black ink had leached into the sky to prevent me reading and fetching a headtorch required an epic trek to the bedroom, so I sat with the coals and the stars and imagined Stephen doing just this, just here, on countless nights just like this.

The cold seeped from the stream; all sound was muted by the rush of water oversheeting the weir. I was thinking about Stephen when he was my age, just three years from his own passing. Our conversations often followed a well-trodden circuit: me still unmarried, largely unemployed and possibly unemployable, still asking the most basic questions about life, writing, women, home, emigration, still finding precious few answers. How I longed for his sage ear. In journalism, you're taught to pursue the five Ws of a story – who, what, when, where and why. But I was increasing drawn to life's sixth, existential W: WTF. The wine bottle had emptied itself and the Milky Way had topped itself up, its stars pressing lower, pressing closer, so near you could almost reach up and brush the glittering curtain aside.

I turned in early. Somewhere in the night's corpulent middle, I was woken by an unsettling light that filled my bedroom. It was the moon. I got up and went outside for a pee, naked save for beanie and fluffy pantoufles, now dewly damp. Top and toe were warm; the rest of me trembled to the tune of the cold. Kromrivier's mountains formed a black dado line around the rim of the sky, enfolding the valley in a serrated embrace. The words of Watson's poem 'The Art of Solitude' floated into my consciousness:

> ... a man alone with his shadow,
> forgetful, beneath the Star River
> that even now, this very night, pours
> its great watershed of stars, the Milky Way,
> into the mountains west of Kromrivier.

I was up before the sun. Dawn and dusk were Stephen's most creative times in the Cederberg and, despite my dopey morning disposition, it was my duty to inhabit both of them for the sake of 'research'. I watched the light slowly change from canary to yellow as the valley appeared to tilt eastwards to welcome the sun. The river smoked its misty spindles and the air was alive with the industry of birds: nest-building weavers, golden bishops droning about like behemoth bumble bees, sunbird agitation, spurfowl scuffling for braai leftovers and all the while the white-noise trilling of turtle doves.

I ate my muesli on the stoep, then donned hiking boots and prepared for a day on foot. Walking was vital to Watson and he hiked many thousands of kilometres in all corners of the globe, but mostly on the Cape Peninsula and in the Cederberg. Solitary and introspective to the point of despair, and often weighed down by existential questions, Watson nevertheless found the act of walking to be life affirming, forging a connection between body, mind, spirit and nature. The essay 'In these Mountains' reveals his early passion for Cederberg hiking: 'If you have known it as a child, nothing can ever quite abolish the memory of what it is like, this rhythmical, sure-footed moving over broken ground, knowing yourself master of your own body.'

His essay 'One Foot-Note' (from *The Music in the Ice*) reaffirms the pleasure and healing solace of walking:

> Heading for the hills, hikers are also heading for a zone in which humanity is not experienced as a series of oppressions. On the trail one is free … One finds again a place where, not least, that rarest commodity of all, a measure of solitude, can be found … There should be a word, though, for that other altered state which walking, unaided by narcotic, so easily induces: a stepping *inside*, not outside of our own experience.

For my first, gentle sortie, I followed the valley floor towards Sugarloaf, giving my city legs the chance to ease back into a walking groove. My plan was to do the ten-kilometre Disa Pool loop, but given the rising heat and my lack of fitness, a shorter amble would have been better advised. Off I strode, relishing the crunch of boots, the swinging pendulums of my legs, trying to find the rhythm and the meter. Before long I was huffing and sweating.

The trail led through lovely stands of proteas, ericas, vygies, mint and fields of everlastings whose papery blossoms caught the sunlight. The riverbanks were thick with restios that parted to offer picturesque glimpses of the Krom. After an hour, I found a fording point, took off my boots and waded into the stream. The water was clear as glass, punctuated by the plop of acrobatic frogs. These Cederberg streams are precious arteries, home to endangered endemics such as Clanwilliam yellowfish, Doring River redfin and spotted rock catfish, of which I saw none. While sitting on a boulder, bathing my feet in the cold water, an orange-breasted sunbird alighted on a nearby branch, eyed me suspiciously and let out a string of chirrupy expletives before flitting off.

Further on, the valley began to narrow, its slopes covered in a chaotic salad of sliced and diced sandstone that came in shades of ochre and grey, its skyline peopled by pinnacles that looked like statues. Disa Pool, when it eventually wobbled into view, lay at the base of a waterfall where I drenched myself and slaked my thirst on delicious water filtered through beds of quartz, sandstone and natural teabags of fynbos.

Back at Kromrivier, I sat nursing my feet on the lawn with a notebook and a tall drink. The light had softened and the valley basked in a honey glow. I was thinking about Watson's love of mountain light and how it became a metaphor for lucidity and clarity of vision, but also for a kind of secular spirituality. His writing repeatedly charts the changing light conditions through the day: from dawn when 'the first light strikes the peaks and is held there, on the surface of the rock-cliffs, its red transparent as paper in flame' ('In these Mountains'); then, as the day progresses, the light becomes 'a property of the rock itself, a stone-light, burning from within, burning steadily outwards'; until sunset when 'one can recognise that the world is not merely revealed by light, but – this being my great pleasure, even love – actually constructed by it' (*A Writer's Diary*).

He goes on to explain why his work is filled with so much light imagery: 'Because love was, and is, above all, this great clarity, transparency of being.' And later: 'This light works as one might wish the imagination would work more often: it takes what is there, even in its poverty, and augments it in such a way that one is convinced that it is merely the latent, but true reality – the thing itself – that is being drawn forth. Thus the stones, the pines, the clouds this afternoon.' He wonders whether light may well be 'my embodiment of the revelation of God's presence on earth? Or what would, in another time, have been seen as such?' Pursuing this thought, he contends that Impressionist painters, Monet in particular, 'besotted as they were by light, were no doubt religious painters'.

The Impressionists also repeatedly recorded the ever-changing play of light upon objects through the day. In this sense, Watson's was a painterly eye, registering the nuances and shades with a similar, precise calibration. In his essay on François Krige in *The Music in the Ice*, he lauds the artist's clarity of vision, how he was able to stare long and hard at an object and then render its essence in paint. Krige was obsessed with mountainscapes, particularly the crags of Cogmanskloof near Montagu, rendering the cliffs in various light incarnations, reworking them in canvas after canvas. Watson writes of Krige: 'It is an image of the almost monotonous persistence of one who was convinced that he had made contact with the real world, perhaps the eternal world, even in a small corner of rural South Africa, and that all he could do thereafter was to revolve around the same few aspects of it that had first caught his attention.'

So too Watson, returning again and again with his limited palette to his narrow subject matter – mountain, weather, light, water, rock – and always with a keen sense of wonder. 'In these Mountains' expresses it more exactly:

> I know that I have spent half a life-time trying to capture such moments; and I know I will need another to do those like them justice. But even in this – no more than a mood, an effect of sun and wind and midday silence – I know that I have made contact with something no less real than anything else, and that I can do worse than continue to chip away at it, however much it might continue to elude such words as I command.

Watson spent a lifetime trying to describe those rocks and the light that played upon them, trying to articulate their 'presence'. Deep down, he knew the landscape would forever hold its silence, but that did not stop him. The futility of his task, I was beginning to understand, elevated it to a form of heroism – of a Sisyphean kind, no doubt, but heroism nonetheless. For fifty years he stared unblinkingly at the light *and did not look away.*

My next hike, Winterbach Peak, was more ambitious. The trail dispensed with any preamble and went straight for the vertical from the outset and I suffered accordingly. Fortunately, as always in these mountains, there was the aural balm of running water, and every time I crossed a stream I drank, refilled my water bottle and soaked my cap.

For a city slicker still daubed with the city's slick, the ascent of Tierkloof was tough. Stone cairns marked the way like goblin guides made diminutive by weather and time, ever receding, ever taunting, luring me upwards. The sun beat my head and back, my knees strained on the upswing of each step. I scrambled over large white boulders, bleached and bloated like beached whales. At every turn, it seemed, another wretched Moby Dick required surmounting. As I climbed, echoes of 'The Mountain Light at Kromrivier' sifted down to me:

> I saw those peaks that brought the range far north,
> the littered stone-mists of their summits glassed
> again by passing cloud-shadows. I saw the oxides
> of the rockfaces, boulders greyed by lichens, iron,
> all ripening in the air …

The path bisected wide bands of sandstone streaked like marble cake. All about me lay the shrapnel of rocks that had been blitzed, tumbling down the slope to form piles of rubble, some of them splashed with the faux blood of iron oxide and looking like rusted machinery. An atom bomb could not have done this; only the slow detonations of time and weather, the gods' immemorial double act, could have wreaked such destruction.

The incline appeared to be leaning towards me, forcing me to grab hold and advance gingerly on all fours, gritty sandstone underfoot and under hand. Glancing back, I saw my car glinting like a speck of mica far below. Just then, a Verreaux's eagle whooshed by, metres from the rock face, all weightless elasticity throwing shade at my clumsy ground hogging. Its primary feathers quivered as the raptor dipped a graceful shoulder and vanished round the cliff wall.

I topped out onto a sandy plateau and made my way along a path that wound through stands of proteas and toothy menhirs, recalling Watson's description of such uplands: 'I climb in the wide stillness, the creak of my pack and rasp of cleated soles on dry stone a cocoon of sound compressed by the hugeness of the wider silence' ('In these Mountains'). For the poet, experiencing wild places such as this was the embodiment of freedom, 'days of walking across high, upland country, the earth open to the sky, the sky raised, pushed back by the elevation of the peaks, and a wind like this one now, raising at our backs, rendering the body as I once knew it, momentarily: something almost bodiless.' My body was feeling anything but bodiless as I tackled the last, short ascent to the summit. Reaching a cleft, I peered through a gap at the world below, a sublime view deftly framed by rock with a bastion koppie – a Martello tower of enormous proportions – as centrepiece.

In his essay 'Recent White English South African Poetry' (*Selected Essays 1980–1990*), Watson laments the fact that local poetry is largely devoid of myth, symbol or any form of the metaphysical. Although he wrote a telling critique of Romanticism, particularly the form it took in colonial poetry, much of his own work is concerned with Romantic themes and ideas, and the quest for a similar transcendence. He certainly had an abiding interest in Wordsworth, whose preoccupation with nature, landscape, weather, solitude, walking and an articulation of various forms of the sublime were close to his own. As poet/academic Peter Anderson suggests, 'The lines in which he shaped the phrase that became the title of his third volume, *Presence of the Earth*, simply cannot be read without hearing and knowing Wordsworth and the Wye at Tintern Abbey.' As Watson intones in 'The Mountain Light at Kromrivier':

> Of all such things that you'll recall from these
> nine weeks, remembering, it is a light drifts in,
> and stills, that goes with you as you go home –
> a mountain light in which all things are stilled
> into their own, and it returns to you as you
> return, as once your own: the presence of the earth.

Romanticism is often defined as a sentimental return to nature by poets reacting to revolutions in the politics, society and literature of their age. Central to their experience of nature was a reawakened sensitivity to the genius loci, the spirit of place that welcomes the visitor but might also avenge any crime committed against such hospitality. English professor Dirk Klopper suggests that Romanticism can be characterised as aspiring towards oneness, wholeness, organic unity and, ultimately, transcendence. It attempts to overcome the Eighteenth-Century dualistic worldview of established dichotomies between spirit and matter, subject and object, content and form. This is nowhere more apparent than in Watson's 'A Kromrivier Sequence'.

A central concern of the Romantic poets was trying to understand 'the sublime' and finding ways to represent it. The development of this concept as an aesthetic quality in nature (as distinct from beauty) was first brought to prominence in the Eighteenth Century by Edmund Burke and Immanuel Kant. Both philosophers envisioned the sublime as a disorienting or overwhelming confrontation with a natural object. Kant suggests that we 'measure ourselves against the apparent almightiness of nature' and experience the consequent realisation of our physical helplessness in the face of power so much greater than ourselves. The Romantics were drawn to the conjoining of wonder and awe with fear and respect inspired by encounters with wild nature, culminating in moments of epiphany or transcendence, perhaps even enlightenment. For them, the sublime involved a dialectic between self and nature, in which the limits to our knowledge are laid bare and nature remains, ultimately, impenetrable to our full understanding.

---— ✱ ———

In 'Bitter Pastoral', Watson defines his childhood response to the Cederberg as an encounter with the pastoral. He contends that the traditional notion of pastoral – bucolic scenes of lush meadows, quiet brooks and shepherds tending their flock – has not died out in our culture 'because it is based on a constellation of human needs that can never be eradicated from the human psyche … to find a place in the world other than the world as we ordinarily know it'. It concerns an escape from reality in search of an ideal in order to nurture our psychological and spiritual wellbeing:

> To return to the Cedarberg and drink its waters again; to hear the night sound of the Kromrivier flowing through its sandstone bed – all this is to know the sweetness of that other world, of that bitter pastoral which is now and ever more the antithesis and necessary complement to our urban worlds. It is to know again that complete sense of being that a seven-year-old child once knew when he first saw the stream at Middelberg and understood, without further thought, that this was *home*.

It is natural beauty, especially encountered at a young age, that lies at the heart of Watson's ideas of freedom and spirituality. In later life, salvation was to be found in returning to those 'encounters' and, by extension, to try to represent or mirror that beauty through language, specifically poetry.

Watson suggests that the pastoral is more needed today than ever before. The idea of London gentry of a previous age hankering after bucolic country scenes has been replaced by the horror of ecocide – 'the systematic destruction of dwelling-places in the name of progress', as defined by Jonathan Bate in *The Song of the Earth*, a book Watson much admired. Like Bate, the poet deplored the contamination by humans of every corner of the planet, taming and destroying nature. 'So total has this domination become, so far-reaching its effects, that it has given rise to a form of loneliness that no one before our time had ever dreamed of.'

Hence the awakening of the human need for wilderness, for untainted places beyond the realm of industrialisation and progress. The pastoral ideal has therefore shifted from gentle, tamed landscapes to those, like the Cederberg, that are 'fiercely inhospitable, absolutely other. It is rock and sand, desert and semi-desert ... that nowadays seem uniquely healing, our most contemporary form of solace. They bear no obvious imprint of our species and its depredations ... Uncolonised, at least for the moment, it is one of those ever fewer parts of the world which still wear the face of Eden' ('Bitter Pastoral').

Where the Romantics sought a living host, a genius loci, to animate their poetry through a form of animism, Watson pursues a different consolation. His poetry seeks to vivify a world of ancient, worn, broken, oxidised rock, a landscape that is an embodiment of time and presence. In 'One Foot-Note', he writes about growing up in Cape Town adjacent to the immense 'otherness of geology'. As Peter Anderson contends, 'Geology, then, for Watson, becomes that sure and certain thing, the massive compound of accreted fact, whose great virtue is the sheer size and duration of the sample.'

Bill McKibben's *The End of Nature* helped Watson understand that man's ecological destruction of the planet had all but annihilated a traditional sense of nature. In a world of such comprehensive devastation, where even the weather could be altered by man, nature as a separate other could no longer stand for God. Watson was profoundly dismayed by the damage being done to that to 'which humanity has always turned in order to confirm its faith and verify its most essential hope ... The destruction of the natural world, eroding as it does that capacity for hope that defines humanity, also undermines the very concept of humanity itself' (*A Writer's Diary*). What is left, then, is geology, the bare rock of our planet that remains largely impervious to human despoliation, and it is in geology that Watson finds solace.

His writing contains infinitely more description of sandstone, shale and granite than anything vegetable (protea, restio, everlasting) or animal (leopard, klipspringer, dassie). *Homo sapiens* (other than the implicit, solitary gazer) is also largely displaced by nature. 'In these Mountains' records his sense of the Cederberg, and indeed the planet, as being a thing of rock: 'We start to feel the earth less as some organism wrapped in its blue mantle of atmosphere, but more as something like the Cedarberg, cobbled together out of huge plates of rock, salted and peppered by scree, flogged by sunlight, splintered by cold.'

He is fascinated by the harshness of the landscape at Kromrivier: 'There is no soil to soften the earth. Here it is all sand, littered shale, ironstone, gravel pits. The hardness of the summers, the poor winter rainfalls, have entered into the very colouring of the sparse vegetation ... The valley gives back no more than a stone can give when squeezed: it gives off dryness' (*A Writer's Diary*).

Watson is also attracted to the notion of geological time, in itself a form of the sublime, the kind of time that 'sleeps on the core of things, in the millennia of geology, unaltered'. He finds himself

> drawn into this other time, which knows no human purpose, in which all things have meaning not because they are situated along some imaginary line extending from the past into the future, but because they *are* ... This is, after all, one of the reasons why I come back to these mountains: to know again ... that the other time exists and can indeed be entered – this time that is pure presence.

On his deathbed, Stephen was asked by Hugh Corder about his thoughts on spirituality and the poet replied that one might find some of the answers in his essay 'The Heart of Albert Camus' (*The Music in the Ice*). In it, Watson repeats the contention, oft stated by Camus, that all who grow up in a colony grow up poor: 'Between this sky and these faces turned toward it, nothing on which to hang a mythology, a literature, an ethic or a religion, but stones, flesh, stars and those truths the hand can touch.'

Camus did, however, find consolatory meaningfulness in the spaces to which his heart gave its instinctive, pre-reflective allegiance – the sea, beaches, sun, sky and the evening light of coastal Algeria – in other words, the natural beauty he loved as a child. As Camus reiterates in *Betwixt and Between*, it was 'those two or three great and simple images in whose presence his heart first opened'. Watson agrees: 'In these mountain dusks I too am in the presence, once again, of that before which my heart opened at the beginning ... A writer needs these two or three images both to fill his heart (to make of it a reservoir) and to steady his heart' (*A Writer's Diary*).

Although Camus lived much of his adult life in Paris,

> he had to return to the Mediterranean world, whether in body or spirit, because this was his real country, his homeland, embodying as such places do the most profound meaning that attaches to place. Back in Algiers, he would remember who he was, rediscover the calm, the security, afforded by that in which one's identity is most deeply founded. ('The Heart of Albert Camus')

These 'first places' became a source – a wellspring – for creativity and inner renewal, perhaps even for a form of absolution. For both writers it was beauty, and the childhood memory of falling for that beauty, as well as a clarity of vision symbolised by light, that were more powerful than any later claims that ideology, politics or history could make on them. This was, 'particularly for those who live outside the embrace of the established religions, perhaps the most they will ever know of moments of redemption or grace' ('The Heart of Albert Camus').

A Writer's Diary develops the idea of a secular, spiritual writing: 'I could never give up on these attempts to know the unknowable, to name the unnameable; that there should still be this rage in me (not to be confused with anger) for a language which might restore to existence the dimensions of depth, and height, and presence.' Indeed, Watson's 'Kromrivier Sequence' was a struggle 'to discern what remains of the "spiritual" these days. At the same time I was trying to find a language that would not simply name or even evoke. I wanted it to incarnate.' His affinity with the Cederberg landscape brought him closer to feeling 'the reality of an ancient faith: the belief that either behind or within these physical features of the world there is something else, a presence that, with long and careful observation, can actually be apprehended ... And that it is among the prime functions of literature, as it is of art, to reveal these presences behind appearances.'

In the poem 'The View from Nowhere' he gazes up the valley at dusk and reaches for the unnameable: 'it's here before him, all else behind – the name / of that which no-one names, almost within reach.' But in the end, he is forced to admit that such moments of engagement with the sublime, with the mountain light 'which I love perhaps above all' and with the Cederberg's 'presence', are perhaps merely an echo of 'the residual, vestigial spirituality to be found in the phenomenological … In other words, a secular transcendence, a spirituality without spirit.' He is compelled to agree with a quote he'd read, stating that 'Immanence, not transcendence, is the truly post-human domain.' And yet … and yet this does not prevent him from reaching, over and over, for the mystical and the transcendent, for 'that which no-one names'.

---***---

One of Stephen's regular hikes was from Kromrivier to the Maltese Cross, an iconic sandstone landmark on the slopes of Sneeuberg. The round trip is more than twenty kilometres and, given the deteriorating weather, I decided to halve the distance by driving the 4x4 trail as far as Sugarloaf before proceeding on foot. I followed the jeep track past the Gonnafontein cottages and along the southern slopes of Dwarsrivierberg. The track turned loose and bouldery, the middelmannetjie bushes raking my 4x4's underbelly with the sound of a scrubbing brush. It was low-range and slow going all the way, past an old leopard trap and along the edge of the Sugarloaf's shale band until the track came to a dead end.

The clouds were low and the temperature on my dashboard read eight degrees. I donned windcheater, beanie and backpack and set off into a gathering gale, hoping to beat the rain to the Cross. After scrambling up a short incline, I traversed heathlands of perdebos and geelbos, heading west around the base of The Pup, its ramparts of sandstone, limestone and slate looming above. The path turned to stream and got mud-sloshy; the air grew icy and clouds settled lower, shrouding Sneeuberg and threatening snow.

Finally, rounding a bend, the thirty-metre Cross hove into view, perched on a crumbly plinth and presiding over a bowl-shaped valley. I approached slowly, reverentially, along a path of white sand lined with whispering dekriet. Finding a rocky seat out of the wind at the base of the Cross, I recalled the strange, doppelgänger incident described in *A Writer's Diary*. While sitting beside the Cross having his lunch, Watson noticed a man approaching with a broad-brimmed sunhat just like his own that obscured his face. Stephen took a swig of water and when he glanced back the hiker had disappeared. He stood up to survey the scrub, but saw no one. Feeling unsettled, he gathered his things and headed back down the mountain, wondering whether the figure had been a stranger or his double, or perhaps 'the hallucination of my solitude … and what was he doing there, at that hour, in this emptiness of mountains, on the edge of nowhere?'

Hunkered down, out of the wind, I saw no sign of my own double, or any other human, for that matter, but I did feel the poet's presence as I sat eating my apple and jotting notes. Was Stephen turning into my own genius loci, I mused? Had he become, for me, the spirit of this place, its host?

Walking back down the mountain, I was propelled by the wind, billowing out of the west, as the sun broke through the clouds and ignited The Pup. Stephen wrote that the /Xam tribe of San believed everyone had a 'wind' associated with them, and when they died this wind began to blow, removing their footprints from the earth. Was Stephen's wind bearing me on, driving me forward, blowing me home? As I walked, I recalled a description of walking these uplands: 'And always at such moments, the desire to live again. In the face of such beauty the sudden hunger to live forever, as if it would be enough – more than enough – simply to be able to see such things over and over, for another fifty years, another hundred, five hundred' (*A Writer's*

Diary). My eyes were stinging as I descended the last stretch to the car, faster now, pursued by rain squalls, chasing the failing light.

Back at Bokmakierie, I sat on my stoep thinking about the email Stephen had sent me from Kingsbury Hospital with 'the worst possible news', a diagnosis of virulent cancers. As Hugh Corder expressed it in his eulogy, Stephen felt that in a sense his illness was the price paid for how hard he'd driven himself in his intellectual pursuits, the emotional toll of forever choosing the hardest route.

I found myself listening again for mountain genii. Stephen's voice had become overlaid by others: that of my late father, of Breytenbach, the poetry of C Louis Leipoldt and anecdotes of Jan Rabie, and behind them the voices of the Khoi and San, singing this land into existence, into beauty. And behind them? Was there, perhaps, a presence? Was I beginning to discern the genius of the Cederberg, or at least its echo?

Walking back from the Cross, I had felt certain that Stephen's ghostly prints were still there on that mountain track and that the path itself was the spirit medium, the way. I'd been walking in Stephen's words, been walked by them. His verses had mediated my experience, measured my responses with their metrics. I'd been all feet and metre, verb and object, rock and way, stumbling along, lost in a cold front of residual grief.

It was Sunday evening and all the weekenders had returned to their city lives leaving Kromrivier blustery and empty – just the way Watson liked it. The wind moaned around Bokmakierie and I sat close to the fire. There was an emptiness inside me too, my mood layered with perennial doubts: my middle age, my South African worries, the choices made and not made, Stephen's spectral presence and his too-soon passing. I drank more, wrote less, ate a bit and went to bed with socks, beanie and an extra blanket, as one does on the Krom of a cold spring night. I woke some time in the heavy hours to the hoot of a spotted eagle owl. Hello, old friend.

'Hu-hoo,' he said.

'Hoo, indeed,' I said.

'Hoo too,' he said.

It felt comforting to have a feathery companion close by as I slid back into sleep.

The next day dawned clear, lifting my spirits, so I decided to drive the 4x4 mountain road to the Biedouw Valley to see its famed spring flowers. I set off early, the jagged rocks of Truitjieskraal casting long shadows and the vygies poking pink faces from the fynbos. I passed Uitsig farm, a cluster of cottages without roofs, their stone and mud-brick walls melting back into a sea of yellow daisies. In *A Writer's Diary*, Watson writes of such isolated, often abandoned, houses or oasis settlements. He was drawn to their beauty: drystone walls, crumbling kraals, ruins sporting the occasional cedarwood log squared off with an adze, perhaps an oak tree or two, and always the sound of water flowing perennially from some nearby spring.

'In such landscapes one of the more elemental human dramas is writ large, vividly. One discerns the actual drama whereby culture was wrested from nature – the rawness, indeed the bitterness, of the material out of which the human realm has been constructed.' And later: 'Almost no lyricism has so archetypal an effect on us as that which embodies, however indirectly, the original culture-making act. Almost nothing seems so authentic as that which still carries in itself some traces of the non-human realm from which it has been wrested.'

Beyond the hamlet of Matjiesrivier, the road led up Trekkloof via Keurbosfontein, an elegantly restored farm where a flock of sheep was emerging from a kraal, followed by a shepherd with staff and veld hat. It was a quintessential Cederberg scene from my childhood – my own 'bitter pastoral' – and I stopped to let the animals flow around my car and up the slope.

The gravel track took me past Wolfberg and Tafelberg, towering on the left, and Tierhoksberg on my right, the lower slopes swathed in flowers, the upper reaches bare rock. I reached Eselbank, the biggest settlement in the high berg, whose semi-detached cottages and vine pergolas line a sand road through the village. Most of the residents were gathered for a funeral and I glided quietly by. In 1973, the exhausted hikers of the Breytenbach party reached Eselbank in the late afternoon, made camp at the edge of the village, then swam naked in a nearby rock pool.

'The sun touched the wide mountain ranges around us, the cedar trees and the red cliffs, the wide basin in which we found ourselves and the sparse cottages and the squealing children and the dogs barking in the dust and the tall rustling poplars beside the stream,' Breytenbach writes in *A Season in Paradise*. The hikers bought a bottle of goat's milk, then picked 'Hottentot bedding' and other fynbos to serve as mattresses for their sleeping bags. Sitting around the fire, they sipped whisky and wine, talked, joked and sang long into the night. At one point, Oom Frederik broke into a hymn, 'harmonising with the dark and holding his hat on his head with a long forearm while looking deeply into the smoke'.

Leaving Eselbank next morning, the hikers made the steep, winding descent towards Wupperthal until, coming over a rise, they saw the mission station laid out below, 'small, almost shy little monuments to man's presence in this vastness: cottages, a church, patches of cultivated earth'. They bought veldskoens at the shoe factory founded by Louis Leipoldt's grandfather, Gottlieb, and had tea with the dominee. Then Yolande arrived to spirit Breyten back to the city where his father had fallen gravely ill and where packs of journalists and interrogation by the authorities awaited, followed by an imminent return to France.

I found Wupperthal undergoing extensive restoration. A recent fire had destroyed forty-five cottages as well as the town hall and school – both partly designed by my father and whose joyous inaugurations I'd attended as a boy. Restoration of the town hall was complete, but renovation of the cottages still had a long way to go and makeshift prefab homes served as temporary accommodation on the rugby field. I pressed on over Kouberg Pass to the Biedouw Valley where the spring flowers were past their prime, but I dutifully sat among the blossoms with my sandwich, along with a handful of day trippers from Clanwilliam, and endured a mouthful of insects for my trouble.

Returning along the mountain's spine, I stopped at Truitjieskraal to view its famed rock paintings. Such art adorns caves and overhangs throughout the Berg, most spectacularly along the Brandewyn River, at Stadsaal and Truitjieskraal. Until as late as the Nineteenth Century, the Cederberg was the realm of the Khoisan, as it had been for thousands of years. Indeed, farmer Rensie Nieuwoudt told Watson that one of his ancestors had been wounded in the calf by a San arrow in the 1840s. But other than rock art, the former residents have left little trace of millennia of habitation. Watson lamented the absoluteness of the San's absence from places such as Kromrivier. 'These are landscapes haunted only by their own geology. The sole signs of bloodshed are the faded stains of iron oxide in the boulders. It is only the peaks up ahead that survive as headstones for a land which is, in reality, one long cemetery' (*A Writer's Diary*).

However, Watson does perform a remarkable act of resurrection and re-imagination of San lore and culture in *Return of the Moon*, a collection of elegiac renditions of /Xam oral accounts, first recorded by linguists Wilhelm Bleek and Lucy Lloyd in the mid-Nineteenth Century. Watson's close association with the Cederberg, homeland of the San, made him well suited to this act of translation and interpretation. His subjects' intimate connection with the sun, moon, stars and weather, and their notions of a unity between humans and nature, and between psyche and cosmos, lay close to the poet's own heart.

I pulled off the track and walked up a sandy path towards a series of pinnacle rock formations glowing orange in the late afternoon light. Entering a sandstone portal, I meandered through a warren of caves and cubbyholes, burrows and overhangs, many of them adorned with exquisite, fine-line paintings: a row of dancers, an elephant, a large eland and strange, half-human, half-spirit-animal therianthropes. The ancient keepers of these mountains seemed palpably present, genii of this wondrous place echoing with pregnant silences. Were those footprints in the sand, leading me along the path, the spoor of ancients? Was that buchu, fat and wood smoke I could smell on the breeze? And could that be the sound of cocoon-rattles shaking on the legs of dancers around a distant fire?

---*---

The short postscript to 'A Kromrivier Sequence' is entitled 'The Spring above Rif Farm'. It's an important poem that distils, in a few apparently simple lines, ideas about art that were fundamental to Watson. I wanted to hike to Rif spring and pay my last respects, so I drove to Driehoek guest farm, set in the shadow of Tafelberg, where I met Lizette Burger at reception. She confided that she was a Watson enthusiast and wanted to establish a small memorial to the poet on the farm. Standing on the lawn, she pointed out Panorama Cave on the northern cliff face where she said the poet sometimes overnighted, then gave directions to Rif farm on a trail that led past the Groothuis and followed a fence line up the side of the mountain.

The first stretch was gentle, but soon the going grew vertical and I was panting once more: metronomic legs, throbbing calves, the metallic clink of boot on stone sounding like a well-struck anvil. I found myself reading the landscape as a Watson text. The paths were sentences tramped by my feet, words in the dust echoing off words on a page of Stephen's notebook, scratched with the nib of his pen in that neat, upright hand, scratched into the spirit of this place, into my heart. Metrical, iambic treading, the slow iamb, the simple 'I am' of this mountain trail. Each foot, each font, each spoor imprinted as I walked the Watson trail, the Watson tale.

The air was filled with the drone of bees and insects in untold numbers going about their springy business. A baboon barked to warn of my presence, his call answered by unseen others. I climbed into a world of unrelenting stone, regiments of weathered rock veined with manganese, slate, granite and iron, the shadows stained with the dark greens of lichen and moss. In 'Bitter Pastoral', Watson refers to this section of the Rif trail as 'one of those places where the world is pared back to its geological origins, to the stone which is the real floor of the world'.

The scene turned architectural, the formations presenting themselves in bastions, turrets and crenellations. Some of the rocks were smooth, marble-like and seemingly squared off, and I had the strange sensation of walking through the ruins of an ancient Mediterranean city. I noticed, too, the remains of burnt cedars – blackened scarecrows, some with their charred bark still attached, others smooth-skinned. The white settlers' greed for timber and the work of veld fires, many started by humans, had stripped the Cederberg of its eponym. As early as 1836, German traveller Wilhelm von Meyer wrote, 'All or nearly all the accessible cedars of commercial value are gone. What are left are either crooked, blemished, too young for the sawyer or inaccessible.' Nearly two centuries later, their continued existence is even more precarious.

On the skyline above, I spotted a young cedar protruding from a crevice, its roots cleaving to the rock, and I recalled that Watson had planted a cedar tree in these mountains on 27 April 1994. Despite his abiding distrust of politics, this small act of faith on the day of South Africa's first democratic election struck me as poignant – planting a rare and endangered tree of hope, high up where it might escape the fires and grow to maturity over the centuries to come.

Following Lizette's directions, I turned left onto a jeep track, then right onto the stone steps of Gabriël's Pass until I came to the remains of Rif farm. Lizette had shown me a photograph of the valley taken in 1934, but the only sign of Rif's fields and groves was a darkening of the fynbos. Just above the farm, I came to a stand of mature cedars, some of them blackened by fire. 'We find cedars with their scent of liniment, their contorted hard-wood smokiness, / drink sparse water with its tang of stone, its dry after-taste of quartz,' Stephen writes in the poem 'Cedarberg'.

Entering their cool shade, I had a memory of coming upon just such a glade one sweltering day on Crete, smelling the dreamy cedar scent and hearing the tinkle of a stream. I heard that same sound now, emanating from the spring that once fed Rif farm. Scrambling down a rocky incline I arrived at the spot, almost. Water gurgled just metres away, but the reeds and ferns were tall and thickly overgrown. I fantasised that perhaps Stephen's ministrations all those years ago had strengthened the flow, allowing the vegetation to thrive. Finding a place to sit, I retrieved *Presence of the Earth* from my backpack and read the lines from his high-Romantic 'The Spring above Rif Farm' once more: 'Traveller, mountaineer, passing through these mountains / and coming on this cedar grove to be delighted by the spring'.

A Writer's Diary tells us that on 14 May 1996 Stephen came here, knelt to clear the vegetation that clotted the spring's mouth and, using a knife, cut a place in the bank for a piece of flat sandstone so the edge would not crumble if someone squatted to scoop water. Then he scattered a handful of quartz pebbles at the mouth: 'white pebbles catching the light, shining as if freshly cut, / so the water would flow clear, still more purely from this spring, / and you'd continue on your way, even in the noonday heat / a clearness lasting in the thirst you've slaked'.

Watson's act had been symbolic and poetic, but also spiritual. In this postscript, the Kromrivier sequence of poems is presented as a set of newly cut quartz chips placed so as to make the water flow even more clearly, so that other travellers may better slake their thirst. Or put another way, life made clearer, 'purer' even, by poetry and by art. It is an act of faith similar to planting a cedar tree on voting day. Perhaps it could be viewed as an offering to the host, the genius, in the same way a devotee might make an offering to the gods or place a votive on a mountain shrine. 'I suppose all worship must have begun with such small, aboriginal acts of tending,' he muses in *A Writer's Diary*. 'In performing such acts, we align ourselves, consciously or not, with the object of our reverence and thereby hope to inherit its characteristics ... It could be a spring like this one, its flow of clear water from out of the darkness of earth into the light of day.'

Sitting beside Rif spring, another Grecian memory came back to me – of a sweltering day in the southern Peloponnese nearly twenty years ago. I'd come upon the remains of a small temple dedicated to Poseidon above a deserted cove. Marble slabs marked the spot where human sacrifices had been made to placate the souls of the dead. Sailors once rowed ashore here from their triremes to listen to the nearby oracle and pray for a safe passage southward to Crete or Africa. Climbing onto the marble plinth, I looked south to Cape Taínaron, the southernmost tip of mainland Greece, and it was then that I noticed the small, domed structure built into the ruined temple. Ducking inside, I found a rustic Christian chapel crudely fashioned from Poseidon's building blocks, like an intruder huddled in the abode of an older god. Beneath the stone lintel lay a few humble offerings: coins, candles and a small Byzantine icon, probably of St Nicholas, the patron saint of sailors.

I understood with a jolt of recognition that 3 000 years on, local fishermen still came here to pray for safe passage. Was Poseidon still deferred to in these matters, just to be on the safe side? As I crouched in the half light, inside a chapel within a temple, the span of millennia seemed both immense and negligible. I followed a gully down the slope until I could find easy access to the stream, where I knelt and drank from its cool water, imagining a line of sailors stretching back into the loom of time doing the same.

On my last evening, I walked the jeep track towards Sugarloaf once more. The sun was balanced on the snout of The Pup as I strode into the Watsonian landscape, the Watsonian light. The poem 'The Sugarloaf' reprises this walk. In it, the mountain is 'not at all the highest peak' and 'far from perfect', but it repeatedly draws him back to capture its light and texture, to describe how at sunset it 'grows weighted with a stillness that outweighs the stone / from which it's grown'. In such moments he is 'reminded of old words, words like "exalted", religious / words which can't be used nowadays, even for such moments.'

I stood watching the last rays enflame the valley walls, the Sugarloaf now blackened against a sky grown pale, like water spritzed with lemon. As the sun disappeared, the kloof slipped into deep shadow like a ship slowly submerging, the sky light of the surface receding as Kromrivier sank into night. Or, in Watson's words, 'This same peak darkens to blackest pitch against the west, which black then thickens while the sky evaporates to almost nothing in the solar fire concentrated above the horizon. Soon the dark of those western mountains will grow so dense that it'll appear compacted of some other substance – made of mountain more than the darkness itself' (*A Writer's Diary*).

The poet's many renderings of this valley at dusk lead one to believe that the act of describing became in itself a solace, a kind of home. 'It is these evening skylines that provide me, repeatedly, with a visual, spatial representation of what I would like a line of poetry to be.' He goes on, 'To write one verse that has both the clarity of line, the poise, as well as the weightiness, that density-in-clarity, of the western slope of the Sugarloaf when the sun has gone down behind it and the sky lifts as it begins to drain; to create, in other words, an aesthetic that would clear the consciousness in the same way that the sky above that same horizon clears the forehead.'

Klopper suggests that 'if, in the Kromrivier sequence of poems, darkness represents division and death, sunset represents that moment when day and night, life and death, consciousness and negation, stand in an articulated relation to each other ... a momentary cosmic stillness and harmony which induces a sense of the sacred'.

I turned for home, crunching back down a track still illuminated by the dusk's embers. The mountains on either side grew in stature with the coming night, as though darkness were a form of densification (of course I was channelling Stephen – how could I not?), just as the farm itself appeared to shrink in the dusk, its pinpricks of light only serving to accentuate the vastness of the wilderness enveloping it (I couldn't help myself).

In 'Descending, Late', Watson returns down this selfsame jeep track: 'It will be dark, in cold, in stars, / stone bedded in the road like iron, / before you reach the final pass, / see far below the small farm lights.' Here he confronts the spectre of his own death, the 'final pass'. His doppelgänger is now his shadow, walking beside him, a shade that has become one with the mountain, with the stone: 'This one who walks, half-shivering, / another, ancient, watching him, / its face a shade, itself a stone.'

The first stars began to sparkle, slowly brightening in their bed of indigo. From the river on my right came the throaty plosives of frogs and the executioners' cry of hadedas beating down the valley to their night roosts. I crossed the bridge over the weir – water gurgling beneath my feet, mountain reflections held in its glassy meniscus – and came finally to Bokmakierie where I sat on the stoep, not yet wanting to go inside, waiting for the full audience of stars to take their own seats. The leafless plane tree on the lawn began to acquire star decorations, like a frugal (bitter) Christmas tree. With the coming of complete dark, the Milky Way began to smoke in its ice and I recalled the words of Watson's /Xam poem 'The Girl Who Created the Milky Way': 'She threw them into the sky, she commanded them then: / "You ashes of wood, which I have held in my hands, / You will lie there, a white arc, encircling the heaven."'

Cold spilled from the river, spreading across the lawn and into my bones, while the Krom continued its sibilant susurration. Was that the spirit of the water I could hear?

> At night
> I listen to the river

> weave its many voices
> into one voice only,
> of water flowing
> channelled
> through the dark.
> ...
> There is
> something that moves
> through water,
> even as it moves,
> that is not water,
> does not
> move – and which
> I hear tonight,
> silent against
> all onrushing,
> not travelling
> through this mountain dark,
> and which I listen to,
> myself not moving,
> not wanting to

This voice, in his poem 'The Water Spirit', uttered from the stream and from the mountains, is what Keats and Bate surely mean by 'the song of the earth' and return the poet to the conviction that without this voice, 'we cannot lead a fully human life' ('Bitter Pastoral').

Later that night, a cold front swept over Kromrivier, rattling the windows and corrugated-iron roof. In the morning, I watched a fast-approaching cloud bank shot through with sunrays, the poplars bending like giant quills to the squalls, the flowers squeezing their petals closed and dancing a demented jig, some even losing their heads. Showers ghosted down the valley and on towards the brighter east to spend themselves in the Tankwa Karoo. In 'On an Ancient Theme', Watson writes of just such a morning:

> This rain that falls
> into a river that, quickened,

>   drains into the long rain-shadow, eastwards,
>   where it too will disappear;
>   these peaks that are stone, leached
>   of all but their stoniness, the ghosts of themselves
>   in a rain that blows white, still
>   white against them –
>   on mornings like these
>   one does not have
>   to go out of one's way,
>   or follow this path much farther, up-river,
>   to remember what it was, years past,
>   that first led one to poetry,
>   what it must have been,
>   in times that seem more ancient still,
>   that once led others
>   to stop, to pray.

In Watson, experience becomes poetry, becomes prayer, becomes a striving towards transcendence. I watched as a rainbow, its colours rinsed by rain, stretched a Herculean span across the valley to plant one foot on each slope. The swollen Krom roared beneath it, threatening to break its banks, as dervish leaves twirled along its flanks. The sound of guinea fowl testing their rusty hinges came and went on the guttering wind.

I packed the car in the gaps between showers, locked the cottage and dropped off the key at reception.

I drove out of the Krom Valley, past Sanddrif and Driehoek, descended Uitkyk Pass until I came to Cape Nature's campsite and reception at Algeria. This is where a seven-year-old Watson came camping with his father and from where the pair climbed the switchback track to Middelberg Hut. Watson was enchanted by the path, the cedar trees, the dressed sandstone masonry, the muleteers and donkeys they passed, and finally the two huts, looking like loaves baked from stone and mud.

I donned my backpack and started walking, through a stand of eucalyptus trees, over a wooden bridge and up the side of Middelberg West. The morning had turned windless and cloudless – a thing of blue magnificence. 'But sometimes a day comes back,' Watson writes. 'The sky above it a blue, unbroken shell from which the world has been poured anew … It is the blue of the blueness recalled from other Septembers … And we walk in that light, bereft of our old questions, unfinished journeys, conscious only of this which links us to other, earlier years, this moment of our homecoming … No longer do we feel ourselves to be nothing in relation to so much existence turned in on itself … I know that I must always return to a day like this, however rare, if I am to remain fully alive.' ('In these Mountains')

After two hours, I emerged into grassy uplands along a path that meandered through a valley until, rounding a bend, I came upon the two huts, 'dumpy as farm-labourers' cottages', looking just as I'd imagined them,

sandstone loaves perfectly in harmony with their rocky surroundings. One of them was derelict, its roof caved in; the other was low-slung with corrugated-iron roof and pane-less windows, its floor – when I peered through the barn door – covered in slangbos bedding for campers. Behind it stood the tall pine trees I had expected, below it the stream, running between oak trees. I crouched to drink from its water, remembering Watson's (and Camus's) words:

> I had never tasted water like this, the coldness flowing in it like another substance, tasting of rinsed stone, not water. Nor in all my seven years had I ever seen anything like the fresh-washed grain

of its bed ... Henceforth this place, Middelberg, would be sacred to me, as are all those places and occasions where we first grow aware of the beauty of the world. Although I did not know it then, henceforth it would be moments like these – and often nothing but these – which would establish my deepest, most lasting allegiance to the world. ('In these Mountains')

For Watson, these unchanging mountains provided a timeless sense of belonging, a form of possession 'which exists not through title-deed, but by right of vision', a world 'as much a matter of mind as geography'. Like my own love of the Cederberg, his had been engendered at a very young age and would stay with him until the end.

It was time to head down the mountain, join the dusty road to the N7 and back to Cape Town. I took the path in the softening light, imagining a seven-year-old Stephen up ahead, striding towards the lip of the descent, and ahead of him, my father, chatting to Breyten as they threaded their way among the protea bushes, and ahead of them, Oom Frederik and his line of donkeys, leading me back into my own memories of the Cederberg and Greece and other places of the heart, waypoints and anchors that tied me to particular geographies with an umbilical cord of reverence and love that was beyond the telling of it. The sun was low; I leant towards the light; my boots sounded their crisp beat on the path.

———✳———

PRAESIDIO

In her article 'Erotics of Place', novelist Deena Linett contends that the human body must occupy some*where*, that it belongs, however momentarily, to that place which in some sense it recognises. Instinctive responses to place are perhaps a function of our inquisitive minds and though we may not be conscious of our examination of the details of our environment, we are constantly looking, listening, evaluating. Linett goes on to suggest that the human need to appreciate is an expression of our affinity with the world of which we are a part, a surge of gratitude that we are alive and aware. The erotics of place runs counter to man's impulse to conquer and can lead to a rapturous response to one's environment.

Looking back over my literary journeys, I've come to think of each one as a secular pilgrimage to loved places made sacred by literature and experience – paying homage, and sometimes rapturously responding, to environments held dear by authors, places of the heart that enshrine their (and my) childhood, and embody their (and my) cultural tastes and origins. I've come to see how all of us understand and define ourselves using landscapes, and how we carry maps – only loosely relating to real maps – within us. These are not dissimilar to songlines or story paths, and are filled with a host of evocative elements, memories and emotions. They are our personal geographies, coloured by literature and by the things we have seen and felt in those locales. The places that are potent to us, that move our spirit and yield up moments of grace, tell us about ourselves and allow us to know and appreciate things that no other environment is able to.

The spirit of place is invested in the flora and fauna, the lie of the land; it can be sensed in the wind, smelt in the earth's musk, overheard in the quirky dialect of a local. It is there in the chime of a distant church bell, the bleat of sheep returning to their kraal, the whisper of wind in the cedars. When you know it and when you feel it, there is an instinctive reaction. To truly get to know a place, you need to listen to the voices of the past, the voices of books and narratives, harvesting them in service to your understanding of the land. Literature about place can transform your experience of the locale, offering greater depth, understanding and emotional engagement. You get to walk in the big, complicated, inspiring boots of artists who have devoted much time and thought to interpreting place.

Prior to the end of apartheid, there was little black writing about landscape, other than in relation to dispossession. Most literary topophilia was produced by white men – all of them products of their class and privilege and wearing a particular set of (often Romantic) spectacles. Indeed, landscape descriptions can offer up as much cultural and political information as they do about geography or topography, with authors such as Reitz and FitzPatrick assuming a white ownership of the land that allowed no alternative. Nevertheless, the black rural idyll persisted in various forms of local pastoral with the kraal, rather than the plaas, as locus. This changed after 1994 with travel writers such as Sihle Khumalo, Lesego Malepe and Fikile Hlatshwayo, and of course in Mda's novels.

In Watson, we have a writer who, even during the height of apartheid, kept his gaze fixed on the landscape. In this respect, he is a version of Michael K, who tells himself, 'Enough men had gone off to the war saying the time for gardening was when the war was over; whereas there must be men to stay behind and keep gardening alive, or at least the idea of gardening.' Liberal and humanist in his inclinations, Watson continued to tend the garden with his landscape poetry throughout the dark days.

———✳———

During my journeys through the texts and terrains of this book, I became increasingly aware of the authors' implicit, at times explicit, appeal to conservation, to halting or deflecting the march of 'progress' … of change in its many guises. The sanctity and genius of place is everywhere under threat in South Africa. On my wanderings, whenever I encountered damaged land – power stations, mine dumps, peri-urban sprawl, polluted spaces – I felt queasiness and anger, sometimes even shame, and registered the desecration as a form of blind and blinding self-harm.

Wild places, old places, places of character and depth are menaced by the multiple threats of development, commercialisation, greed, corruption, crime and neglect – forces that disconnect people from the environments they hold dear. The cult of endless economic growth and consumption has left a trail of destruction across South Africa's landscapes, ecosystems and cultures. Thankfully, the places celebrated in this book have escaped the worst of these ravages and retained a degree of wildness, for now.

The essayist Scott Russell Sanders, quoted in the journal *Windfall*, says: 'Many of the world abuses – of land, forest, animals and communities – have been carried out by people who root themselves in ideas rather than places.' A literature of place is one that cherishes particular locales and conveys the spirit of place in such a way that should make its desecration unthinkable. Even when focused on a specific area, it is nevertheless able to address broad social and environmental issues and be emblematic of some of the greatest challenges of our age.

We recall the Wordsworthian idea of the sanctity and vulnerability of the spirit of place and how a host's vengeance for 'killing the albatross' may come in many guises, be it a cyclone, virus, flood or wildfire. Nature, for Wordsworth, represents what we might now call an ecological unity that it is our duty to preserve and protect. If we modernise the Romantic notion of awe in the face of the sublime, a contemporary 'ecological sublime' might serve to remind us of the importance of a sense of wonder at a time when nature is everywhere being tamed or destroyed. In our age of ecocide, we need less ego and more awe, enchantment and perhaps even some of Watson's striving for transcendence through nature.

In her article 'Dissolution and Landscape in Olive Schreiner's *The Story of an African Farm*', Hannah Freeman observes that imperial pastoral narratives, such as those of Rider Haggard, viewed the natural world as a resource to be mastered and exploited for the brave (British) adventurer. She notes how Schreiner exposed this practice as harmful not only to the landscape and the colonised, but also to the coloniser. Schreiner deplored the senseless slaughter of wildlife and called for the establishment of game reserves. She also cautioned against imperial power with its tendency to dominate and segregate, and instead celebrated the Karoo of her imagination as a form of inclusive antidote. Indeed, her great book can be viewed as an ecological text in that it blurs the hierarchy of human, fauna, flora and mineral, forcing us to acknowledge that we are all part of Nature.

One of the most problematic and racist scenes in *Jock of the Bushveld* involves a meeting between FitzPatrick and a rival 'Bushman-Hottentot' storyteller. One of Jantje's tales concerns an incident in which a man robs a honeyguide bird of too much honey, and must subsequently offer compensation, before nature forgives him. FitzPatrick can't understand Jantje's 'garble' of fancy and superstition; however, critic Stephen Gray argues that this is perhaps the most beautiful and moral story of the entire book: 'Jantje's fable about how to live as part of the balance of nature and harvest man's share of it effectively is abundantly clear, and is far more in tune with modern humankind's view of ecology and preservation than FitzPatrick's own aggressively exploitative attitudes.'

Gray goes on to note that, to his credit, FitzPatrick had a change of heart and worldview. In 1909 he wrote an article, 'Jock of the Bushveld and Those Who Knew Him', in which he called for a more conservation oriented approach to nature and strict controls on poaching and trophy hunting – a belated recognition that the game was not endless and that limits on human greed needed to be set.

The natural conclusion to Marais's pioneering research on primate minds is the idea that the differences in psychology between humans and the other great apes is too small to justify their different treatment. This opens the door to granting apes the same ethical consideration as humans. The wider implication for the conservation of fauna and habitats is immediately clear. It's the kind of protection of the natural world that Matthee alludes to in *Circles in a Forest* and passionately campaigned for during her life. She presents Old Foot as symbol of the forest and of conservation, standing as counterpoint to the rapacious quest for ivory, timber and gold. Matthee's novel is a lament for the loss of the great elephant herds of Knysna and a cry for the preservation of indigenous forests. Her books also recognise the contribution of woodcutters – people who lived in tune with nature – to the culture and spirit of the forest, just as Bosman's tales honour the bushveld world of the Marico farmer.

Life & Times of Michael K offers a frugal metaphor for a way to survive in a country ravaged by civil strife. An isolated man, alone on a Karoo farm, lowers a teaspoon into a well to retrieve water in order to irrigate a meagre subsistence crop. Perhaps this is also a metaphor for how to live in a post-apartheid, post-*Disgrace*, South Africa? Maybe in a nation plagued by corruption and criminality, state capture and disintegration, one survival option might be to adopt a frugal, self-reliant, off-grid existence – a humble, agrarian life beyond the bounds of any camp or ideology. Not the colonising of a Robinson Crusoe (killing and taming goats, subjugating Man Friday), nor the establishment of a new order that replicates the old regime's thievery. Better a gardener and nurturer than an old-style farmer or settler be. Gardening for Michael is an existential position that places him outside politics, outside history, outside time itself. He is an escape artist who refuses to be defined and, as such, stands for intellectual and artistic freedom, even (or especially) in a time of war.

The novel also offers an ecological message. Michael thinks 'only of growing enough for the seed not to die out' and pumping from the borehole only as much water as his garden needs. He wants what is best for the land and builds his hut of biodegradable material that will melt back into the soil. Academic Derek Wright suggests that in *Michael K*, Coetzee is concerned with founding 'a new myth of the land: the myth of earth minus man, or at least of Western Technological Man (white), as distinct from Vegetarian, Macrobiotic Man (here, black), who eats only what nature supplies and is not damaged by'.

Saving wild places is also central to *The Heart of Redness*. Mda recognises that in post-apartheid South Africa, decisions about land, its ownership and uses are critical to our future. He understands that in a region like the Wild Coast, protecting the natural environment is essential for the spiritual, cultural and psychological wellbeing of its inhabitants. Mda posits that a sensitive, controlled form of ecotourism – rather than the exploitation symbolised by a casino complex – is the way forward for the Wild Coast.

Building a sustainable future requires addressing the needs of the people without compromising the needs of future generations. It's an indigenous, postcolonial environmentalism that balances the requirements of humans and the land, and seeks to retain the unique spirit of place. The victory of Camagu and the Believers results in a village-owned cooperative venture and is a triumph for those who respect the land. It's an example of the kind of people-centred conservation that is required throughout Africa, where local communities need to be integrally involved in, and benefit from, protection of the land.

The Heart of Redness presents Camagu and Qukezwa as contemporary incarnations to Nongqawuse. The goals and vision of the young prophetess were no match for the power of imperial Britain; however, the two modern heroes do have the tools to protect their community. In so doing, they provide hope for similar rural societies and environments facing the onslaught of global capital.

PLACE - SOUTH AFRICAN LITERARY JOURNEYS

Great journeys enacted on a sublime stage form an integral part of our nation's defining narrative, from Khoi migrations to the Great Trek odyssey and Mfecane diasporas, pioneer and transport-rider journeys, Anglo-Boer War raids, migrant-worker and miner narratives, and the peregrinations of the forcibly removed under apartheid. All these stories are set against the epic backdrop of the land, whose splendour is embedded in our national anthem – those 'ewige gebergtes / Waar die kranse antwoord gee'. I could spend the rest of my days chasing such cultural and literary lines, walking in the footsteps of Poppie Nongena and Sol Plaatje, through the pages of *Cry, the Beloved Country* and *The Quarry*, following the highways of *To Every Birth Its Blood* or sailing to the island of *The Keeper*.

National identities are forged around land narratives. Given our history of colonial and apartheid dispossession and the ongoing 'land question', this notion is as potent as ever. However, each individual's identity is an agglomeration of personal responses to the land, be it through childhood memories of special places, through a Pierneef painting or a Langenhoven poem, a Zulu troubadour song or a hike in the Drakensberg. Personal myths and narratives about land and homeland – forged in one's very own spiritual terroir – are continually being formed.

This book was partly conceived as a love letter to South Africa, an excuse to spend a lot of time on the road exploring favourite haunts. Over the course of a long period of research, my vision about the country's future has darkened. Much of what I hold dear, and sought to venerate in these pages, is under threat. Crime, and rural crime in particular, is emblematic of the problem. The rendering unsafe of pastoral and wild South Africa – traditionally a refuge from city strife – leaves nowhere secure. What remains when safety is taken away? We move towards a low-grade form of warfare, a narrowing of horizons, even if it is only waged in the head and heart.

A counterweight to my topophilia is Coetzee's injunction to not get too hung up on the land. 'Better to cut yourself free and hope the wounds heal,' he writes in *Summertime*. My own concerns about South Africa's future and flirtation with emigration provided the counterpoint to these journeys. Like Coetzee, like Watson, I have been experiencing a heartstring tug of war: to leave or not to leave this promised, beloved, broken land.

My thoughts have been coloured by the books I've been immersed in. Journeys to Mpumalanga, the Waterberg and Marico reignited my love of the bushveld in all its guises, but stories of farm murders, hollowed-out municipalities and corrupt land redistribution that has seen the Zanufication of once prosperous farms cast a shadow. While Mda paints a positive picture of a local community fighting off the depredations of big capital, the story elsewhere on the Wild Coast has been darker with unscrupulous miners bent on destroying the land. But there is hope: large swathes of Knysna Forest now form part of a national park, the heart of the Cederberg has gained protected status, rural communities have taken up the fight for environmental justice in many regions, and plenty of Karoo farms are remote enough to withstand most of the ravages.

But my doubts remain. Colonial South Africa destroyed so much of what indigenous South Africa held dear, and it seems inevitable that one way or another, whether by intent or as collateral damage, the new custodians will destroy much of what conservationist South Africa holds dear. Such is history. I am a product of (white) pax apartheid, and (rainbow) pax Mandela – paxes that were largely won by force. Now that pervasive violence and corruption are back, what does it mean for one's relationship with the land, for one's engagement with its spirit?

'Ah, but your land is beautiful,' they say, but is beauty enough in this land of damaged people? Through Watson, I've begun to believe that perhaps beauty *is* enough. This place is home, and one's attachment to the first places one learns to love, one's sacred places, is unshakeable. From Odysseus to the present day, homecoming is synonymous with peace and healing. For the traveller, even an inveterate traveller like me, home still offers the clichés of belonging and wholeness. All the writers dealt with in this book, whether born into those landscapes or not, are patently, palpably at home in them. Their passionate attachment underlines, as Watson avers in *A City Imagined*, 'why it is that the word "home" is freighted with as many connotations as any in the language; and why its polar opposite, exile, has always been regarded as perhaps the most bitter of the deprivations a human being can be forced to suffer'.

When, in *A Writer's Diary*, Watson contemplates leaving South Africa, he is reminded that the bond he feels for the Cape is similar to the 'primordial, tenacious' bond between a child and its mother. 'In how many lives, though, has this same bond been transferred, then re-enacted, in relation to a landscape ... This is borne out by the crisis that has closely followed whenever you've considered – seriously considered – the possibility of breaking that attachment.' For him, the spirit of place and the bonds forged by landscape were enough to forestall emigration.

My thinking about the land brought me reluctantly, via many byways, to the notion of patriotism. How much is love of country about landscape and how much about people? If it's only about the land, is it truly patriotism: beautiful land, troubled citizens? These issues become thornier in a kleptocratic state like South Africa. How to separate love's grain from cynicism's chaff? A nation's worth is surely underpinned by its cultural legacy and natural beauty/bounty; hence the importance of these writers who are implicitly patriotic in their transmogrification of (our) place into gold through the alchemy of art. Their writing elevates, deepens and transforms our understanding and love of the land. To borrow from Watson's 'Rif Farm' poem, these texts are quartz chips placed at the spring of culture, enhancing the clarity of its flow.

My own 'patriotism' is irrigated by these waters. Perhaps there is a lesson in localism here: to be locally patriotic, to love the spirit of a certain corner of the land rather than biting off the whole nation, which is indigestible. I can be fiercely patriotic about a stream or a forest or a local community, and yearn to 'belong' to it. Like Schreiner, who felt a sense of disempowerment in the new South Africa of the early Twentieth Century, and turned away from politics and urbanity, engaging instead with landscape and nature as a way of existing here, of being content here. Another option is to hunker down like Michael K, find niches, cathartic retreats, places with cracks that let the light in: locales that offer beauty and solace, and deserve our full immersion, veneration and protection.

In *The Heart of Redness*, the whites who are bent on selling their Qolorha properties and emigrating to Australia and New Zealand remonstrate with Dalton: 'You are the only one who will remain in this mess, John ... Everyone is leaving.' 'Not everyone,' says Dalton ... 'I am staying here ... I am not joining your chicken run. This is my land. I belong here. It is the land of my forefathers.' This commitment to a local ecosystem and indigenous culture is set against the forces of capitalism that seek to neutralise endemism and commodify the land. In this light, reimagining a specific place through literature, appreciating and understanding its uniqueness, is a weapon in the fight for preservation.

The authors who inspired my literary journeys have all become genii loci,

PRAESIDIO

custodians of landscape memory. It is to the shrines of their texts that I have been drawn for a fuller appreciation of the heart-land and I must assume that, barring a radical change of heart, I will go on making such pilgrimages until I am no longer able to do so. When one's roots are sunk too deep, and one's attachment to the land is too strong, then leaving becomes a species of impossibility.

> The car is packed, the tank is full once more,
> my Slingsby maps are in the glove compartment,
> my tent, sleeping bag and surfboard are in the back,
> an old kitbag filled with books sits on the seat beside me.
> And so it's time to take the road,
> to take the road once more.

———※———

BIBLIOGRAPHY

GENERAL WORKS (INTRODUCTION AND CONCLUSION)

Basso, KH. 'Wisdom Sits in Places: Notes on a Western Apache Landscape' in Feld, S. and KH Basso (eds). *Senses of Place* (School of American Research Press, Santa Fe, 1996)

Bell, MM. 'The Ghosts of Place' in *Theory and Society* 26, 6 (December 1997)

Bosman, HC. 'Paris: Sidelights and Half-Laughs' in *The South African Opinion* 3 (April 1936)

Breytenbach, B. *A Season in Paradise*, translated by R. Vaughan (Persea Books, New York, 1980)

Bulpin, TV. *Discovering Southern Africa* (Discovering Southern Africa Productions, Muizenberg, 2001)

Chatwin, B. *The Songlines* (Vintage, London, 2005)

Collocott, EEV. 'The Spirit of Place' in *The Australian Quarterly* 23, 2 (June 1951)

Consiglio, MC. 'Art and the Spirit of Place: DH Lawrence Translates Giovanni Verga' in *Études Lawrenciennes* 44 (2013)

Durrell, L. *Spirit of Place: Letters and Essays on Travel* edited by AG Thomas (EP Dutton & Co, New York, 1971)

Friedman, AW. 'Place and Durrell's Island Books' in *Modern Fiction Studies* 13, 3 (Autumn 1967)

Heffernan, JAW. *Hospitality and Treachery in Western Literature* (Yale University Press, New Haven, 2014)

Hillis Miller, J. *Topographies* (Stanford University Press, Stanford, 1995)

Lawrence, DH. *Studies in Classic American Literature* (Thomas Seltzer, New York, 1923)

Linett, D. 'Erotics of Place' in *The Georgia Review* 67, 3 (Fall 2013)

Macfarlane, R. *The Old Ways: A Journey on Foot* (Penguin, London, 2013)

Mandoki, K. 'Sites of Symbolic Density: A Relativistic Approach to Experienced Place' in Light, A. and J Smith (eds) *Philosophy and Geography III: Philosophies of Place* (Rowman & Littlefield Publishers, New York, 1998)

Meynell, A. *The Spirit of Place and Other Essays* (CreateSpace Independent Publishing Platform, February 2017)
Moffett, H. (ed) *Lovely Beyond any Singing: Landscapes in South African Writing* (Double Storey, Cape Town, 2006)
Pocock, DCD. 'Place and the Novelist' in *Transactions of the Institute of British Geographers* 6, 3 (1981)
Sanders, SR. quoted in *Windfall: A Journal of Poetry of Place* (Fall 2017)
Schama, S. *Landscape and Memory* (Vintage, New York, 1996)
Sheldrake, P. *Living Between Worlds: Place and Journey in Celtic Spirituality* (Darton, Longman and Todd, London, 1995)
Stiebel, L. 'Hitting the Hot Spots: Literary Tourism as a Research Field With Particular Reference to KwaZulu-Natal, South Africa' in *Critical Arts* 18, 2 (2004)
Winton, T. *Island Home: A Landscape Memoir* (Picador, London, 2017)
Wynn, M. 'Knowledge of Place and Knowledge of God: Contemporary Philosophies of Place and Some Questions in Philosophical Theology' in *International Journal for Philosophy of Religion* 62, 3 (December 2007)

OLIVE SCHREINER

Barsby, T. *Olive Schreiner: An Introduction* (NELM, Grahamstown, 1995)
Coetzee, JM. *White Writing: On the Culture of Letters in South Africa* (Radix, Johannesburg, 1988)
Cronwright-Schreiner, SC. (ed) *The Letters of Olive Schreiner* (Fisher Unwin, London, 1924)
Cronwright-Schreiner, SC. *The Life of Olive Schreiner* (Fisher Unwin, London, 1924)
Cronwright-Schreiner, SC. Unpublished diaries (Amazwi South African Museum of Literature, Grahamstown)
Driver, D. 'Invoking Indigeneity: Olive Schreiner and the Poetics of Plants' in *The Journal of Commonwealth Literature* 56 (2021)
Driver, D. *Olive Schreiner's Poetics of Plants* (Amazwi, Grahamstown, 2019)
Eve, J. *A Literary Guide to the Eastern Cape* (Double Storey, Cape Town, 2003)
Freeman, H. 'Dissolution and Landscape in Olive Schreiner's *The Story of an African Farm*' in *English Studies in Africa* 52, 2 (2009)

BIBLIOGRAPHY

First, R. and A Scott. *Olive Schreiner: A Biography* (Rutgers University Press, New Brunswick, 1990)

Fogg, J. *The Schreiner House: Cradock* (NELM, Grahamstown, 1993)

Hardy, T. *Return of the Native* (Oxford University Press, Oxford, 2005)

Hardy, T. *The Woodlanders* (Cambridge University Press, Cambridge, 2019)

Klopper, D. 'Between Man, Woman and Dog: Olive Schreiner's *The Story of an African Farm*' in *The Journal of South African and American Studies* 19, 4 (2018)

Knechtel, R. 'Olive Schreiner's Pagan Animism: An Underlying Unity' in *English Literature in Transition 1880–1920* 53, 3 (January 2010)

Krige, U. *Die Naamlose Muse* (Protea Boekhuis, Pretoria, 2002)

Mcmurry, A. 'Figures in a Ground: An Ecofeminist Study of Olive Schreiner's *The Story of an African Farm*' in *English Studies in Canada* 20, 4 (December 1994)

Mill, JS. *A System of Logic:, Ratiocinative and Inductive* (Longmans, London, 1879)

Mills, B. 'Klein Gannahoek: An Archaeo-architectural Investigation of an African Farmhouse' in *Southern African Field Archaeology* 1, 1 (1992)

Monsman, G. *Olive Schreiner's Fiction: Landscape and Power* (Rutgers University Press, New Brunswick, 1991)

Rive, R. (ed) *Olive Schreiner: Letters 1871–99* (David Philip, Johannesburg, 1987)

Ruden, S. 'Olive Schreiner in the New South Africa' in *The Antioch Review* 57, 2 (1999)

Schoeman, K. *Olive Schreiner: A Woman in South Africa 1855–1881* (Jonathan Ball, Johannesburg, 1991)

Schreiner, O. *From Man to Man, or, Perhaps Only* (UCT Press, Cape Town, 2015)

Schreiner, O. *The Story of an African Farm* (AD Donker, Johannesburg, 1986)

Schreiner, O. *Thoughts on South Africa* (Fisher Unwin, London, 1923)

Spencer, H. *First Principles* (Williams & Norgate, London, 1893)

Stanley, L. (ed) *Olive Schreiner's The Dawn of Civilisation & Other Unpublished Wartime Writings* (X Press, Edinburgh, 2018)

Van Niekerk, M. *Agaat* (Tafelberg/Jonathan Ball, Cape Town, 2006)

Van Wyk Smith, M. 'From "Boereplaas" to Metamyth: The Farm from Thomas Pringle to JM Coetzee', unpublished paper presented at AUETSA Conference (Unisa, Pretoria, 1999)

Vivan, I. *The Flawed Diamond: Essays on Olive Schreiner* (Dangaroo Press, Sydney, 1991)

Walters, P. and J Fogg (eds). *Olive Schreiner: Her Reinterment on Buffelskop* (NELM, Grahamstown, 2005)

The Olive Schreiner Letters Online, www.oliveschreiner.org

PERCY FITZPATRICK

Cartwright, AP. *The First South African: The Life and Times of Sir Percy FitzPatrick* (Purnell, Cape Town, 1971)

Coetzee, DJ., BP Simmons and W Knoesen. 'In FitzPatrick's Footsteps: Jock of the Bushveld's Paradise Camp' (self-published pamphlet for the Lowveld Diggers' and Transport Riders' Society, 1987)

Coetzee, DJ. and BP Simmons. 'Macmac Diggers & Transport Riders Memorial' (self-published pamphlet, 1992)

De Souza, BJL. *Lost Trails in the Makhonjwa Mountains* (Kiaat Creations, Pietermaritzburg, 2009)

Dubow, S. 'Colonial Nationalism, the Milner Kindergarten and the Rise of "South Africanism", 1902–10' in *History Workshop Journal* 43, 1 (Spring 1997)

FitzPatrick, P. *Jock of the Bushveld* (AD Donker Publishers, Johannesburg, 2009)

FitzPatrick, P. 'Jock of the Bushveld and Those Who Knew Him' in Niven, C. (ed) *Jock and Fitz* (Longmans, Cape Town, 1969)

Gray, S. 'Domesticating the Wilds: J. Percy FitzPatrick's *Jock of the Bushveld* as a Historical Record for Children' in *English in Africa* 14, 2 (October 1987)

Jock, the movie, directed by G Hofmeyr (1986)

Pienaar, U de V. *Neem Uit die Verlede* (Protea Boekhuis, Pretoria, 2007)

Simmons, BP. 'In FitzPatrick's Footsteps: Through the Present White River District' (self-published pamphlet, 2000)

# BIBLIOGRAPHY

DENEYS REITZ

Burgess, M. 'How Jan Smuts Cheated Death' in *Farmer's Weekly*, 7 September 2018
Couzens, T. *South African Battles* (Jonathan Ball, Johannesburg, 2013)
Delport, S. *Uit My Hart se Kontrei: Sestig Stukkies vir Sestig Jaar* (Rietberg, Kirkwood, 2007)
Gouws, J. 'Deneys Reitz and the Boundaries of Self-Understanding' in Viljoen, H. (ed) *Cross/Cultures 157: Crossing Borders, Dissolving Boundaries* (Rodopi, Amsterdam, 2013)
Pakenham, T. *The Boer War* (Jonathan Ball, Johannesburg, 2011)
Penn, N. 'Into the Cape' in *Getaway*, October 1999
Reitz, D. *Commando: A Boer Journal of the Boer War* (Faber & Faber, London, 1932)
Reitz, D. *Memoirs of the English War, 1899–1902*, translated by M Reitz (Unpublished manuscript, Brenthurst Library, Johannesburg)
Shearing, T and D. *General Smuts and his Long Ride* (self-published, Sedgefield, 2000)
Smith, RW. 'Modderfontein 17 September 1901' in *Military History Journal* 13, 1 (June 2004)
Stretton, S. *Smuts in the Stormberg* (The Anderson Museum, Dordrecht, 2001)
Tomlinson, R. 'Britain's Last Castles: Masonry Blockhouses of the South African War, 1899–1902' in *Military History Journal* 10, 6 (December 1997)
Uys, S. 'Dit is My Kontrei' on SABC radio, 10 July 1956
Uys, S. 'I Remember Three Wars' on SABC radio, 29 December 1963

EUGÈNE MARAIS

Marais, E. *Keurverhale* (Afrikaanse Pers Boekhandel, Johannesburg, 1948)
Marais, E. *My Friends the Baboons* (Methuen, London, 1939)
Marais, E. *The Road to Waterberg and Other Essays* (Human & Rousseau, Cape Town, 1972)
Marais, E. *The Soul of the Ape* (Human & Rousseau, Cape Town, 1969)

Marais, E. *The Soul of the White Ant* (Methuen, London, 1938)
Mieny, CJ. *Leipoldt en Marais: Onwaarskynlike Vriende* (Joan Lötter, Pretoria, 1988)
Opperman, DJ. *Senior Verseboek* (Tafelberg, Cape Town, 1980)
Rousseau, L. *The Dark Stream: The Story of Eugène Marais* (Jonathan Ball, Johannesburg, 1982)
Rousseau, L. (ed) *Die Beste van Eugène Marais* (Rubicon, Cape Town, 1986)
Swart, S. '"Bushveld Magic" and "Miracle Doctors": An Exploration of Eugène Marais and C Louis Leipoldt's Experiences in the Waterberg, South Africa, c. 1906–1917' in *The Journal of African History* 45, 2 (2004)
Die Wonderwerker, the movie, directed by K Heyns (2012)

HERMAN CHARLES BOSMAN

Bosman, HC. *Bosman at his Best* (Human & Rousseau, Cape Town, 1981)
Bosman, HC. *The Collected Works of Herman Charles Bosman* (Southern Book Publishers, 1992)
Bosman, HC. *The Complete Voorkamer Stories* (Human & Rousseau, Cape Town, 2011)
Bosman, HC. *Homecoming: Voorkamer Stories II* (Human & Rousseau, Cape Town, 2005)
Bosman, HC. *Idle Talk: Voorkamer Stories I* (Human & Rousseau, Cape Town, 1999)
Bosman, HC. *Mafeking Road and Other Stories* (Human & Rousseau, Cape Town, 1991)
Bosman, HC. *Marico Moon* (The House of Emslie, Edinburgh, 2018)
Bosman, HC. *Seed Time and Harvest and Other Stories* (Human & Rousseau, Cape Town, 2001)
Goldblatt, D. *Some Afrikaners Revisited* (Umuzi, Cape Town, 2007)
Gray, S. *Life Sentence* (Human & Rousseau, Cape Town, 2005)
MacKenzie, C. *The Oral-Style South African Short Story in English* (Rodopi, Amsterdam, 1999)
Rosenberg, V. *Herman Charles Bosman: Between the Lines* (Struik, Cape Town, 2005)
Rosenberg, V. *Sunflower to the Sun: The Life of Herman Charles Bosman* (Human & Rousseau, Cape Town, 1976)

Sachs, B. *Herman Charles Bosman as I Knew Him* (Dial Press, Johannesburg, 1974)
Kannemeyer, JC. *Die Goue Seun: Die Lewe en Werk van Uys Krige* (Tafelberg, Cape Town, 2002)
Krige, U. *Versamelde Gedigte* edited by JC Kannemeyer (JL van Schaik/Human & Rousseau/Perskor, Cape Town, 1985)

JM COETZEE

Attwell, D. *JM Coetzee and the Life of Writing: Face to Face with Time* (Jacana, Johannesburg, 2015)
Attwell, D. *JM Coetzee: South Africa and the Politics of Writing* (David Philip, Cape Town, 1993)
Breytenbach, B. *Dog Heart: A Travel Memoir* (Human & Rousseau, Cape Town, 1998)
Coetzee, JM. *Boyhood: Scenes from Provincial Life* (Secker & Warburg, London, 1997)
Coetzee, JM. *Doubling the Point: Essays and Interviews* (Harvard University Press, Cambridge, Massachusetts, 1992)
Coetzee, JM. *Dusklands* (Raven Press, Johannesburg, 1974)
Coetzee, JM. *In the Heart of the Country* (Secker & Warburg, London, 1977)
Coetzee, JM. *Life & Times of Michael K* (Vintage, London, 1998)
Coetzee, JM. 'Nietverloren' in *Ten Years of the Caine Prize for African Writing* (New Internationalist, Oxford, 2009)
Coetzee, JM. *Stranger Shores: Essays 1986-1999* (Secker & Warburg, London, 2001)
Coetzee, JM. *Summertime: Scenes from Provincial Life* (Vintage, London, 2010)
Coetzee JM. *White Writing: On the Culture of Letters in South Africa* (Radix, Johannesburg, 1988)
Dovey, T. *The Novels of JM Coetzee: Lacanian Allegories* (AD Donker, Johannesburg, 1988)
Gallagher, SV. *A Story of South Africa: JM Coetzee's Fiction in Context* (Harvard University Press, Cambridge, Massachusetts, 1991)
Fox, J. *The Life and Art of François Krige* (Fernwood, Cape Town, 2000)

Kannemeyer, JC. *JM Coetzee: A Life in Writing* (Jonathan Ball, Johannesburg, 2012)

Krige, U. *Versamelde Gedigte* edited by JC Kannemeyer (JL van Schaik/Human & Rousseau/Perskor, Cape Town, 1985)

Mitchell, E. 'Towards the Garden of the Mothers: Relocating the Capacity to Narrate in JM Coetzee's *Life & Times of Michael K*' in *Theoria: A Journal of Social and Political Theory* 91 (June 1998)

Smuts, E. '"The Country of His Heart": JM Coetzee, Wordsworth and the Karoo Farm' in *English in Africa* 42, 2 (September 2015)

Smuts, E. *Displaced Romanticism: Searching for the Self in JM Coetzee's Autobiographical Fiction* (UCT doctoral thesis, 2014)

Vital, A. 'Toward an African Ecocriticism: Postcolonialism, Ecology and *Life & Times of Michael K*' in *Research in African Literatures* 39, 1 (Spring 2008)

Wright, D. 'Black Earth, White Myth: Coetzee's *Michael K*' in *Modern Fiction Studies* 38, 2 (Summer 1992)

DALENE MATTHEE

Cloete, W. and M Wenzel. 'Translating Culture: Matthee's *Kringe in 'n Bos* as a Case in Point' in *Literator* 28, 3 (December 2007)

Franks, A. 'A Forest Killed for Greed' in *The Times*, 28 August 1984

Matthee, D. *Circles in a Forest* (Penguin, Johannesburg, 2005)

Matthee, D. *Dreamforest* (Penguin, Johannesburg, 2004)

Matthee, D. *Fiela's Child* (Penguin, Johannesburg, 2005)

Matthee, D. *The Mulberry Forest* (Michael Joseph, London, 1989)

Pretorius, G. 'Walking with Words' in *South*, Spring 2016

www.dalenematthee.co.za

ZAKES MDA

Burton, AW. *Sparks from the Border Anvil: A Record of Remarkable and Inspiring Events and of Progressive Enterprise on the Long-contested Cape Frontier, Now the Border districts of the Cape Province* (Provincial, King William's Town, 1950)

DeLoughrey, E. and GB Handley (eds) *Postcolonial Ecologies: Literatures of the Environment* (Oxford University Press, New York, 2011)

Epril, T. 'The Shock of the New' in *The New York Times*, 11 August 2002

Fincham, G. *Dance of Life: The Novels of Zakes Mda in Post-apartheid South Africa* (Ohio University Press, Athens, 2012)

Mda, Z. *The Heart of Redness* (Oxford University Press, Cape Town, 2000)

Mda, Z. *Sometimes there is a Void: Memoirs of an Outsider* (Penguin, Johannesburg, 2011)

Mda, Z. 'Zakes Mda: The Story Behind *The Heart of Redness*' and 'Zakes Mda: The naming of *The Heart of Redness*' on *YouTube*, 22 May 2013

Mtshali, OM. *Sounds of a Cowhide Drum* (Jacana, Johannesburg, 2012)

Peires, J. *The Dead Will Arise: Nongqawuse and the Great Xhosa Cattle-Killing Movement of 1856–7* (Jonathan Ball, Johannesburg, 2003)

Pillay, P. and C Addison. 'Organic Intellectuals in Zakes Mda's *The Heart of Redness*' in *English in Africa* 42, 3 (December 2015)

Rossouw, H. 'Mda's Twin Peak' in *Mail & Guardian*, 12 January 2001

Sosibo, K. 'Cows: The Sacred and the Profane' in *Mail & Guardian*, 7 April 2016

Vital, A. 'Situating Ecology in Recent South African Fiction: JM Coetzee's *The Lives of Animals* and Zakes Mda's *The Heart of Redness*' in *Journal of Southern African Studies* 31, 2 (June 2005)

STEPHEN WATSON

Anderson, PR. 'This Late Place: Stephen Watson (1954–2011), Poet, Essayist, Critic and Scholar' in *English in Africa* 39, 1 (May 2012)

Bate, J. *The Song of the Earth* (Picador, London, 2001)

Breytenbach, B. *A Season in Paradise*, translated by R. Vaughan (Persea Books, New York, 1980)

Corder, H. 'Eulogy for Stephen Watson' in *New Contrast* 159, 40, 3 (2012)

Heffernan, JAW. 'Wordsworth on the Sublime: The Quest for Interfusion' in *Studies in English Literature, 1500–1900* 7, 4 (Fall 1967)

Hitt, C. 'Toward an Ecological Sublime' in *New Literary History* 30, 3 (Summer 1999)

Klopper, D. 'On the Edge of Darkness: Stephen Watson and the Return of the Romantic Imagination' in *English in Africa* 25, 1 (May 1998)

Rabie, J. *Droomberge – Sederberg* (Saayman & Weber, Cape Town, 1985)

Symons, S. 'Dreaming a New Land: An Exploration of the Topographical and Landscape Poetry of Stephen Watson, Kelwyn Sole, Ingrid de Kok & Joan Metelerkamp in the Post-Apartheid Era' (unpublished essay, UCT, 2013)

Tyfield, D. 'Remembering Stephen Watson: A Legacy at Risk' in *Stellenbosch Literary Project*, 11 April 2013

Watson, S. (ed) *A City Imagined* (Penguin, Johannesburg, 2005)

Watson, S. *In This City* (David Philip, Cape Town, 1986)

Watson, S. *The Light Echo and Other Poems 2000-2006* (Penguin, Johannesburg, 2007)

Watson, S. *The Music in the Ice: On Writers, Writing & Other Things* (Penguin, Johannesburg, 2010)

Watson, S. *The Other City: Selected Poems 1977-1999* (David Philip, Cape Town, 2000)

Watson, S. *Presence of the Earth: New Poems* (David Philip, Cape Town, 1995)

Watson, S. *Return of the Moon: Version from the /Xam* (Carrefour, Cape Town, 1991)

Watson, S. *Selected Essays 1980-1990* (Carrefour, Cape Town, 1990)

Watson, S. *A Writer's Diary* (Queillerie, Cape Town, 1997)

---※---

ACKNOWLEDGEMENTS

Special thanks to ANFASA (Academic and Non-Fiction Authors Association of South Africa) for its generous grant to assist with the research for this project. A heartfelt thank-you, also, to all those who helped me on the journey of this book: Lesley Marx, Sandra Antrobus, David Attwell, Marius Bakkes, Deoni Barnard, Lydia Barrella, Fourie Botha, Breyten Breytenbach, Ann Bryan, Lizette Burger, Christopher Cawood, Carrol Clarkson, Gerald Coetzee, JM Coetzee, Hugh Corder, Sandra Dodson, Nick Dover, Jacques du Plessis, Willie du Plessis, Mike English, Martha Evans, Cameron Ewart-Smith, Marida Fitzpatrick, Grethe Fox, Revel Fox (jnr), Suzanne Fox, Brenda Goldblatt, James Haupt, Klaas Havenga, Katinka Heyns, Michaela Howse, Rufus Hulley, Kevin Jacobs, Annetjie Joubert, Michael Kepe, Elsabe Koen, Kobus Kok, Mandla Langa, Aoife Lennon-Ritchie, Kallie le Roux, Zakes Mda, Sidney Mikosi, Basil Mills, André Nel, Rinda Nieuwoudt, Carlos Nkonki, Wilfred Oraai, Gareth Patterson, Don Pinnock, Hermanus Potgieter, Pete Reinders, Catriona Ross, Peet Rossouw, Daantjie Schoeman, Sonya Schoeman, Louis Strauss, Sandy Stretton, Stephen Symons, John Theunissen, Egbert van Bart, Santa van Bart, Annari van der Merwe, Meagan Vermaas, Mariëtte van Wyk, Crystal Warren, Gillian Warren-Brown, Stephen Watson, Trevor Wigley, Brian Wilmot, Tanya Wilson and Tracey Younghusband.

---*---

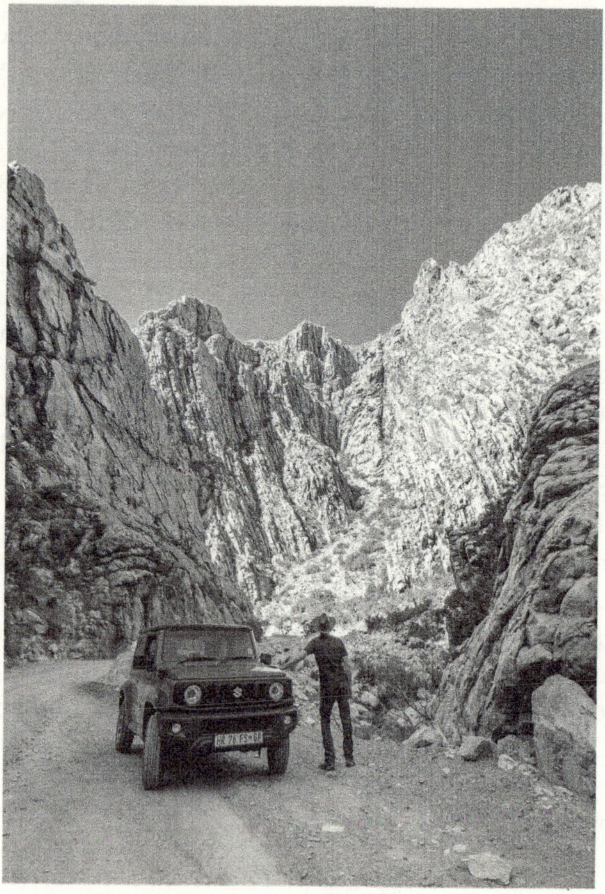

Petersoen